LANGUAGE, SEMANTICS AND IDEOLOGY

LANGUAGE, DISCOURSE, SOCIETY

Editors: Stephen Heath and Colin MacCabe

LANGUAGE, SEMANTICS AND IDEOLOGY
Stating the Obvious

Michel Pêcheux

Translated by Harbans Nagpal

MACMILLAN

© François Maspero 1975
English translation © Harbans Nagpal 1982

References, bibliography and index by Ben Brewster

First edition 1982
Reprinted 1983, 1986

Published by
THE MACMILLAN PRESS LTD
Houndmills, Basingstoke, Hampshire RG21 2XS
and London
Companies and representatives
throughout the world

Printed in Hong Kong

ISBN 0–333–24564–4 (hardcover)
ISBN 0–333–35263–7 (paperback)

Contents

Translator's Note

The publishers and I are grateful to all the publishers who have allowed the use of quotations from their publications. For this purpose I have used the standard English editions when these are available. Where no English translation is available or when the author's use of a quotation requires it, I have translated directly from the French or adapted the available English translation.

For help with the translation, especially some difficult philosophical passages, I am grateful to Dr Grahame Lock; and to Mr Jean-Jacques Lecercle, especially for help with technical linguistic terms. I would also like to thank Mme Michèle Guenoun.

HARBANS NAGPAL

Paris, 1979

Little Prefatory Note

The term *semantics* is often found today in the company of those of *semiotics* and *semiology*; in this connection, I should like to review a few of the characteristic aspects of these different disciplines.

Semiotics, or the science of signs, introduced by John Locke in the context of an empiricist philosophy of language, was developed in the United States by the philosopher Charles Sanders Peirce (1839–1914), with his distinctions between the iconic, the indexical and the symbolic. In their recent *Dictionnaire encyclopédique des sciences du langage* (1972), from which I have taken the gist of this note, Oswald Ducrot and Tzvetan Todorov quote the following admission of Peirce himself as to the universal goals of semiotics as he understood it: 'It has never been in my power to study anything, – mathematics, ethics, metaphysics, gravitation, thermodynamics, optics, chemistry, comparative anatomy, astronomy, psychology, phonetics, economics, the history of science, whist, men and women, wine, metrology – except as a study of semeiotic' (Peirce 1953, p. 32). This typically American empirical universality can paradoxically be linked however with Ernst Cassirer's 'philosophy of symbolic forms', in which the symbolic, the distinguishing feature of man as opposed to animals, constitutes the common spring of myth, religion, art and science, each of which is a 'language'. Next, the logician Charles Morris, basing himself on the notion of ideal language (Frege, Russell, Carnap), developed the relationship between logic and semiotics, notably by proposing a distinction between syntax (the relations between signs and other signs), semantics (the relation between signs and what they designate) and pragmatics (the relation between signs and their users). Note finally that, beginning in the 1960s, investigators in the Soviet Union and other socialist countries have started to develop research in semiotics. For this, they have drawn especially on the theory of dual signalling systems, and on cybernetics and information theory.

Completely independently, the term *semiology* was introduced by the linguist Ferdinand de Saussure to define the object of linguistics inside a much larger field; he wrote:

> *Langue* is a system of signs that express ideas, and is therefore comparable to a system of writing, the alphabet of deaf-mutes, symbolic rites, polite formulas, military signals, etc. But it is the most important of all these systems. *A science that studies the life of signs within society* is conceivable; it would be part of social psychology and consequently of general psychology (Saussure 1974, p. 123).

As is well known, with the help of the celebrated distinction between signifier and signified and other linguistic oppositions such as paradigm and syntagm, a series of semiological studies of the systems of fashion, advertising, road signs, kinship relations, myths, etc., have been developed under the aegis of this statement of Saussure's.

Whether or not semiotics and semiology designate one and the same discipline – a point that is still in dispute – it remains the case that they are both concerned with all signs, whether they be by nature linguistic or extra-linguistic (images, sounds, etc.). By contrast, *semantics*, most generally defined as concerning meaning or sense,[1] seems to refer especially to linguistics and logic; the word semantics emerged at the end of the nineteenth century, but what it designates concerns both very ancient preoccupations of philosophers and grammarians, and recent linguistic research; there was a period (roughly the first half of the twentieth century) when linguists were reluctant to recognise semantics as 'a part of linguistics'. Since the advent of Chomskyism, semantics ('interpretative' or 'generative') has been at the centre of linguistic controversy, especially in respect to its relationship with syntax (is the deep structure exclusively syntactic, or is it both syntactic and semantic?). These controversies depend, as we shall see, on philosophical questions which themselves involve the problem of universality and ideal language. Finally, some authors (such as Adam Schaff) identify *semantics* with *semiology*, a clear sign of the theoretical proximity of the three disciplines.

1. The straightforward translation of '*sens*' into English is 'meaning'. However, the French word is also used in contexts where the normal English word would be 'sense' or, in the negative form '*non-sens*', 'nonsense'. Moreover, in their translations of the writings of Frege, Black and Geach adopted 'sense' for Frege's '*Sinn*' in the opposition *Sinn/Bedeutung* (sense/reference), which French translations of Frege render *sens/dénotation*. In this translation '*sens*' has mostly been translated by 'meaning'; sometimes, when the context seemed to demand it or a Frege translation was concerned, as 'sense', and occasionally, at the risk of a certain clumsiness, as here with both English words [Translator's Note].

Acknowledgements

The author and publishers wish to thank the following who have kindly given permission for the use of copyright material: George Allen & Unwin Ltd and Basic Books Inc., for the extract from 'Interpretation of Dreams' in *The Standard Edition of the Works of Sigmund Freud*, vols IV and V; Basil Blackwell Publisher Ltd, for the extracts from *Translations from the Philosophical Writings of Gottlob Frege* (ed. Peter T. Geach and Max Black), and from *Logical Investigations* by Gottlob Frege, translated by Peter T. Geach and R. H. Sloothoff; Éditions Gallimard, Paris, for the extract from *Leibniz: Critique de Descartes* by Yvon Belaval (1960); Walter de Gruyter and Co., Berlin, for the extract from *Wilhelm von Humbolts Werke*, vol. V (1968); Harper & Row Publishers Inc., for the extract from *The History of Rationalist Thought* by N. Chomsky (1966); Éditions Klincksieck, Paris, for the extracts from *Le Mauvais outil* by Paul Henry (1977); Lawrence and Wishart Ltd, for the extracts from *Marx and Engels: Selected Works in 3 Volumes*, vol. III, and *Collected Works of Lenin*, vol. XIV; Éditions François Maspero, Paris, for the extracts from *Une Crise et son enjou* by Dominique Lecourt (1973); *Philosophie et Philosophie spontanée des savants* by Louis Althusser (1967); *Cahiers Marxistes-Leninistes* (1966) and *Cinq études du materialisme historique* by Étienne Balibar (1972); Les Éditions de Minuit, Paris, for the extract from *L'Établi* by Robert Linhart (1978); New Left Books, for the extracts from *Reading Capital* by Louis Althusser and Étienne Balibar, translated by B. Brewster (1965); *Lenin and Philosophy and other Essays* (1964) and *Politics and History: Montesquieu, Rousseau, Hegel and Marx* by Louis Althusser, translated B. Brewster (1968), and *Essays in Self Criticism* by Louis Althusser, translated by Grahame Lock (1972); Open Court Publishing Co., for the extract from *The Science of Mechanics* by Ernest Mach, translated by T. J. McCormack (1960); Pergamon Press Ltd, for the extract from *Introduction to Semantics* by A. Schaff (1962); Presses Universitaires de France, for the extract from *l'Empirisme Logique* by Louis Vax (1970); Routledge & Kegan Paul

Ltd and Humanities Press Inc., for the extracts from *Logical Investigations* by E. Husserl, translated by J. N. Findlay, and with W. W. Norton & Co. Inc., for the extract from *The Standard Edition of the Works of Sigmund Freud*, vol. VIII; Éditions du Seuil, Paris, with Basil Blackwell Publisher Ltd and Johns Hopkins University Press, for the extract from *Dictionnaire encyclopédique des sciences du langage* by Ducrot and Todorov (1972); Éditions du Seuil, Paris, with Tavistock Publications Ltd and W. W. Norton Inc., for the extract from *Écrits* by Jacques Lacan (1957); and VEB Deutscher Verlag der Wissenschaften, Berlin, for the extracts from *Moderne Logik* (1965) and *Sprache der Politik* (1971) by G. Klaus.

Every effort has been made to trace all the copyright-holders but if any have been inadvertently overlooked the publishers will be pleased to make the necessary arrangement at the first opportunity.

Introduction

According to anecdote, Stalin one day exclaimed: 'I am surrounded by a lot of blind kittens!', without suspecting for a moment his own participation in that blindness.

Today, with the worsening of the imperialist crisis, the crisis in the international Communist movement is becoming ever more marked, laying bare for all to see the contradiction that has been smouldering in the world workers' movement since the beginning of the 1930s: at its most profound, the contradiction between the political effects of October 1917, the Soviet revolution and the victory of Stalingrad on the one hand, and on the other, everything that has imperceptibly undermined, diverted and buried them in the practical horror of Stalin's regime, many of whose features survive in the repressive system of the USSR today.

With the Twentieth Congress of the CPSU, the workers' movement thought nonetheless that it had dealt with this contradiction by criticising the 'cult of personality' and the crimes of the subject-Stalin, hoping thus to put a period to the story of Stalinism: but since the deeper-lying causes of the 'Stalinist deviation' remained opaque, they continued intact to produce their effects. . . . In its own way, the 'humanist' explosion of the 1960s prolonged this ignorance of the causes through a concentration on their effects; nevertheless, for better or for worse, a new space was opened up in the Communist movement, attempting to question the relationship between proletarian politics and the bourgeois state, the methods for conquering that state, transforming it and smashing the mechanisms by which it reproduces itself.

The workers' movement of the capitalist countries (especially in Italy, France and then Spain) rediscovered the question of whether it is not absolutely indispensable, precisely to achieve these objectives, to play the game of the bourgeois state as it were, to take it 'at the word' of its own legality, so as to turn that legality against it. At the same time, in the 'existing socialist countries', the Twentieth Congress encouraged a fresh interrogation of the nature of socialist society and the proletarian state.

Obviously, ideology was one of the crucial issues in this new interrogation; Marxist scholars thus set off on reconnaissance in theoretical regions which, during the period of historical Stalinism, Zhdanov and his henchmen had simply forbidden them. Semantics constitutes one of these taboo regions.

In 1960, the Zhdanovian ghosts haunting the 'proletarian' pseudo-sciences had disappeared, and the Polish Marxist philosopher Adam Schaff could set out to reconcile Marxism with semantics – 'a branch of linguistics . . . concerned with the meaning and the changes of meaning of words and expressions' according to the dictionaries (Schaff 1962, p. 5). He concluded his *Introduction to Semantics* by observing:

> We are now witnessing its ['semantics'] rehabilitation. Not only in linguistics, where the development of semantic researches has never faced major difficulties, but also in logic. For it has turned out that the study of logical syntax and metalanguage have very practical applications in the construction of translating machines, mechanical memory devices, etc. It is also worthwhile to draw attention to another field of applications of semantics, unfortunately neglected in socialist countries, which is a scientific theory of propaganda (1962, p. 364).

In other words, the re-emergence of semantic investigations in the light of Marxism is contemporaneous with the Twentieth Congress of the CPSU and also with the beginning of the so-called 'computer and space age'. A considerable period has elapsed since this rehabilitation and, in the East as in the West, more and more studies have been produced in this domain.

I do not intend to consider here Adam Schaff's theoretical positions separately and in their own right, nor to make a survey of the works which have resulted from this re-emergence in the context of 'Western' studies which had meantime gone their own way (by-passing Marxism or eyeing it suspiciously). I think, indeed, that the very possibility of a *history* of all these studies (whether or not undertaken under the banner of Marxism) is conditional on *a prior question which is both theoretical and political in character*: the possibility (and the profound necessity) of initiating within Marxism and Leninism a critique of this rehabilitation without for all that raising the ghosts of Zhdanov or Marr. I refuse the rhetorical trap constituted by the dilemma (in the mode 'either-or' and 'if not one, then the other') into which some people would like to *corner* Marxist research or *drown* it like a blind kitten, preventing it from constructing new problematics. I therefore demand the right to *challenge the philosophical opportunism* which today gives its blessing to the 'Marxist' coexistence of Pavlovism, cybernetics, semiotics, applications of formal logic to the theory of language and to semantics, *and at the same time to struggle against a voluntarist Stalinist conception of science* in which 'Marxism' would dictate in advance to a science its principles and results, in the name of Dialectical Materialism or the Laws of History.

But this is only a good intention: it must be judged by its results. . . .

Let me begin by examining how Schaff exploits the evident proposition that semantics, as a part of linguistics, is a modern and complex science which Marxism has every interest in 'incorporating'.

The book I have just referred to starts with a *definition*, presented as a piece of information: 'Semantics (semasiology) is a branch of linguistics' (Schaff 1962, p. 3); as one might say 'Paris is in France' – an evident fact. But, reading on, we discover that this branch of linguistics has some remarkable extensions, towards 'logic' on the one hand, and also towards something described in the phrase cited above, 'the scientific theory of propaganda', which thus, via politics, involves what was classically called rhetoric.

Thus the inclusion of semantics in linguistics endows the latter with two extensions, viz.:

'logic', that is, *evidently*, that part of mathematics called mathematical logic, but also and above all (the first guaranteeing the second) the 'theory of knowledge' as a theory of the 'laws of thought';

and its apparent counterpart, 'rhetoric' as a reflection on the techniques of argument, the manipulation of beliefs, bluff and deceit. Thus 'rhetoric' (*not to speak* of politics) is the inevitable supplement counterbalancing 'logic' (mathematics unites men, politics divides them, as Hobbes said).

How can all this be held together as semantics, a branch of linguistics? Idealism naturally has its solutions (we shall see which), but Schaff claims he can find the answer to this question in Marxism, to be precise in *The German Ideology* (Marx and Engels 1976b), from which he quotes abundantly and extracts the notion of the 'communicational function of language', developed as follows:

> The communication process and the related sign-situation, i.e., the situation in which material objects and processes become signs in the social process of semiosis, have served us as the starting point and the basis of the analysis of such semantic categories as sign and meaning. But such analysis shows that in order to understand not only the communication process but also what sign and meaning are, it is necessary to refer to language by means of which we communicate with one another on the social plane and within which material objects and processes may, under definite circumstances, function as signs, that is, acquire definite meanings. That is why language and speech are raised to the role of fundamental categories in all semantic research. Moreover, the linguist, the logician, the psychologist, the anthropologist, etc., likewise refer to language and speech (Schaff 1962, p. 311).

With the help of this rather long quotation I can extend the list of 'evident' propositions that Schaff has run across en route:

there are *things* ('objects' and 'material processes') and *persons*, subjects endowed with the intention to communicate ('we' communicate 'by means of . . .');

there are objects which become *signs*, that is to say which refer to other objects, by the 'social process of semiosis';

finally there are the *human sciences*, each of which has something to say about language and speech, which constitute a real point of intersection of different disciplines.

If, to round all this off, I add that for Schaff, language is 'a system of verbal signs which serves to formulate thoughts in the process of reflecting objective reality by subjective cognition, and to communicate socially those thoughts about reality, as also the related emotional, aesthetic, volitional, etc., experiences' (1962, p. 315), the list can be topped up with two last 'evident' propositions:

there is an opposition between the *emotional* and the *cognitive* (an image for the opposition rhetoric/logic);

and, above all, thought and knowledge have a *subjective* character.

Without trying to settle the extent to which these various

'evident' propositions are Schaff's own projections into his reading of *The German Ideology*, I am forced to admit that such a reading is at least possible, and even one found more and more frequently today, with the result that this text, like the *Theses on Feuerbach* (Marx 1976) and *a fortiori The 1844 Manuscripts* (Marx 1975), appears as a way of avoiding reference to the concepts present in *Capital* (Marx 1961–2) and to the two-fold rupture (rupture in theory *and* rupture in practice) that goes with them, a rupture extended in Lenin's work (theoretical *and* practical) and continuing today in what is called Marxism-Leninism.

This is to say that my purpose here is to challenge *the evident propositions that underlie 'semantics'*, while attempting, as far as my means will allow, to lay the bases for a materialist theory.

My point of departure is two-fold. I intend to show:

(1) that *semantics*, which, as we have just seen, presents itself as a 'part of linguistics' – with the same status as phonology, morphology and syntax – constitutes in reality *for linguistics* the nodal point of the contradictions that criss-cross and organise that discipline in the form of tendencies, research programmes, linguistic 'schools' and so on which, at one and the same time, *reveal and conceal* (attempt to bury) those contradictions;

(2) that if semantics constitutes for linguistics such a nodal point, it is because it is at this point that linguistics, usually without knowing it, is concerned with *philosophy* (and, as we shall see, with *the science of social formations, historical materialism*).

I am therefore going to bring together linguistics *and* philosophy, to speak about linguistics *and* about philosophy, to speak of the linguistics in philosophy *and* of the philosophy in linguistics. This requires a detour, so that the linguists and the philosophers, to whom I am addressing myself in particular, can both become familiar with the way in which I am going to speak to them about philosophy and linguistics – or rather, so that they can become familiar with one another through the way I am going to speak to them.

To reveal the conditions, the terrain and the objectives of this detour, a rapid characterisation of the present situation in linguistics is necessary. Without going into more detail than is useful for the non-specialist, it is legitimate to identify three main tendencies which oppose, combine with and dominate one another in various forms:

(1) The formalist-logicist tendency, essentially organised today in the Chomskyan school, as a critical development of linguistic structuralism via 'generative' theories. It so happens that this tendency has sought philosophical credentials in the works of the Port-Royal school. I shall return to this point.[1]

(2) The historical tendency, formed in the nineteenth century as 'historical linguistics' (Ferdinand Brunot, Antoine Meillet), its modern descendants being theories of linguistic variation and change (geo-, ethno-, socio-linguistics).[2]

(3) The last tendency could be called the 'linguistics of *parole*' (of 'enunciation', of 'performance', of the 'message', the 'text', of 'discourse', etc.); in this tendency certain preoccupations of rhetoric and poetics are reintroduced, via a critique of the linguistic primacy of communication. This leads to a linguistics of style as deviation, transgression, disruption, etc., and to a linguistics of dialogue as a game between partners.[3]

It is clear that today, at least in the so-called 'West', in the balance of forces between these different tendencies, *the first tendency dominates the other two*: it is above all in relation to the formalist-logicist tendency that the other two tendencies define themselves; rather they usually depend on it (borrow from it, rework it, reappropriate it) in order to separate themselves from it. In fact, they are both related to it by contradictory bonds: the historical tendency is connected in a contradictory way to the formalist-logicist tendency by various intermediary forms (functionalism, distributionalism,[4] etc.); the linguistics of *enunciation* also has a contradictory bond with this tendency, in particular through the analytic philosophy of the Oxford school (John Langshaw Austin, John Rogers Searle, Peter Frederick Strawson, etc.), and its examination of the problems of presupposition.

Finally, the historico-sociological tendency is also bound to the

1. Apart from Chomsky, let me mention Charles J. Fillmore on the one hand, and George Lakoff and James McCawley on the other, and also the Soviet formalist Sebastian Konstantinovich Shaumyan.
2. E.g. Marcel Cohen, Uriel Weinreich, William Labov and, from a less theoretical point of view, Basil Bernstein.
3. In particular Roman Jakobson and Émile Benveniste, Oswald Ducrot, Roland Barthes, Algirdas Julien Greimas and Julia Kristeva.
4. Most important here are the studies of Leonard Bloomfield, and their consequences for the works of Zellig Harris, which will frequently be evoked in this work. See, on this point, Appendix 2 and also Pêcheux and Fuchs (1975).

third tendency in so far as it invokes 'the facts of *parole*' to break down the homogeneity of 'competence', the key notion of linguistic formalism. Simultaneously, studies which are purely 'generativist' (Robert Desmond King, Paul Kiparsky) or would like to be (William Labov, Uriel Weinreich) are trying today to 'explain' linguistic change.

I should add that the main contradiction, which opposes the formalist-logicist tendency to the other two tendencies, has repercussions inside each of them (and also inside the dominant tendency itself) in the form of secondary contradictions: the *explicit* form this contradiction takes is that of a contradiction between linguistic system (the *langue*) and *non-systematic determinations* which, *on the fringes of the system, oppose it and affect it*. Thus *langue* as a system turns out to be linked in contradictory fashion both to 'history' and to 'speaking subjects', and this contradiction is currently at work in linguistic researches in different forms which constitute precisely the object of what is called 'semantics'.

It is within this work that the present study aims to intervene, not in order to open up a mythical *fourth tendency* which would 'resolve' the contradiction(!), but in order to contribute to the development of that contradiction on a material basis within historical materialism. So let me explain how I am going to approach this contradiction and set it to work.

In my opinion, the fundamental thesis of the formalist position in linguistics can be summed up in two points, viz.:

(1) *Langue is not* historical, precisely to the extent that it is a system (the term 'structure' is also used);

(2) It is to the extent that *langue* is a system, a structure, that it constitutes the theoretical object of linguistics.

This being so, system (or structure) is opposed to history as the explicable is opposed to its inexplicable residue, and the systemic or structural explicable comes first, so there is no need to ask under what conditions it becomes explicable: for *linguistic structuralism*, but also for functionalism and even generativism, their object is 'given' in the general form of *langue* (or grammar). To this extent, and especially where 'semantics' is concerned, linguistic structuralism cannot completely avoid falling into a *philosophical structuralism* which attempts to include in the explicable its inexplicable residue.

Faced with this thesis and its consequences, the historical position responds by posing the problem of the genesis, the evolution, the transformations of the object which, for the formalist tendency, is 'given' in the first place. Thus the contradiction can take the well-known form of an irresolvable conflict between 'genesis and structure' . . ., to the ultimate advantage of the formalist tendency. However, things are not always so simple, in so far as the reference to history as a response to the formalist theses conceals a serious ambiguity:

When one speaks of history vis-à-vis linguistics, is it a matter of the vague commonplace that 'social factors influence the *langue*' (the *langue* 'enriching itself' progressively in the course of the 'evolution' of technical and social progress)?

Or is it a matter of something quite different, beyond this evolutionist and sociologistic historicism, which structuralism can easily recuperate via the *parole* of the 'speaking subjects'?

I believe that a reference to history vis-à-vis linguistic questions is only justifiable in the perspective of a materialist analysis of the effect of class relationships on what can be called the 'linguistic practices' inscribed in the operation of the ideological apparatuses of a given social and economic formation; given this, it becomes possible to explain what is going on today in 'the study of language' and to help to transform it, not by repeating its contradictions but by grasping them as derivatory effects of the class struggle in a 'Western country' under the domination of bourgeois ideology.

Here I shall draw from recent work by Renée Balibar and her colleagues on 'national French' (Balibar, R. and Laporte 1974) and 'fictional varieties of French' (Balibar, R. 1974), a distinction which greatly clarifies the material and historical basis of these contradictions; this distinction concerns two historical processes, periodised by transformations in class relationships in France (the anti-feudal struggle of the bourgeoisie to conquer and secure political domination, and its anti-proletarian struggle to maintain it).

The first of the these processes dates from the French Revolution itself, and consists of a *uniformisation* aiming politically and ideologically to set up a national language against the dialects and Latin which were, in different ways, obstructing the *free linguistic communication* necessary for the economic, juridico-political and ideological realisation of capitalist relations of production.

The second historical process, realised by the imposition through the education system of elementary French as the common language, consisted of *an inegalitarian division inside the egalitarian uniformisation*, aiming politically and ideologically to impose an antagonistic differentiation in class linguistic practices, within the use of the national language, so that the free linguistic communication required by capitalist relations of production and their reproduction *was at the same time also a definite non-communication*, erecting 'inside language' class barriers equally necessary for the reproduction of these same capitalist relations.

Let me point out straight away that such a distinction is completely absent from the work of Schaff, who does, in his own way, speak of the first process ('language as communication'), but never of the second (the definite non-communication imposing class barriers 'inside language'). In short, evolutionist historicism (to which Schaff is not averse to referring) does not take it into account that the arena of struggle has shifted over time: at the beginning of the bourgeois revolution there was a directly linguistic struggle for the phonological, morphological, syntactic and lexical unification of the *langue* inscribed in the nation-form, a unification which structuralism, functionalism, generativism, etc., were to grasp in the twentieth century as the unity of a system; but in time capitalist relations gave rise to a new struggle between 'realisations' of this *langue*, in which are reproduced, of course, morphophonological, lexical and syntactic differences in the handling of the *langue* – these differences are today the object of socio-linguistics and ethno-linguistics – but these differences are re-inscribed in differences of meaning such that, on either side of the 'linguistic and ideological divide that separates in France the two educational levels, primary and secondary-higher' (Balibar, R. 1974, p.281), there are contrasting 'vocabularies-syntaxes' and 'arguments', which lead, *sometimes with the same words*, in different directions depending on the nature of the ideological interests at stake. *It is precisely this point that the present work aims to develop.* It is thus not an attempt at a 'Marxist' socio-linguistics tending towards a kind of revenge of the concrete, setting the empirical variations of performance, the plurality of levels of communication, the different modalities of 'social interaction' etc. . . . against 'grammatical abstraction'. A recent article (Gadet 1977) makes a remarkable critique of the very basis of the socio-linguistic enterprise (which has been growing steadily since the beginning of the 1970s), revealing in it a psycho-social theory of linguistic behaviour that provides the foundation for a correlationist method and inevitably leads to a profoundly reformist conception of politics.

The present work aims to understand how what is *tendentially* 'the same *langue*' in the linguistic sense of the term allows antagonistic operations of 'vocabulary-syntax' and 'arguments'. In a word, the point is to set to work the contradiction which runs through the formalist-logicist tendency, behind the evident propositions that constitute its façade

It would be neither just nor possible from a linguistic point of view to write off the domination of this tendency, in which, in different respects, the majority of linguists concur today in the *concept of langue as a linguistic system*, and it seems to me that it would be a misunderstanding of the *historical* nature of Renée Balibar's work to see it as an encouragement to multiply fictional languages meta-phorically ('*langue*' of the bourgeoisie, of the proletariat, of the petty bourgeoisie, and '*langue*' of the law, of administration, etc.) as *new linguistic objects* counterposed empirically to French as the language imposed by the national education system: the tendential unity of what contemporary linguistics defines as *langue* constitutes the basis for antagonistic processes at the level of 'vocabulary-syntax' and at that of 'arguments'. We shall see why I have been led speak in this connection of *discursive processes and discursive formations*, in the perspective of a materialist analysis of the practices 'of language'.

The reader will already have understood that the question of the discursive division behind the unity of *langue* is in reality, via the intermediary of communication/non-communication, what takes on the appearance of the logic/rhetoric couple, through the various 'functions' fulfilled by that division in the capitalist social formation in which its presence can be detected everywhere:

in the economic base, within the very material conditions of capitalist reproduction: the necessities of the organisation of labour, of mechanisation and of standardisation imposing an unambiguous *communication* – 'logical' clarity of instructions and directives, apt-ness of terms used, etc. – a communication which is at the same time, through the socio-technical division of labour, a *non-commmunication* separating the workers from the organisation of production and making them subject to the 'rhetoric' of authority;

the division is also found in capitalist relations of production, and in their legal form, whose job it is to clear away ambiguities in contracts, commercial exchanges, etc. (linguistico-legal equality between contracting parties) and at the same time to foster the fundamental ambiguity of the 'labour contract', which can be summarised by saying that in bourgeois law 'all men are equal but some are more equal than others'!

Finally, the same division (equality/inequality, communication/ non-communication) is found in political and ideological social relations: dependence in the very forms of autonomy. I shall be returning to this point later.

So we find, combined in the divided and contradictory unity communication/non-communication, the elements whose theoretical study has, as we have seen, been split up, as if by chance, into different schools and tendencies (the logico-formal tendency and the rhetorico-poetic tendency). This split hides in reality the fact that these elements only exist in combination, in tendential forms corresponding to what Christian Baudelot and Roger Establet have characterised as the *two networks of the bourgeois education system* (Baudelot and Establet 1971). Without providing all the necessary proof here and now, I shall propose that these two tendential forms of combination of logic and rhetoric are *concrete realism* on the one hand and *idealist rationalism* on the other.

In *concrete realism*, logic is present in the form of simple, indestructible elements, constituting the essence of objects, without any extraneous addition. The rhetoric of the concrete and of the situation 'catches the attention' of the children (. . . and of the workers who, as everybody knows, are 'grown-up children'!) and with difficulty raises them to the 'essential' level, that is to say to the minimum they need to know in order to find a useful place for themselves, to avoid complete confusion. In other words, 'primary' concrete realism concerns that without which an object ceases to be what it is. The composition-comprehension is the school form of concrete realism.

In *idealist rationalism*, on the contrary, realism is transformed, because thought adds to reality, and, one could go so far as to say, recreates it in fiction. Logic must therefore remain open to all the interpolations, adjunctions and all the supplements through which the mind (I mean, of course, the mind of one of those who have advanced from the 'primary' to the 'secondary-higher' level) represents reality to itself. Thus logic is no obstacle to poetry, to that without which 'things would only be what they are': some will even go so far as to say that logic is the sublimest form of poetry. The essay-appreciation is the school form of idealist rationalism.[5]

5. Composition-comprehension/essay-appreciation: the French school exercises the author refers to – *rédaction-narration* and *dissertation-explication de texte* – have no *direct* correlates in the English education system; I hope that the English exercises chosen, which occupy equivalent places in the school system, are reasonably appropriate to the author's argument [Translator's Note].

We shall see later the manoeuvre whereby these two curricular forms are projected, reorganised, in the specialised philosophical forms of metaphysical realism and logical empiricism. In the meantime I think I have said enough to allow the reader who is not a specialist in linguistics to grasp why I have been led to take as the raw material for my study, as the constant exemplar during the necessary detour of the first two chapters, the 'linguistic' phenomenon classically designated by the opposition between 'explicative apposition' and 'determination', in particular the case of relative constructions of the type: 'L'homme qui est raisonnable est libre', which linguists describe as 'ambiguous' because of this opposition.[6]

As for the reader who has had some training in linguistics, I expect he or she will have recognised in this opposition between explicative and determinative one of the major difficulties encountered by current linguistic theories, whether 'structuralist' or 'generative'.[7] In fact, this opposition condenses and manifests in the linguistic domain the effects of the duality of logic and rhetoric, whose suspiciously evident character I have just remarked upon; or rather it *calls irresistibly* into linguistic reflection considerations as to

6. This example presents a problem for translation that we shall encounter many times in this book: the differences between the systems of determiners (articles, quantifiers, demonstratives, etc.) in French and English mean that many French sentences illustrating, in particular, phenomena of determination fail to demonstrate the same features when translated directly into English: thus the author's example translates into the *two* 'unambiguous' English sentences 'Man who is rational is free' and 'The man who is rational is free' (ignoring, as I have generally done, the thesis that differences in intonation, rendered by differences in the use of commas in writing, will distinguish between determinative and explicative relative clauses, e.g.: 'The horse which is brown is the fleetest' vs. 'The horse, which is a quadruped, is fleet-footed'). Moreover, simply to seek in English for a sentence which will illustrate the 'same' ambiguity – e.g., 'The horse which is of old-world origin is fleet-footed' – implies a logico-linguistic formalism which *Language, Semantics and Ideology* sets out to subvert; can this ambiguity really be called 'the same'? As a result the author's examples have been translated as literally as possible, at the cost of forcing English usage on occasion and the need to resort to explanatory footnotes when all else fails. The terms of the opposition between 'determinative' and 'explicative' or 'appositional' relative clauses adopted in this book are those of the Port-Royal logicians (see Arnauld and Nicole 1685). Linguistics written in English today more usually uses 'restrictive' and 'non-restrictive' relative clauses respectively, but the older terms more readily convey the way the terms have ramifications beyond linguistics in logic and philosophy [Translator's Note].

7. This aspect is systematically explored in Henry (1975). See also Fuchs and Milner (1979).

the relationship between object and properties of the object, between necessity and contingency, between objectivity and subjectivity, etc., which constitute a veritable philosophical ballet around the duality of logic and rhetoric. In Aristotelian terms, the opposition between explication and determination overlaps with the distinction between the two types of connection that can exist between an *accident* and a *substance*: where a certain accident is linked by an essential connection to a substance, the substance cannot continue to exist if the accident in question is lacking. Thus, for example, a man cannot continue to exist without his head or his reason (so Aristotle's conception of the relative construction cited above is spontaneously explicative, since a man without reason is not a man). But there are accidents which can be removed from an entity without affecting its existence, for example, the fact that a man is dressed in white is an accident which, if suppressed, does not destroy the substance, to which it is linked by an 'inessential' connection; whereas one cannot conceive of 'a man who is not reasonable', one can conceive of 'a man who is not dressed in white'; the relative clause thus *determines* the one entity among others to which it applies, without at the same time denying the existence of entities to which it does not apply, an existence which, on the contrary, it presupposes.

So we see how the relationship between *necessity* (as linked to the substance) and *contingency* (expressing the incidence of 'circumstances', 'points of view' and 'intentions'[8] which may or may not attach some property to some object) is articulated in this 'linguistic' question.

As will have been observed, the 'evident' propositions on which Schaff builds and which I set out above, not because I want to attribute any special importance or responsibility to this author, but because he represents a particularly clear 'symptom', these 'evident' propositions (for example, that *words* communicate a *meaning*, that there is a division between *persons* and *things*, between *subjectivity* and *objectivity*, between *the emotional* and *the cognitive*, etc.) thus confront us straight away.

The reader who is a philosopher will already have seen one consequence of this which it is worth making explicit for those who work in other 'specialisations': this is the fact that the 'linguistic'

8. Remember that, for Aristotle, rhetoric is a technique which allows the artificial production of a result which is only '*in potentia*', i.e., capable of being or not being indifferently, as opposed to the 'necessary' properties of the substance.

questions I am discussing here are at the same time inscribed in a philosophical problematic, broadly speaking that of 'modern' empiricism and subjectivism; the contradictory sign of this 'modernity' is the *logico-mathematical formalism* which is so prominent today (Chomsky, Piaget, Lévi-Strauss) and seems radically opposed to 'primary' empiricism and subjectivism, although it is its continuation: today, Bishop Berkeley's empiricism is dead and buried,[9] but in modern neo-Kantianism, its empirico-logical descendant is doing quite well, as we shall see.

A theoretical question, therefore, which I shall try to grasp both in its philosophical development and in its linguistic ramifications; but we shall find that this question is also, directly, a *political* question: the fact that in his time Lenin was concerned to intervene in the question of empirio-criticism is a first indication of this.[10] The political conditions through which contemporary Marxism has, amongst other things, regained contact with 'semantics' – as noted above, the Twentieth Congress of the CPSU and the beginning of the 'computer and space age' – constitute another; the cold spaces of semantics conceal a burning subject.

One point in passing that the reader might like to bear in mind during the long 'detour' of the first two chapters: semanticists, as we shall see, are always using dichotomous classifications of the type abstract/concrete, living/non-living, human/non-human, etc., which, if they were exhaustively and rigorously applied, would constitute a kind of *natural history of the universe*:

For example, for Jerrold Katz (1972, p. 40), a *chair* is characterised by the following features: (Object), (Physical), (Non-living), (Artifact), (Furniture), (Portable), (Something with legs), (Something with a back), (Something with a seat), (Seat for one).

Similarly, a *bachelor* is characterised (p. 278) as: (Object), (Physical), (Human), (Adult), (Male), (Unmarried), which would sanction the highly suspect *lapalissade* that if a man is not married, that is because he is a bachelor![11]

Strange how the classifying machine jams all of a sudden . . . and

9. Although even today the experimental psychology of perception is still seriously discussing George Berkeley's theses with a view to proving or refuting them, especially in the United States.
10. I am indebted to Dominique Lecourt for the light he has recently cast on this question (Lecourt 1973). I shall make extensive use of his book in this work.
11. The French title of this book, *Les Vérités de La Palice*, was intended to render to Monsieur de la Palice the place he deserves as the semanticist's patron saint. According to the song:

yet it worked so well on *persons* and *things*! Is it an accident that in order to operate it needs the abstract universal space of the law as produced by the capitalist mode of production? Bernard Edelman's work (1979) is particularly revealing as to this point.

At any rate, the reader will have smelt a rat by now; and, if he has read one of Louis Althusser's recent texts, he will know that, although there is no mention of 'semantics' in it, it does raise the question as to whether, like man (with a small m or capital M),

Messieurs vous plaît-il d'ouïr	Gentlemen, would it please you to hear
L'air du fameux La Palice	The song of the famous La Palice
Il pourra vous divertir	You ought to find it entertaining
Pourvu qu'il vous réjouisse	So long as you enjoy it
La Palice eut peu de bien	La Palice had little wealth
Pour soutenir sa naissance,	To support his natural talents,
Mais il ne manqua de rien	But he never lacked for anything
Tant qu'il fut dans l'abondance.	So long as he had plenty.
Bien instruit dès le berceau	Well brought up from the cradle
Jamais, tant il fut honnête,	Never, such a well-bred fellow was he,
Il ne mettait son chapeau	Did he put on his hat
Qu'il ne se couvrît la tête,	Without covering his head.
Il était affable et doux	He was gentle and sweet
De l'humeur de feu son père,	Just like his late father,
Et n'entrait guère en courroux	And never lost his temper
Si ce n'est dans la colère.	Except when he was angry.
Il épousa, ce dit-on,	He married, so they say,
Une vertueuse dame;	A virtuous woman;
S'il avait vécu garçon	If he had remained a bachelor,
Il n'aurait pas eu de femme.	He would have had no wife.
Il en fut toujours chéri	She was his constant comfort,
Elle n'était point jalouse;	And never jealous;
Sitôt qu'il fût son mari,	As soon as he became her husband,
Elle devient son épouse.	She became his wife.
Un devin, pour deux testons,	For two pennies, a fortune teller
Lui dit d'une voix hardie	Told him boldly
Qu'il mourrait delà les monts	That he would die beyond the mountains
S'il mourait en Lombardie.	If he died in Lombardy.
Il y mourut, ce héros,	Our hero did die there,
Personne aujourd'hui n'en doute,	No one any longer doubts it,
Sitôt qu'il eut les yeux clos	The moment he closed his eyes,
Aussitôt il n'y vit goutte.	He no longer saw a thing.

history, the masses, the working class are or are not *subjects*, with all the consequences that follow . . .[12]

As we shall see, the text 'Reply to John Lewis' (Althusser 1976b), together with the 'Notes toward an Investigation' published in 1970 in the journal *La Pensée* under the title 'Ideology and Ideological State Apparatuses' (Althusser 1971b) and also the recent 'Elements of Self-Criticism' (Althusser 1976a), go to the heart of the problem, *even if* and probably *because* they are only very incidentally concerned with the question of 'the meanings of words': Althusser says very little about linguistics, and nothing, to repeat, about 'semantics'. By contrast, he does talk about the *subject* and *meaning*, and here is what he says:

> Like all evident facts, including those that make a word 'name a thing' or 'have a meaning' (therefore including the evident fact of the 'transparency' of language), the 'evident fact' that you and I are subjects – and that that does not cause any problems – is an ideological effect, the elementary ideological effect (1971b, p. 161).

In other words, the evident fact states: words have a meaning because they have a meaning, and subjects are subjects because they are subjects: but behind the evident character there is the absurdity

Il fut par un triste sort	By a sad fate
Blessé d'une main cruelle.	He was wounded by a cruel hand.
On croit, puisqu'il en est mort,	Since he died of it, it is thought
Que la plaie était mortelle.	That the wound was a mortal one.
Il mourut le vendredi	He died on Friday,
Le dernier jour de son âge.	The last day of his life.
S'il fût mort le samedi	If he had died on Saturday
Il eût vécu davantage.	He would have lived longer.

12. For example, for the problem, opened up by the Twentieth Congress of the CPSU, of the 'cult of personality', and also for humanism, and the fusion of Marxist theory with the workers' movement. What Althusser says on this last point is in itself a 'reply' to the text by Schaff I quoted at the beginning:

> The union, or fusion of the Workers' Movement and Marxist theory is the greatest event in the history of class societies, i.e., practically in all human history. Beside it, the celebrated great scientific-technical 'mutation' constantly resounding in our ears (the atomic, electronic, computer era, the space-age, etc.), is, despite its great importance, no more than a scientific and technical fact (1972, pp. 164f.).

of a *vicious circle* in which one seems to be lifting oneself into the air by pulling on one's own hair, like Baron von Munchausen, a character less well-known to the French than Monsieur de la Palice, but one who is also worthy, in another way, of a place in semantics.[13]

This then is the framework of this study, which takes further a preliminary investigation into the relation between *linguistic system* and 'semantics' (Haroche, Henry and Pêcheux 1971): we shall find the anti-psychologistic positions of the logician Gottlob Frege[14] extremely precious, *up to a certain point which constitutes, as we shall see, the 'blind spot' of his idealism*. In addition, some aspects of the work of Jacques Lacan – in so far as he has made explicit and enriched Freud's materialism – will turn out to overlap with what I have said constitutes the essential element here, namely the directions opened up by Althusser, especially in the texts by him of 1970, 1973 and

---

13. La Palice, of course, delights in the evident. Munchausen, on the other hand, specialises in the absurd, which, as we shall see, comes strangely close to the evident:

> On another occasion, I wanted to get over a bog which did not initially strike me as so broad as I found it when already in the midst of my jump. Swinging round in mid-air, I returned to my starting point, in order to make a longer run up. Nonetheless, the second time as well I jumped too short, and fell not far from the other bank up to my neck in the mire. Here I would certainly have died, had I not dragged myself (together with my horse, which I held fast between my knees) out again by pulling with all the strength of one arm on a lock of my own hair (Raspe and Bürger 1786, pp. 54f.)

[This anecdote is not to be found in Raspe (1786), or in most subsequent English editions of Munchausen's memoirs; French and German versions, which usually have it, seem to derive from this first German translation: the German phrase 'sich am eigenen Schopfe aus dem Sumpfe zu ziehen' gave rise to (derives from?) this tale. Its English equivalent is 'to pull oneself up by one's own bootstraps'. Cf. n. 14 below – *Translator's Note*.]

14. Discussing the approach in psychological terms to logical questions, Frege wrote: 'This view leads necessarily to an idealist theory of knowledge (*zum erkenntnistheoretischen Idealismus*); for if it is correct, then the parts that we distinguish in a thought, such as subject and predicate, must belong as much to psychology as do thoughts themselves. Now since every act of cognition is realised in judgements, this means the breakdown of any bridge to the objective. And all out striving to attain to this can be no more than an attempt to draw ourselves up by our own bootstraps' ('*sich am eigenen Schopfe aus dem Sumpfe zu ziehen*' – literally 'pull ourselves out of the bog by our own hair') (Frege 1979, pp. 143f.).

1974 already quoted (Althusser 1971b, 1976b and 1976a respectively).

I shall examine first the historical development of the problem of *determination* (the relation between the determinative relative clause and the explicative relative clause) in its logico-philosophical and rhetorical aspects, from the seventeenth century to the present, demonstrating at the level of linguistics the consequences that have followed for the relation between 'theory of knowledge'[15] and rhetoric, this circular relation implying in various ways the covering up of the discontinuity between scientific knowledge and ideological effect of miscognition.

I shall then try to develop the consequences of a materialist position, in the element of a Marxist-Leninist theory of Ideology and Ideologies, for what I shall call here 'discursive processes'. The scientific elements (still only in an embryonic state) which I shall propose for the analysis of these processes will here be designated by the global name 'theory of discourse', without, I repeat, taking this for the claim to have founded a new discipline, between linguistics and historical materialism. Finally, I shall examine the effects these elements have, in their specificity, on two questions which are central to Marxism-Leninism, namely:

the question of the production of scientific knowledges,
the question of revolutionary proletarian political practice.

In Appendix 3, the English reader will find a text written during the French political winter of 1978–9. This text begins the necessary process of correcting certain aspects of the theses developed in the third and fourth parts and conclusion of the present book.

---

15. I have put this phrase in quotation marks to remind us of the ideological character of what it designates: 'The whole history of the "theory of knowledge" in Western philosophy, from the famous "Cartesian circle" to the circle of the Hegelian or Husserlian teleology of reason *shows* us that this "problem of knowledge" is a closed space, i.e., a vicious circle (the vicious circle of the mirror relation of ideological recognition)' (Althusser 1970, p. 53).

PART I

LINGUISTICS, LOGIC AND PHILOSOPHY OF LANGUAGE

I A Glance at the Historical Development of the Relationship between 'Theory of Knowledge' and Rhetoric in regard to the Problem of Determination

The seventeenth-century position on the logico-philosophical relationship between determination and explication is supplied by a passage from the Port-Royal *Logic*, which Noam Chomsky has recalled to attention with the following commentary:

> The theory of essential and incident propositions . . . is extended in the Port-Royal *Logic* with a more detailed analysis of relative clauses. There, a distinction is developed between *explicative* (non-restrictive or appositive) and *determinative* (restrictive) relative clauses. The distinction is based on a prior analysis of the 'comprehension' and 'extension' of 'universal ideas', in modern terms, an analysis of meaning and reference. The comprehension of an idea is the set of essential attributes that define it, together with whatever can be deduced from them; its extension is the set of objects that it denotes: 'The comprehension of an idea is the constituent parts which make up the idea, none of which can be removed without destroying the idea. For example, the idea of a triangle is made up of the idea of having three sides, the idea of having three angles, and the idea of having three angles whose sum is equal to two right angles, and so on. The extension of an idea is the objects to which the word expressing the idea can be

applied. The objects which belong to the extension of an idea are called the inferiors of that idea, which with respect to them is called the superior. Thus, the general idea of triangle has in its extension triangles of all kinds whatsoever' (Arnauld and Nicole 1964, p. 51). In terms of these notions, we can distinguish such 'explications' as *Paris, which is the largest city in Europe* and *man, who is mortal* from 'determinations' such as *transparent bodies, wise men* or *a body which is transparent, men who are pious* (Chomsky 1966, pp. 35f.).

To this philosophico-logical statement of the problem corresponds explicitly the exposition in the *General and Rational Grammar* of Arnauld and Lancelot, as the *Avertissement* added to its second edition in fact points out: 'We are pleased to announce that since the first edition of this book, there has appeared a work called *Logic, or the Art of Thinking*, which, being founded on the same principles, can very usefully serve to cast light on it and to prove various things which are treated in it' (Arnauld and Lancelot 1664, p. 157). On reading this latter book, it is indeed clear that grammar (or the art of speaking) is homogeneous with logic (or the art of thinking), in so far as the same principles are set to work in both.

In Part Two Chapter IX, 'Of the Pronoun Called Relative', the authors of the *General and Rational Grammar* propose that this pronoun, while having something in common with the other pronouns (the fact that it can be put in the place of a noun), also has 'something particular' which can be considered in two ways:

The 1. is, that it always has a relation to another noun or pronoun, called the antecedent; as, *God who is holy*: . . . The 2. thing particular to the relative, and which I don't remember to have ever been observed, is, that the proposition into which it enters (and which may be called accessary) may constitute part of the subject, or of the attribute of another proposition, which may be called the principal.

This cannot be rightly understood, without recollecting what has been mentioned already in the commencement of this discourse: that in every proposition there is a subject, namely, that of which something is affirmed; and an attribute, that which is affirmed of something. But these two terms may be either simple, as when I say *God is good*; or complex, as when I say, *an able magistrate is a man useful to the republic*. For that, of which I affirm in this last proposition, is not only *a magistrate*, but *an able magistrate*. And what I affirm, is, that not only he is a man, but moreover, *that he is a man useful to the republic* (Arnauld and Lancelot 1753, pp. 62f.).

Referring to the *Logic* ('On Complex Propositions', Part Two Chapters iii, iv, v and vi), the authors go on to state that this union of several terms in the subject or the attribute does not prevent the proposition from being simple from a logical point of view, so long as it contains *only one judgement or affirmation*: it is as if an entity (or class of entities) were labelled by its union with a substance of characteristic properties, the entity (or class of entities) being thus determined as a species within a genus. This being so, the relative proposition does not make the 'intire subject' or 'intire predicate'; 'but we must join with it the word, whose place the relative supplies, in order to make the subject intire'. The reader will have recognised here the principle of the *relation of determination* which Arnauld and Lancelot implicitly recognise as realisable equally well by a relative construction, an adjectival phrase (the example above) or by a noun complement (Arnauld and Lancelot's example, p. 63: '*The valour of Achilles has been the cause of the taking of Troy*').

They go on:

But at other times these propositions, whose subject or attribute are composed of several terms, include at least in the mind, several judgements, out of which so many propositions may be formed: as when I say; *the invisible God has created the visible world*; there are three judgements formed in my mind, all included in this proposition. For 1. I judge that *God is invisible*. 2. That *he has created the world*. 3. That the *world is visible* . And of those three propositions, the second is the principal and essential. But the first and third are accessary ones, which form but a part of the principal, the first constituting the subject, and the last the attribute (p. 64).

Such then, for the Port-Royal grammarians, is the definition of the *explicative relation* as opposed to the former; it is immediately visible that these two relations do not have the same status with respect to seventeenth-century ontology. In fact, it can be said that the determinative relation, through the action of the relationship between comprehension and extension, is concerned exclusively with the order of being, the world of essences, *without any addition from thought*: we are on a level at which being itself designates itself.

The explicative relation intervenes, on the contrary, as an *incidence of thought* on the order of essences. (The term 'accessary' – '*incidente*' in the French – used by Arnauld and Lancelot in the passage quoted above, should strictly speaking henceforth be reserved for explication.) It is here that light can be cast on the relationship between 'theory of knowledge' and rhetoric as far as the seventeenth century is concerned: as Michel Foucault shows in his introduction to the Port-Royal *Grammar*: 'Grammar is not to be taken as the prescriptions of a legislator, at last giving the chaos of utterances (*paroles*) their constitution and laws . . . it is a discipline which states the rules to which any language (*langue*) must conform for it to be able to exist' (Foucault 1969, p. XIII). In other words, logic (and the 'theory of knowledge' that corresponds to it) is the first foundation, and 'the art of speaking' has no other aim than to conform to the rules that constitute that logic, as rules immanent in the very order of essences. In this view, the *correct use of speech* is to bring the subject back to the truths of the world of essences: the 'art of speaking' is constitutively pedagogical: *explication* thus becomes *the means by which to reduce the discrepancy* between my thought and the entities to which my discourse refers, i.e., at the grammatical level, between what Foucault calls the 'mother tongue' (or at least that part of the mother tongue which is acquired in childhood) and the language to be learned (or at least the rules of the mother tongue that have as yet been neither used nor understood).

In so far as explication thus consists in 'restoring the rules to their foundation', one can say that good rhetoric is at the service of a pedagogy of truth: the *rhetoric of figures* then appears at one and the same time as a system of errors pedagogically necessary to attain the truth, and coextensively as the constant danger of straying from the truth, of an anabasis of man at the mercy of his imagination (and of non-being).

This subordination of speaking to the order which alone allows it to be formulated, i.e., the subordination of the fields of grammar and rhetoric to that of knowledge, is marked, finally, in the seventeenth-century conception of the relationship which the speaking subject maintains with his discourse. I think it permissible to see this restrospectively as the absolutely deliberate absence of any theory of enunciation (I define this term on p. 39), as is clear from the beginning of Part Two Chapter VIII of the *Grammar* ('Of Pronouns'):

> As men are obliged to mention frequently the same things in discourse, and it would have been *troublesome* to repeat always the same nouns; they have invented certain words to supply the places of those nouns, and which are therefore called *pronouns*. In the first place they perceived, that it was often *needless and indecent* to name themselves: Hence they introduced the pronoun of the first person, to supply the name of the person that speaks: *Ego, I* (Arnauld and Lancelot 1753, p. 54 – ['troublesome' and 'needless and indecent', emphasis mine, M.P.]).

The position of the subject is simply the effect of a rule, one both of etiquette and of economy, it is completely dependant on the enounced and is logically reduced to it.

Let us now examine the shift that has taken place since the seventeenth century. I shall take for a reference point the philosophy of the eighteenth century (and the theory of language which corresponds to it) to demonstrate that they constitute a true 'transitional form' in the shift I am analysing. The distinction between *essential properties* and *contingent properties* did not disappear with the seventeenth century: Leibniz is appealing to it when he separates truths of reasoning (or necessary truths) and truths of fact (or contingent truths):

> There are also two kinds of *truths*: truths of *reasoning* and truths of *fact*. Truths of reasoning are necessary and their opposite is impossible; those of fact are contingent and their opposite is possible. When a truth is necessary, the reason for it can be found by analysis, that is, by resolving it into simpler ideas and truths until the primary ones are reached . . . But a *sufficient reason* must also be found in the case of *contingent truths* or *truths of fact*; that is to say, in the case of the series of things spread over the universe of created things; otherwise resolution into particular reasons might go on into endless detail on account of the immense variety of things in nature and the division of bodies *ad infinitum*. There are an infinite number of shapes and motions, both present and past, which enter into the efficient cause of my present writing; and there are an infinite number of minute inclinations and dis-

positions of my soul, both present and past, which enter into its final cause (Leibniz 1973, p. 184).

Let me begin by recalling what Leibniz means by resolving a necessary truth into simpler ideas and truths: it is in fact to bring out the *determinations* of an idea. Yvon Belaval writes:

> For Leibniz to understand means to analyse, and . . . since the idea God has of the triangle is expressed in me, analytically contained in this expression must be *all* the properties of the triangle, and, known or unknown, knowable or unknowable to us, they must all have their effects in it: and that is why the idea is defined by the ability to 'recollect', according to the doctrine of the *Meno*, the various properties of the triangle, when the occasion to do so arises (Belaval 1960, p. 151).

What then is the status of 'contingent truths', which precisely cannot be reduced to axioms, concatenating by calculus definientes to their definitions according to the law of the substitution of identicals? What relationships do the irreducible truths of religion, ethics, diplomacy and history have to mathematical truths, which are reducible to their axioms? It is at this point, for our purposes here, that eighteenth-century philosophy made the shift, a shift that Leibniz achieved in his own way, with respect to the concepts of seventeenth-century rationalism: formulated in the terms already introduced, we can say that, for Leibniz, this shift consists in *reducing, from God's point of view, all explicative relations to determinative relations*; the 'sufficient reason' which, unlike analytic reason, man cannot grasp in all its details in his thought, is thus referred to this super-calculus which is inaccessible to man and determines the secret necessity of contingent facts.

Let me explain, using an example adapted from Leibniz. Take the statement: 'Sextus Tarquinius, who insisted on going to Rome, contributed (by his rape of Lucretia) to the fall of the monarchy.' The 'accessary' relative clause explains the historical role of Sextus by his contingent decision to go to Rome. If he had not gone, the face of the world would have been changed. Now this contingent fact 'Sextus insisted on going to Rome', which seems separate from Sextus's real 'substance', is treated by Leibniz as a *determination*, by means of the fiction of the infinity of possible worlds; and here is what is said by the goddess Pallas as she shows human visitors round the pyramid of possible worlds:

Thus you can picture to yourself an ordered succession of worlds, which shall contain each and every one the case that is in question, and shall vary its circumstances and its consequences . . . I will show you some, wherein shall be found, not absolutely the same Sextus as you have seen (that is not possible, he carries with him always that which he shall be) but several Sextuses resembling him, possessing all that you know already of the true Sextus, but not all that is already in him imperceptibly, nor in consequence all that shall yet happen to him. You will find in one world a very happy and noble Sextus, in another a Sextus content with a mediocre state, a Sextus, indeed, of every kind and endless diversity of forms (Leibniz 1951, p. 371).

So if Sextus' decision to go to Rome seems contingent to us, that is because our minds are incapable of discerning *which Sextus we are dealing with*, that is, of recognising all the determinations which characterise it, in contrast to all the other possible Sextuses. Note the grammatical effects of this logical fiction; the proper name Sextus cannot as such support grammatically any relative clause but an appositional one; the appearance of indefinite pronouns (*one of the Sextuses who* . . . etc.) and determiners such as *a* Sextus, *some* Sextuses, *the other* Sextuses, etc., like the appearance of the determinative relation itself are produced by the fiction of a series of characters with the same name, which is the common noun for them. It is as if grammar here, in a certain sense, masked the truth and bore the traces of our lack of discernment, our 'blindness'. And, in fact, Leibniz's theory of language starts from the principle that there was once an 'Adamic language' which plainly revealed the natural order common to angels, to men and to all intelligences in general, but of which contemporary languages only retain a distorted trace in partial correspondences between logic and grammar. An immense effort of decoding is therefore necessary to ascend to the lost origin, and in this sense Leibniz clearly belongs to the same theoretical configuration as the 'empiricist' philosophers of the eighteenth century,[1] despite his quarrels with them about the

---

1. By his introduction of the problematic of the 'possible worlds', Leibniz decentred the seventeenth century's world of eternal truths. He thereby introduced a *principle of variation* which is the rationalist counterpart to the empirical principle of the *tabula rasa*, according to which there are no *a priori* truths.

origins of ideas (cf. Leibniz 1896), as can be seen, moreover, in this quotation from an essay by Maupertuis of 1748:

> Since languages have departed from this original simplicity, and there are perhaps no longer people in the World savage enough to instruct us in the search for the pure truth which each generation has obscured, and on the other hand, the first moments of my existence cannot help me in this search . . . , since, then, I am deprived of these means for my instruction and am obliged to accept a multitude of established expressions, or at least to use them, let us try to make out their meaning, their force and their scope; let us ascend to the origin of languages and see by what stages they have been formed (Maupertuis 1970, p. 31).

This question of the origin of languages, which so preoccupied all science and philosophy in the eighteenth century, will in fact lead us gradually to *the 'modern' problem of enunciation*; indeed, it is here that the infinite variety of languages and ideas (a variety which disputes the edifice of seventeenth-century reason) will find its unique origin, via a sensualist and utilitarian anthropology whose essential thesis is that our ideas come from our senses and our needs. It is therefore necessary, in order to understand the origin of language, associated with the faculty of thought, to ascend to the 'state of nature', a new and empiricist fiction that can be said to mirror Leibniz's rationalist fiction (concerning the relationship proper name/common noun). Here is one of the countless examples of this fiction, from Adam Smith:

> Two savages, who had never been taught to speak, but had been bred up remote from the societies of men, would naturally begin to form that language by which they would endeavour to make their mutual wants intelligible to each other, by uttering certain sounds, whenever they meant to denote certain objects. Those objects only which were most familiar to them, and which they had most frequent occasion to mention [a cave, a tree, a fountain] would have particular names assigned to them . . . Afterwards, when the more enlarged experience of these savages had led them to observe, and their necessary associations obliged them to make mention of, other caves, and other trees, and other fountains, they would naturally bestow, upon each of these new objects, the same name, by which they had been accustomed to express the similar

object they were first acquainted with . . . And thus, those words, which were originally the proper names of individuals, would each of them insensibly become the common name of a multitude (Smith 1767, pp. 437f).

The beginning of language is therefore the production of those sounds emitted in relation to immediate objects, and at the command of needs; but this language itself is the natural extension of what Condillac in 1775 called the *language of action*, namely 'that which nature imposes on us by virtue of the configuration she has given our organs' (Condillac 1970, p. 197). Now, the way Condillac conceives the combination of the gestures of the 'language of action' and the sounds of articulated language provides a résumé of how the rudiments of a theory of enunciation are now beginning to emerge:

> It is clear that each man, while saying for example *fruit eat*, could show, by the language of action, whether he was speaking of himself, of the person he was addressing, or of somebody else; and it is no less evident that his gestures then were the equivalent of the words *I, you, he*. He thus had distinct ideas of what we call the first, the second and the third person; and he who understood his thoughts had the same ideas of these persons as he did. Why could it not then be that sooner or later they agreed together to express these ideas by certain articulated sounds? (1970, pp. 204f.).

I shall return to the consequences of this shift, by which the subject, *subordinate* to the truth of his discourse in the seventeenth century, gradually became the *source* of that discourse, in so far as he was a bundle of needs, fears and desires; I now have to expound the last link in the historical development I am examining, namely the appearance of philosophies of subjectivity, with a corresponding 'theory of knowledge' and, we shall see, a new function for language and rhetoric.

The philosophies of the nineteenth and twentieth centuries have developed fully the contents that had appeared in what I have called the 'transitional form' of the eighteenth century, with respect both to the 'theory of knowledge' and to the philosophy of language and the linguistics that corresponds to it: the resultant new conceptual form, dominated by the category of *subjectivity*, appears in the reworking that Kant and his successors performed on the Aristotelian opposition between contingent and necessary, via the question of the inherence of the predicate in the subject (or concept) to which it applies. Remember the distinction Kant introduced between *analytic* judgements and *synthetic* judgements in these terms:

> In all judgements in which the relation of a subject to the predicate is thought . . . this relation is possible in two different ways. Either the predicate B belongs to the subject A, as something which is (covertly) contained in this concept A; or B lies outside the concept A, although it does indeed stand in connection with it. In the one case I entitle the judgement *analytic*, in the other *synthetic* (1933, p. 48).[2]

It is worth emphasising that for Kant the *analytic* judgement consists of the awareness of a *necessary* relation, inscribed in the concept itself (i.e., a truth by definition or one reducible by calculus to an identity), whereas, and this is the decisive new element, the *synthetic* judgement is an *act* of the subject who posits a connection between the concept and something outside it. Hence Kant's claim: 'Judgements of experience, as such, are one and all synthetic' (1933, p. 49).

This new conception of the relationship between necessary and contingent, and the notion of *an act of the subject* that came to be attached to it, linking subjectivity and contingency, constitute the common foundation of 'modern' thought, in which the links between logico-philosophical reflection and preoccupations with the nature of language become ever closer, as is shown by the otherwise so divergent writings of Husserl on the one hand and Frege on the other. Here is a short quotation from the latter, showing how the category of subjectivity is introduced into the problematic of the necessary and the contingent:

> But we may be inclined to distinguish between essential and inessential properties and to regard something as timeless if the changes it undergoes involve only inessential properties. A property of a thought will be called inessential if it consists in, or follows from, the fact that this thought is grasped by a thinker (Frege 1977c, p. 28).

2. Remember that Kant conceives of the existence of 'synthetic *a priori* judgements' (linked to the transcendental forms of the intuition of space and time), which the logical empiricists were to reject, identifying the analytic with deduction and the synthetic with observation.

I shall have to return later to the specificity of Frege's work and the anti-subjectivism it manifests.[3] But it will do for the moment to emphasise the *apparent similarity* between this statement and Husserl's reflections in his *Logical Investigations* which, as it were, take us to the heart of the matter, for there Husserl makes explicit his relationship with what I have called the 'transitional form' of Leibnizianism:

> There is undeniably a subjective, experiential distinction which corresponds to the fundamental objective-ideal distinction between law and fact . . . Leibniz's *vérités de raison* are merely the laws, i.e., the ideal truths in the pure and strict sense, which are solely rooted in our concepts, which are given and known to us in pure, apodeictically evident generalisations. Leibniz's *vérités de fait* are individual truths; they form a sphere of propositions which, even if expressed in universal form, e.g. 'All Southerners are hot-blooded', are, above all, assertions of existence (Husserl 1970b, vol. 1, p. 154).

This passage, which clearly reveals Husserl's phenomenology's descent from Port-Royal theses, also suggests the nature of the historical shift that has taken place; without destroying the seventeenth-century opposition between necessary and contingent, a new opposition, characteristic of modern philosophical idealism, has been superimposed on it, an opposition that can be summed up in the couple: objective/subjective. It is best here to give the definitions provided by Husserl himself:

> *Definition 1* ('objective expression'): We shall call an expression *objective* if it pins down (or can pin down) its meaning merely by its manifest, auditory pattern, and can be understood without necessarily directing one's attention to the person uttering it, or to the circumstances of the utterance . . . Among objective expressions we have, e.g., all expressions in theory, expressions out

3. Reviewing Husserl's *Philosophie der Arithmetik*, Frege concluded as follows: 'If a geographer were to read a treatise on oceanography in which the origin of the oceans was explained in psychological terms, he would surely gain the impression that the author had missed the point in a very odd way. That is exactly the impression I have of this book. Certainly the sea is something real, which number is not; but that does not prevent the latter being something objective; and that is the important point' (1967, p. 192).

of which the principles and theorems, the proofs and theories of the 'abstract' sciences are made up. What, e.g., a mathematical expression means, is not in the least affected by the circumstances of our actual use of it (1970b, vol. 1, pp. 314f.).

Definition 2 ('subjective expression'): On the other hand, we call an expression essentially subjective and occasional, or more briefly, *essentially occasional*, if it belongs to a conceptually unified group of possible meanings, in whose case it is essential to orient actual meaning to the occasion, the speaker and the situation (1970b, vol. 1, p. 315).

This reveals the close link I mentioned between logic, 'theory of knowledge' and philosophy of language, the notion of enunciation being at the centre of this new configuration.[4] It is impossible not to recognise in this text of Husserl's the direct 'philosophical' correlate of the 'linguistic' opposition between situational properties and permanent properties, expressed, for example, in the use of the 'be – ing' test applied to utterances to determine whether or not they are situational.[5]

We shall see later that this correspondence is not at all accidental, and that Husserl's philosophical consideration of subjective expressions leads him to formulate remarks strangely similar to those

4. An example of this link between theory of knowledge and philosophy of language is provided by Oswald Ducrot's attempt to define contrastively presuppositions and implicature (Ducrot 1969). Ducrot counterposes *langue* (seen as a 'tool') and *parole* (seen as the use of that tool), presuppositions belonging to the former and implicature to the latter. A reading of the article reveals the following oppositions:

IMPLICATURE	PRESUPPOSITION
fact of *parole* (or discourse)	fact of *langue*
enunciation	*enounced*
to be treated in a	to be treated in a
rhetorical component	*linguistic* component
bound to the *situation*	always *true*
notions of the *speaking subjects*	*arbitrary*
later (both in actual production and at the level of the model)	*earlier*

5. (a) the postman hurries by → the postman is hurrying by; (b) the three perpendiculars of a triangle intersect in one point → *the three perpendiculars of a triangle are intersecting in one point.

   The second example is from Husserl, who comments: 'What this assertion asserts is the same whoever may assert it, and on whatever occasion or in whatever circumstances he may assert it' (1970b, vol. 1, p. 285).

made by linguists[6] dealing with the problem of the relationship between situation, enunciation and determination.

Indeed, commenting on what he has defined as subjective expression, Husserl goes on: 'every expression, in fact, that includes a *personal pronoun* lacks an objective meaning' (1970b, vol. 1, p. 315), and he adds a little later: 'what is true of personal pronouns is of course also true of demonstratives' (1970b, vol. 1, p. 316), and then: 'In the sphere of essentially occasional expressions one has also the subject-bound determinations "here", "there", "above", "below", "now", "yesterday", "tomorrow", "later", etc.' (1970b, vol. 1, p. 317).

He adds further:

> An essentially occasional character naturally spreads to all expressions which include these and similar representations as parts: this includes all the manifold speech forms where the speaker gives normal expression to something concerning himself, or which is thought of in relation to himself. All expressions for percepts, beliefs, doubts, wishes, hopes, fears, commands belong here, as well as all combinations involving the *definite article*, in which the latter relates to something individual and merely pinned down by class– or property– concepts. When we Germans speak of *the* Kaiser we of course mean the present German Kaiser. When we ask for *the* lamp in the evening, each man means his own (1970b, vol. 1, p. 318).

6. Some linguists explicitly formulate the opposition objective/subjective. For example, Klaus Heger (1964, 1965) establishes a classification of concepts on the basis of an opposition between deictic concepts expressing 'the subjective point of view of the speaker' and definitional concepts expressing 'objective differences between events'.

   The first type of concepts should be conceived, argues Heger, as fixed points linked to the enunciating subject (the 'I-here-now'), while the second may be designated by 'formal categories'. But this latter point seems much less clear when it is realised that Heger classifies as deictic concepts the phenomena of tense and aspect (marked grammatically in Russian by morphological oppositions), and as definitional concepts those known as phenomena of mode of action or order of process (lexicographic oppositions), which, even ignoring the philosophical position that such a procedure presupposes, reveals a considerable lack of understanding of the relationship between lexicon and grammar.

   I have taken these remarks from Fuchs (1970). More extended analyses of this question can be found there, especially pp. 50ff.

Finally, Husserl gives other examples of 'fluctuating' (essentially occasional) expressions: 'No one would understand the sentence "There are cakes" as he understands the mathematical sentence "There are regular solids". In the first case we do not mean that cakes exist absolutely and in general, but that there are cakes *here* and *now* – for coffee' (1970b, vol. 1, p. 319). It is well known that Husserl distinguished between the 'psychological experience' and the ideality of logico-mathematical objects, this to avoid the trap of 'sceptical relativism' in the sciences and especially mathematics.[7] Yet can we say that Husserl is on the same epistemological positions as Frege, with his notorious Platonic intransigence? 'A traveller who crosses a mountain-range does not thereby make the mountain-range; no more does the judging subject make a thought by acknowledging its truth' (Frege 1952c, p. 127; 1977b, p. 43). It seems that Frege marks himself off from Husserl vis-à-vis a decisive point to which I shall return: *the relationship between the subject and his representations*. Husserl expresses this relationship in terms like 'unity of consciousness' or 'experience of consciousness', etc., making consciousness the zero point, the 'origin' of representations; Frege, by contrast, constantly insists that, if representations are linked to the subject, that is only in so far as he is their *bearer*, which suggests that they could not find any origin in him:

> The field and the frogs in it, the sun which shines on them, are there no matter whether I look at them or not, but the sense-impression I have of green exists only because of me, I am its bearer. It seems absurd to us that a pain, a mood, a wish should go around the world without a bearer . . . The inner world presupposes somebody whose inner world it is (Frege 1977c, p. 14).

Now, of these two conceptions – Husserl's conception of subjectivity as *source and unifying principle of representations*, and Frege's conception of the subject as *bearer of representations* – it is clear that historically the first has constantly dominated and obscured the second, from Kant to the present, so that the romantic myth of creation and the author (the unique 'ego' who expresses himself, etc.) emerges as the literary reflection of this philosophical subjectivity; subjectivity becomes both the contingent surplus that overflows the concept, and the indispensable precondition for the

7. On this point, see Husserl's critique of the principle of 'economy of thought' so dear to Mach and Avenarius (Husserl 1970b, vol. 1, pp. 204–7).

expression of the concept – a position suggested in the following passage by Wilhelm von Humboldt:

> The bare idea, devoid of all it derives from expression, offers at best a dry instruction. The most remarkable works, analysed in this fashion, would give a most mediocre result. It is the way the ideas are rendered and presented, the mind is encouraged to meditation, the soul is moved, and new channels of thought and emotion are revealed to it, which transmits, not just the doctrines, but the very intellectual force which has produced them, from age to age down to a remote posterity. What, in the art of writing, intimately linked to the nature of the language in which it is practised, expression lends to the idea cannot be detached from it without appreciably weakening it; the thought is the same only in the form in which it was conceived by its author (Humboldt 1906, p. 288).

It can be said that the sanitary operation whereby 'living experience' is separated from concepts has had the indirect consequence of installing subjectivity as the principle of explanation for what Husserl calls 'occasional', non-objective expressions; it is as if in this domain the rule that: 'for each man that is true which seems to *him* true, one thing to one man and the opposite to another, if that is how he sees it' (Husserl 1970b, vol. 1, p.138) had been restored to full authority, and thereby left open the possibility of a *rhetoric* in which even the terms *situation, enunciation* and *determination* would reappear with a new function, linked to the expression of the subject in confrontation with another subject. I say that this is a *rhetoric*, although it is no longer one in the sense of the seventeenth-century theory of figures, which presupposed a distance between thought and expression and a dependence of the latter on the former; in this sense rhetoric did indeed disappear in the nineteenth century, but gave way to an *art of expression* which, as von Humboldt says in the passage quoted, is 'intimately linked to the nature of the language in which it is practised', which is another way of saying that language (*langue*) is created in expression.

It is not surprising, then, to find, on the border between linguistics and literary studies, the erection of *theories of the speaking subject in situ*, mixing romantic expressions with the 'modern' terminology of communication: Maurice Dessaintes' study *La Construction par insertion incidente* (1960) provides a good example. Wishing to characterise the phychological bases of the insert (or explication), he writes:

> It is the situation, the ambience, the act of communication which leads to the momentary interruption of a proposition or a sentence, i.e., of a global representation. The content of such an act is of an intellectual order, it appeals to the intelligence. But the two poles, speaker and hearer, are not only an emitting mind and a receiving mind, they are also temperaments, bodies, souls which *vibrate*, at different intensities and to different degrees, at the contact with the reality communicated (1960, p. 152).

It is worth adding, finally, that this theory of the speaking subject in situ applied to the problem of accessary (or 'explicative') relatives leads Dessaintes to formulations which constitute a kind of *psychologistic counterpart to Husserl's positions*, as can be seen from the following assertions:

> Accessary insertion plays an interesting part in the expression of subjectivity . . . We take the adjective 'modal' in the sense of: relating to the way (*modus*) that the speaking and writing subject presents the fact stated, or the way that subject is affected by what he states. We call *modalities* the sum of linguistic procedures which make this subjective expression possible; the repercussion of a fact stated on he who states it (1960, p. 59).

This expressive function of the accessary clause is accompanied by one of reaction to:

> the presence of another, listener or reader, to be convinced, persuaded, enlightened. And it is in this psychological perspective that one must interpret the accessary clauses I have called objective: it is his concern to enlighten the other, to pre-empt his objections or reactions, that compels the speaker to interrupt the discursive development of his utterance, to insert into it circumstantial details, objective in themselves, but subjective in relation to the motive which induced their introduction into this unwonted place (1960, p. 58).

The reader familiar with contemporary research in the semantic domain will no doubt object that the historical panorama I have just given is incomplete, if not futile; surely, with Saussure, then Harris and Chomsky, the relations between logic and linguistics have been transformed, and semantic studies so revolutionised that the history of this discipline only began, properly speaking, some fifteen years ago? The article I referred to at the beginning (Haroche, Henry and Pêcheux 1971) sets out (in the case of Saussure) the reasons why such a conception must, it seems, be rejected: these reasons are to be found in the effects of the break made by Saussure in linguistics, in so far as that break reinforced substantialist and subjectivist illusions in the domain of semantics, in the form of the ideological couple creativity/system. This is only apparently a paradox:

> If the Saussurian break was sufficient to allow the constitution of phonology, morphology and syntax, it could not prevent a return to empiricism in semantics. On the contrary, it seems even that the development of phonology made this return possible by providing a *model* which allowed the reinterpretation in a formalist framework of very traditional conceptions of semantics (p. 94).

In short, a return to empiricism, refurbished by formalism. I shall not re-examine here the reversal in the relationship between *signification* and *value* which followed from the role which Saussure assigned to *parole* with respect to 'analogical creation'; I shall simply recall the conclusion we reached: Saussure left open a door through which flowed formalism and subjectivism; this open door was *Saussure's conception of the idea as something impossible except as completely subjective and individual.* Hence the opposition between the creative subjectivity of *parole* and the systematic objectivity of *langue*, an opposition which has the circular properties of an ideological couple:

> Creativity presupposes the existence of a system it can destroy, and every system is only the resultant effect of a previous creativity. The notion of system, whether it characterises a realist classification of the objective properties of reality, or designates a principle of vision, an organisation of reality for a subject (psychological, anthropological, historical, aesthetic, etc.), thus seems the indispensable complement to creativity in the 'field of language' (Haroche, Henry and Pêcheux 1971, p. 98).

In short, in the couple *langue/parole*, the term *parole* reacts on that of *langue*, overloading the systematicity characteristic of the latter (phonological, morphological and syntactic) with the supposedly extra-linguistic systematicity of thought as a reflection or vision of 'reality'. The 'subject of science' is not far away.

I believe these remarks could be extended in this domain to the *semantic* studies of Chomsky and his school, even though, as is well known, the opposition between competence and performance does not exactly parallel that between *langue* and *parole*: in fact, its presuppositions are the same as those I have just examined, as is shown, moreover, by the present convergence of the *structural semantics* inspired, mainly in Europe, by Saussurian structuralism, with *generative semantics*, the most recent development of Chomskyism. The sceptical reader can refer, for example, to Ferenc Kiefer (1966, 1973 and 1974; cf. also Bierwisch and Kiefer 1969).

It could also be shown that the couple creativity/system continues to haunt the ideas of the linguist Zellig Harris, including his most recent works, which incidentally are very interesting for the linguistic perspective within which I would locate myself (see Appendix 2); here I would refer the reader to his 1969 paper 'The Two Systems of Grammar: Report and Paraphrase' (Harris 1970) in which the author, wishing to characterise the difference between 'incremental transformations' (in which a non-equivalent utterance is produced by adding something to an utterance) and 'paraphrastic transformations' (which reformulate an utterance in another equivalent one), suggests that this difference 'is roughly that between the directly useable activities of life and the institutional apparatus which channelizes these activities' (p. 677).

I shall not examine this point in detail to show how the different historical elements I have identified are reincorporated, with different emphases and alternations, in current semantic theories, but rest content to insist on two essential aspects which suggest that these theories are in fact still on the old terrain whose fundamental components we have examined (from Port-Royal to phenomenology).

The first point common to structural and generative semantics is the idea of a semantic combinatory capable of determining by a calculus the meaning or meanings of an utterance; the system of *semantic markers* (in the sense of Katz and Fodor) is in principle homogeneous with the system of *langue* and has the same functional characteristics (destruction of the system if an element is removed, etc.) transposed to the conceptual level. But this Cartesio-Leibnizian perspective, for which the speaking subject spontaneously calculates, has a limit in the existence of the 'context' and the 'situation', which prevent the 'closure of the system' by constituting a *residue* whose reduction is radically impossible (hence the resort to contextual semantic features, the recognition of the non-systematic uniqueness of *distinguishers* as opposed to the systematicity of *semantic markers*, etc.). This already introduces the second characteristic point of current semantic theories, designated to us as it were by duality: in fact this is the theory of enunciation[8] as the *theory of this residue* inherent in the existence of the 'speaking subject' in situ; it contains a mixture of elements, some relating to anaphoric designation,[9] others to indexical (extra-linguistic) designation,[10] and others concerning the position of the subject with respect to the situation and/or the enounced produced in this situation (evaluative and emotive modalisations, etc.). In other words, enunciation designates both the fact that the subject is the support for his enounced *and* the set of subjective effects (different psychological contents) which underlie that enounced.

It is sufficient for my purposes to emphasise the fact that the ideological circle system/speaking-subject constitutes the invariant of the different forms taken by 'semantics' today. This explains why contemporary linguistics spontaneously conceives the field of language as distributed along an axis whose two poles are respectively the set of scientific statements on the one hand, and, on the other, conversation (or everyday language). I may add that the spontaneous philosophy which dominates linguistic researches today presupposes that this distribution occupies a continuum

---

8. *Enunciation* (*énonciation*): the act by which enounced utterances (*énoncés*), sentences, sequences, etc., are realised, assumed by a particular speaker, in precise spatio-temporal circumstances. The presence in the enounced of linguistic elements such as *I, You, here, now*, . . . manifests the link between enounced and enunciation (cf. Ducrot and Todorov 1972, pp. 405f.).

9. *Anaphore*: 'A segment of discourse is said to be anaphoric when it is necessary, in order to give it an interpretation, . . . to refer to another segment of the same discourse' (Ducrot and Todorov 1972, p. 358). As well as the trivial example: 'I saw *Peter. He* told me that . . . ', there are others which are much more complex.

10. *Indexical designation*: the term indexical designation is used when an understanding of an utterance necessitates 'information' about the 'situation', for example when it is essential to know who 'I' and 'you' are, and what 'this' is, in the sentence 'I am going to show you this'.

running from the perceptible to the intelligible, or, if you prefer, from *situational properties* to *permanent properties* (or else from practical language to theoretical or formulation language, to use the expressions of the Prague Linguistics Circle).[11]

Let me sum up: an immensely long trajectory, throughout whose length, from the philosophy of Aristotle to the 'scientific' discipline that goes today by the name *semantics* (via the writings of Port-Royal and phenomenology), two threads have constantly intersected: that of *analytics* (the rules of demonstrative reasoning which give access to knowledge) and that of *rhetoric* (the art enabling one to convince by use of the verisimilitudinous); a trajectory which, *in its very development*, seems condemned constantly to retrace its own steps.

What is the reason for this strange circularity produced within the appearances of a development? 'One may well ask,' as they say. Allow me to attempt an answer.

11. 'Two centres of gravity: one in which language is "situation-bound", i.e., relies on the complement of extra-linguistic elements (practical language), the other in which language aims to constitute as closed a whole as possible, tending to constitute itself as complete and precise, to use terminological words and judgement-sentences (theoretical or formulation language)' (cit. Ducrot and Todorov 1972, p. 409).

2 Metaphysical Realism and Logical Empiricism: Two Forms of the Regressive Exploitation of the Sciences by Idealism

A first observation: the philosophical position according to which thought and language derive first from experience and second from deduction is not restricted to the spontaneous effects it has in the practice of the linguist: it exists in an autonomous philosophical form with its own 'solution to the problem' of the relationship between 'theory of knowledge' and 'rhetoric'. Hence the spontaneous continuism of linguistics in epistemological matters is based on a philosophical continuism running from the 'given' to the 'deduced', with the proviso that one can *apprehend the given correctly or incorrectly* and that one can *deduce correctly or incorrectly*, which provides a means by which to distinguish between what is science and what is not, and to decide, by internal criteria, whether or not a discourse is scientific. In order to understand the effects of this spontaneous philosophy[1] (and as we shall see later, in order to attempt to protect oneself from it), it remains therefore to examine how its categories operate in relationship to the two spaces which I have hitherto called 'theory of knowledge' and 'rhetoric'.

The theoretical problem of the relationship between the two 'spaces' considered was not *explicitly* singled out for discussion by seventeenth-century philosophy; but, by virtue of the historical

1. For the expression 'spontaneous philosophy', see Althusser (1974a, pp. 99f.): 'By the spontaneous philosophy of scientists I mean not the set of ideas that scientists have about the world (i.e., their "conception of the world") but only the ideas they have in their heads (consciously or not) which concern their scientific practice and science.'

review carried out above, it can be said that the question was implicitly raised both in the perspective of Cartesian realism and in that of empiricism and subjectivism. To be more precise, it seems that these two branches of philosophical idealism have constantly tried to provide 'solutions' enabling them to impose a unity on these two heterogeneous spaces, by destroying the discrepancy between them.

As has just been shown, the solution of rationalist idealism lay in principle in the ideal subordination of the contingent to the necessary, even though this subordination has taken different forms historically:

The Port-Royal school, as I have said, was concerned to suppress the discrepancy between thought and truth, not so much 'by classifying all possible objects into broad predefined types, but by multiplying ad libitum the forms and levels of the representation of an object, so as to be able to analyse it, setting out to decompose, combine and arrange it. A logic of ideas, signs and judgements replaced the logic of concepts, categories and proofs' (Foucault 1969, p. xviii).

Leibnizianism took further the development of this 'logic of ideas' (not without making in certain respects a paradoxical regression to scholasticism and the theories of the 'schoolmen') into a theory of representation that would allow us to conceive the secret necessity of what appears to us to be contingent.

Finally, the principle of the subordination of the contingent to the necessary takes, in the element of modern idealism, the form of the subordination of the subjective to the objective:

> *Ideally* speaking, each subjective expression is replaceable by an objective expression which will preserve the identity of each momentary meaning-intention . . . Everything that is, can be known 'in itself'. Its being is a being definite in content, and documented in such and such 'truths in themselves' . . . To being-in-itself correspond truths-in-themselves, and, to these last, fixed, unambiguous assertions (Husserl 1970b, vol. i, pp. 321f.)[2].

The result of this subordination is the apparent possibility of treating all entities (including those belonging to the domains of

---

2. And Husserl adds immediately: 'We are infinitely removed from this ideal' (1970b, vol. i, p. 322).

ethics, religion, politics, etc.) as analogous to logico-mathematical entities, and of applying to them the same operations.

Indeed, Frege indirectly implies this same confused unification in which the sciences, religion and ethics 'come under the same rubric': commenting on the need to venture to judge about 'things in the external world', he wrote: 'Would there be a science of history otherwise? Would not all moral theory, all law, otherwise collapse? What would be left of religion? The natural sciences too could only be assessed as fables like astrology and alchemy' (1977c, p. 24).

Consider the effects of what I have called the subordination of the contingent to the necessary (and of the subjective to the objective) in a domain like 'ethics'. Take the sentence:

'Men who run away are cowards.'

It is clear that the 'difficulties' raised by the interpretation of this sentence bear on:

(1) the relationship between extension and comprehension vis-à-vis the notion 'man who runs away';

(2) the distinction between essential and contingent properties;[3]

(3) the nature of the *link* between the properties 'running away' and 'being cowardly'.

It is also clear that there is no way to resolve these three 'difficulties'! It is now more comprehensible that we are, as Husserl said, 'infinitely removed' from the ideal of a *universal theory of ideas*, in the sense given by the Port-Royal *Logic*: this is due to the fact that the various operations dependent on the extension/comprehension relationship lose their meaning and validity if it is attempted to

3. These 'difficulties' are clearly revealed by an analysis of Husserl's concerning an example of the same type:

> If we say 'A soldier should be brave', this does not mean that we or anyone else are wishing or willing, commanding or requiring this. One might rather oppose that a corresponding wishing and requiring would be generally justified, i.e. in relation to every soldier, though even this is not quite right, since it is surely not necessary that we should here be really evaluating a wish or a demand. 'A soldier should be brave' rather means that only a brave soldier is a "good" soldier (1970b, vol.I, p. 82).

> In other words, the subordination of the subjective to the objective implies that a 'value judgement' is necessarily based on a 'judgement of reality' apparently devoid of any normative character. The (clearly extra-logical) question raised by Husserl's remark is ultimately whether 'only a brave soldier is [truly] a soldier', i.e., is bravery an *essential property* of the idea soldier?

apply them outside the domain of the scientific disciplines existing at a given historical moment, so the idealist ambition to achieve a universe of 'fixed and unequivocal' statements embracing the whole of reality is no more consistent than a dream, an imaginary satisfaction in the mode 'as if' (to act as if the operations mentioned above were definite everywhere).[4]

Of course, this has not prevented this dream from having been developed vis-à-vis certain entities particularly apt to fulfill a wish in the imaginary mode: the idea of the triangle in seventeenth-century philosophy functioned as the prototype from which one could analogically arrive at *the idea of God* and at *the inventory of the essential properties* of that idea. Spinoza seems to have been the only one to have seen the joke at the time when he wrote: 'I believe that a triangle, if only it had the power of speech, would say in like manner that God is eminently triangular, and a circle would say that Divine Nature is eminently circular' (Spinoza 1928, p. 288).

All this leads me to a new observation: it seems indeed that any universal theory of ideas such as is presupposed by the project of a 'semantics' is necessarily neutral with respect to the opposition between *science* on the one hand and *ignorance, superstition or myth* on the other, precisely because it operates in the mode 'as if'; and this brings us to the place of the *second (empiricist) solution* I announced above. It constitutes in reality the cynical and pragmatico-sceptical counterpart to the metaphysico-realist dream just described, in so far as empiricism purely and simply inverts the relation of subordination between the space of the 'theory of knowledge' and the space of 'rhetoric', to the advantage of the latter.

Empirio-criticism, which was the spontaneous philosophy of physicists during the years of the 'crisis of physics', is, as we shall see, not so dissimilar from the spontaneous philosophy of linguistics today: here too we find 'variants, mixtures, combinations, some-

---

4. Lewis Carroll showed amusingly what happens when this universality of operations is presupposed irrespective of the terms used. Take the following logically irreproachable syllogism cited in Grize (1969, p. 63):
   'Every prudent man avoids hyenas
   But no banker is imprudent
   Hence no banker ever fails to avoid hyenas.'
   The comic effect arises from the fact that the property 'be prudent' is not fixed and unequivocal in the sense of a logico-mathematical property, except in relation to a theory abstractly studying human behaviour in general in the face of risk in general. 'Game theory', which knows neither peasants nor bankers, apparently constitutes an example of such a study.

times extremely ingenious ones, of empiricism, nominalism, pragmatism and criticism, etc., i.e., *idealism*'. Once again it is the same
'philosophical constellation of themes from eighteenth-century
English *empiricism*, dominated by Kantian *criticism*' (Althusser
1974a, p. 74). In other words, empirio-criticism is on the trajectory
from radical empiricism (discredited today and practically in-
defensible as such) to the logical empiricism of today.

In *Materialism and Empirio-criticism*, Lenin sets out the
philosophical, and in the end political, 'ins and outs' of this *regression*
in which the possibility of a knowledge of objective reality vanishes
together with objective reality itself (Lenin 1962).[5] And it turns out,
something particularly important in this connection, that this
conception depended on a link between subjectivist empiricism and
certain categories of rhetoric (above all that of *conviction*), as indeed
the empirio-criticists stated themselves: 'Subjective conviction, not
objective certainty is the only attainable goal of any science' (cit.
Lenin 1962, p. 221), wrote Dr. Hans Kleinpeter, a fervent disciple
of Mach's.

This position of principle is explained and developed in these
assertions quoted by Lenin: 'All my (outer and inner) experience,
all my thoughts and aspirations are given to me as a psychical
process, as part of my consciousness' (p. 221); and: 'that which we
call physical is a construction of psychical elements' (p. 221).

Thus the sciences become 'convenient instruments',[6] pragmatically and rhetorically effective 'ways of speaking',[7] this effectiveness
not being in itself anything more than a reflection of the deductive
and classificatory effectiveness of what one can therefore call *logico-
mathematical rhetoric*. 'Science' is then reduced to the procedures of
logical reasoning, and is thus confounded with the system of
operations (which may become very complex and logically very
abstract) that can be applied to any catalogue of facts, objects or

5. I would remind the reader that Dominique Lecourt's recent *Une Crise et son enjeu*
   (1973) patiently and lucidly examines the various aspects of the 'empirio-
   criticist' enterprise and the way in which Lenin intervened in the affair.
6. This theory, according to which the laws of nature are conventions created by
   man for his convenience was developed in France especially by Henri Poincaré,
   in the same philosophical context as empirio-criticism. It is worth stressing here
   that Lenin distinguished between the 'great physicist' (spontaneously materialist in his scientific practice) and the 'puny philosopher', bearer of the idealism of
   his time. The same remark could be applied to Mach himself.
7. For Karl Pearson, 'The reality of science is symbolic' (*The Grammar of Science*,
   1892 – cf. Lecourt 1973, p. 92).

events. In other words, 'science' is conceived as a set of administratively effective procedures, as Karl Pearson, the English disciple of Mach commended by Lenin for his uncompromising clarity, asserted: 'Like space, it [time] appears to us as one of the plans on which that great sorting-machine, the human perceptive faculty, arranges its material' (cit. Lenin 1962, p. 183).

Note that this conception of the human mind as a 'great sorting-machine' is the regressive re-inscription in the element of modern idealist philosophy of the empiricist myth of the eighteenth century, linked in its time to the ideological struggle against metaphysics: the passage from Adam Smith quoted above (pp. 28f.) goes on to define 'those classes and assortments, which, in the schools, are called genera and species' as 'merely a number of objects, bearing a certain degree of resemblance to one another, and on that account denominated by a single appellation, which may be applied to express any one of them' (1767, p. 440).

Thus once again, but in the opposite form to that of the theologico-metaphysical dream of a universal science peculiar to the seventeenth century, it seems that there is no distinction between what is science and what is not, in so far as any catalogue can be the object of a logical administrative procedure so long as this procedure is of some 'interest', albeit as a game. This empiricist-behaviourist position, today the cornerstone of many of the 'social sciences', has found an expression even within the polemic which has historically opposed different conceptions of logic: Wittgenstein's constructivist and anti-Platonic theses – calculus for him being 'an anthroponomic technique founded on consensus' (Bouveresse 1971, p. 146) – constitute one example of this position. Logical necessity thus becomes a mere consequence of the decision that *we*[8] take to regard a statement as unassailable, the constraint of 'science' is identified with a social constraint.[9]

The struggle 'against metaphysics' conducted by logical empiricism and 'analytical philosophy' thus conceals an attack on materialism, itself identified with a metaphysics (the religion of 'holy matter' according to the empirio-criticist Bazarov – cit. Lenin

8. Note, from the linguistic point of view, the reappearance of a 'shifter' whose function it is to support the universal orator's unlimited persuasive power over himself as universal audience.
9. Marcuse provides a contemporary example of the political consequences that may follow from this sceptical opportunism.

1962, p. 23): if the truth of a statement for a subject were indeed no more than the class of moments during which the subject accepted it, that would mean that 'the elements of the world' are nothing but pure representations, which comes down to saying, as Frege so lucidly explains, that 'psychology would contain all the sciences within it, at least it would be the supreme judge over all the sciences' (1977c, p. 25).

The only flaw in Frege's lucidity, one might say the limit of his materialism, is that he appeals, as has already been pointed out, to the sciences *and* to 'institutions' (law, religion, ethics, etc.) indifferently in his criticisms of subjectivist theses: 'Trial by jury would assuredly be a silly arrangement if it could not be assumed that each of the jurors could understand the question at issue in the same sense' (1952c, p. 121; 1977b, p. 36). I shall return to this point. In the argument that follows, Frege's investigations will put to use more than once; even as we use one or other of his formulations, we must never forget the existence of this 'blind spot' in Frege, what I have called the limit of his materialism.

We have just reached, *beneath the 'philosophy of language'* as spontaneous philosophy of linguistics, the *philosophical core of idealism* which, in its double form, counterposes it to the philosophical position of materialism, marked by the recognition of the existing scientific disciplines.

I can sum up my investigation so far by making the following observation: *empiricist theories of knowledge just as much as realist ones seem to have an interest in forgetting the existence of the historically constituted scientific disciplines, to the advantage of a universal theory of ideas, whether this takes the realist form of a universal and a priori network of notions, or the empiricist form of an administrative procedure applicable to the universe, considered as a set of facts, objects, events or acts.*

These two types of theories can be called *ideological* in so far as they *exploit* the existence of scientific disciplines *while at the same time masking* that existence, such that the distinction between science and non-science is obscured.

It should be emphasised in passing that these two apparently contradictory ideological forms are in reality linked together by a secret necessity: as an example, take the historical destiny that led Husserl 'as if by the hand' from the Platonism of the *Logical Investigations* of 1913 (cf. p. 32 above) to the sceptical pragmatism of *The Crisis in the European Sciences and Transcendental Phenomenology* of 1936, where we find that 'in geometrical . . . mathematisation,

... we measure the life-world ... for a well-fitting garb of ideas' (Husserl 1970a, p. 51).[10]

This last point casts a new light on the *strange circularity* I noted above (p. 40).

One ambiguity still needs to be resolved: if the theories in question 'forget' the existence of the historically constituted scientific disciplines, this is no unfortunate accident of history. To speak anthropomorphically (and inadequately, in this case), one would rather have to say that they were 'designed to do so', i.e., to obscure the scientific knowledges available at a given historical moment. Let me correct the anthropomorphism of the formulation: in saying this I do not want to imply that this fictional existence of knowledges in the imaginary, in the mode 'as if', is the result of a deliberate intention. It should rather be seen as the material effect of what Engels called 'blind necessity' on a historical state of ignorance, specifically determined by the state of development of the sciences (of nature and of history): this ignorance is anything but an initial void of thought, it is on the contrary the ideological 'fullness' by which the unthought is hidden from thought in thought itself. Now the fundamental discovery of Marxism-Leninism consists precisely in the recognition that the effect of this necessity is not restricted to 'nature' and its laws, but includes also the conditions in which 'man', as part of nature, enters into relation with it; namely the *productive forces* and the *relations of production* which have determined the history of 'human societies', with the class struggles corresponding to them and the material forces thereby brought into play, since the beginning of that history.

The ideological, as imaginary 'representation', is thereby necessarily subordinate to these material forces which 'guide men' (the practical ideologies in Althusser's terminology), and is re-inscribed in them. Lenin wrote:

For Engels all living human practice permeates the theory of knowledge itself and provides an *objective* criterion of truth. For until we know a law of nature, it, existing and acting independently of and outside our mind, makes us slaves of 'blind necessity'. But once we come to know this law, which acts (as

10. We are greatly indebted to Jean Cavaillès for his clear demonstration of the necessary link between what might seem superficially to be two contradictory 'moments' in Husserl's philosophy (Cavaillès 1960, p. 66).

Marx repeated a thousand times) *independently* of our will and our mind, we become the masters of nature (1962, p. 190).

The extension of materialism to history, the emergence of a science of history which allows us to start 'mastering history', is based on the same necessity: *the real object* (in the domain of the natural sciences as in that of history) *exists independently of the fact that it is or is not known*, i.e., independently of the production or non-production of the object of *knowledge* which 'corresponds' to it.

I can now set out the fundamental theses of materialism and comment on them in the domain which concerns us:

(a) the 'external' material world exists (real object, concrete-real);

(b) objective knowledge of this world is produced in the historical development of the scientific disciplines (object of knowledge, concrete-in-thought, concept);

(c) objective knowledge is independent of the subject.

Note straight away that these theses are not independent of one another. Thus thesis (a) and thesis (b) are indissociable and even literally indistinguishable. ' "Belief" in the objectivity of science is the same as "belief" in the objective existence of external objects', that is materialism, wrote Lenin (1962, p. 292). In the same way thesis (b) is identical with thesis (c), as is clear from the affirmative answer Lenin gave to the following question: 'Is there such a thing as objective truth, that is, can human ideas have a content that does not depend on a subject, that does not depend either on a human being or on humanity?' (1962, p. 122). The materialist character of these theses lies therefore both in their *content* AND in their *unity*, i.e., *in the order in which they come into relationship with one another*. Thus for example if one were to 'forget' thesis (c) and to invert the relationship between thesis (a) and thesis (b) by making the external world a mere correlate of scientific knowledge one would fall at once into idealism. This interdependence of the three theses was expressed by Frege in a formula which is at once ambiguous and surprisingly lucid: 'If man could not think and could not take as the object of his thought something of which he is not the bearer, he would have an inner world but no environment' (1977c, p. 23). Ambiguous because thesis (a), the existence of the external world, might seem *subordinate* to thesis (c), the independence of knowledge from the subject, leading to a Platonic idealism; but surprisingly lucidly materialist if understood to mean that if man can think and take as the object of his thought something of which he is not the bearer, that is only because the external world exists.

The main materialist gain in Frege's formula is that it makes explicit thesis (c) which asserts the independence of objective knowledge with respect to the subject. By saying that the subject is not the bearer of the object of his thought, Frege was, without quite naming it, pointing to the 'process without a subject' intolerable to all idealist philosophy, from Avenarius to Sartre: Lenin quoted and criticised this sentence of Avenarius': 'We can think of a region where no human foot has yet trodden, but to be able to *think* [Avenarius' italics] of such an environment there is required what we designate by the term *self, whose* [Avenarius' italics] thought it is' (cit. Lenin 1962, p. 78). Frege's critique of Husserl's *Philosophie der Arithmetik I* goes along with Lenin's critique of empirio-criticism in this matter: it consists of a *denunciation of the confusion between representation and concept*, the confusion that tends to the position 'that everything is a representation' (Frege 1967, p. 181). Frege writes vis-à-vis Husserl's theses:

> Thus we have a blurring of the distinction between representation and concept, between imagination and thought. Everything is transformed into something subjective. But just because the boundary between the subjective and the objective is obliterated, what is subjective acquires in its turn the appearances of objectivity (1952b, p. 79; 1967, p. 182).

'The subjective acquires . . . the appearances of objectivity': in the terminology I have used hitherto, the subjective *simulates* the objective; the representation operates *as if* it were a concept, and, simultaneously, the concept is reduced to the state of pure representation. I shall return to this point. What is important here is to understand that this simulation is itself entirely determined by the 'blind necessity' Engels mentioned: the two operations, that of the *notion* (necessary effect of the real in the imaginary, image spontaneously imposing itself, 'figurative-concrete') and that of the *concept* (necessary effect of the real in what Frege calls 'thought') are each effects of *the same necessity*, distributed according to the historical conditions in which they are realised (the historical state, i.e., the nature of class relations with the interests that they bring into play, *and* the state of development of such and such scientific disciplines).

To sum up I shall say that the essential thesis of materialism is to posit the independence of the external world (and of the objective knowledge of its laws which I shall henceforth call the scientific-conceptual process) with respect to the subject, *while at the same time positing* the dependence of the subject with respect to this external world (hence the necessary character of the effects on that subject which I shall henceforth call the notional-ideological process). In other words, the materialist proposition that 'matter is independent of the mind' cannot be converted to read 'the mind is independent of matter' without completely overturning the very bases of materialism.

Let me stress once again that the distinction between scientifico-conceptual process and ideologico-notional process is not a metaphysical opposition establishing a kind of Great Wall of China between two eternally fixed 'regions', each with its own laws and its own necessity. Later on I shall have occasion to go into detail on this point, but let me say straight away that if, in Lenin's words, 'knowledge is born from ignorance', that is because at any given historical moment all ideological forms *are not equivalent*, and the effects of simulation-repression which they generate *are not homogeneous*: the forms that 'the imaginary relation of individuals to their real conditions of existence' can take are not homogeneous, precisely because those 'real conditions of existence' are 'distributed' by the economic relations of production, with the different types of political and ideological contradictions that result; at any given historical moment the 'ideological forms' present fulfil their dialectical role of *raw material* and *obstacle* to the production of knowledges, to pedagogical practice and to proletarian political practice itself, in a necessarily uneven fashion.

Let us stop here for the moment: we have just had our first encounter with the philosophical category of the *process without a subject* to which this study will constantly return. We shall next encounter it after a rather long and inevitably 'specialised' detour via which, armed with the materialist theses I have just stated, we shall be able to ascend from the *(logico-linguistic) evidentness of the subject*, inherent in the philosophy of language as the spontaneous philosophy of linguistics, to what will enable us to think *the 'subject form' (and specifically the 'subject of discourse') as a determinate effect of the process without a subject.*

So at the same time we shall also return to the two problems, of the production of knowledges, and of proletarian political practice, which I am leaving 'in suspense' here.

PART II

FROM THE PHILOSOPHY OF LANGUAGE TO THE THEORY OF DISCOURSE

3 *Langue* and Ideology

The reader may be thinking: 'Whether or not there are sciences, whether or not there are philosophies, idealist or materialist, it remains the case that men speak, that languages exist, that their objective (scientific) study is possible, and indeed partly achieved today' – a declaration by which he implicitly attests to the spontaneously materialist character of linguistics, as a scientific practice *within the limits of its own domain*, which is to recognise, as I said at the beginning of this work, that linguistics is *constantly solicited outside its own domain*, on a certain number of points about which, it is thought, linguistics must surely have 'something to say' (and, above all, semantics, logic and rhetoric). Basing myself on all I have argued hitherto, I now want to show that linguistics cannot avoid the issue simply by saying 'I am not what you think I am!', i.e., by reinforcing the defences at its frontiers. If the solicitations brought to bear on linguistics inevitably concern the questions I have just recalled, this is no accident: 'the tongue finds the aching tooth,' said Lenin, meaning that the constant return to a teasing question indicates that there is 'something behind it', it bears witness to the non-resolution of the question.

In other words, if linguistics is solicited on this or that point outside its own domain, it is because inside its own domain (in its specific practice), linguistics meets these questions in some way, in the form of questions which *do* concern it ('you would not look for me if you had not already found me'). Linguistics would not be drawn by solicitations towards 'semantics' if it had not in some sense already encountered it . . . inside itself.

It could even be suggested that the way linguistics was constituted as a science (in the form of phonology, then morphology and syntax) was precisely by a constant discussion of the question of meaning and of the best way *to banish the question of meaning from its domain* (cf. Haroche, Henry and Pêcheux 1971).

The 'semantic questions' encountered by linguistics today thus constitute what might be called the return of the origins of a science (of what it had to separate itself from to become what it is) within that science itself. And we now know that the modality in which the origins of linguistics are present inside it today is precisely the 'philosophy of language' (with its realist or empiricist variants of a common idealism) which I have examined in the first chapter of this book.

This re-emergence manifests itself in linguistic practice itself in different forms which there can be no question of analysing here in detail, but which can be said to consist essentially either of *denegations of the origin* ('linguistics today has nothing to fear from philosophies of language, whether idealist or no, thank goodness') or of *repetitions of the origin* ('linguistics today finds just what it needs in the Port-Royal *Logic*, or in logical empiricism, or in a mixture of the two').

'Just as I thought,' some readers may say, 'Everything said so far was leading up to this point: he is now going to try to persuade us that materialist (Marxist-Leninist) philosophy contains "just what linguistics needs" to solve its problems. Once again linguistics is being solicited outside its own domain to be exploited to the profit of a philosophy, and the fact that it is materialist is neither here nor there. In the name of materialism prohibitions are going to be imposed on linguistics, utterances are going to be classified as "scientific" or "ideological", and languages are going to be remade on the basis of the opposition between notion and concept. Thank you very much!'

Such misgivings need unequivocal reassurance, in so far as they constitute (theoretically and politically) the crux of a number of important problems: to start with, I will say that what is emerging in this objection is an idealist conception projected on to materialist philosophy, and one which has not failed to have disastrous effects, in linguistics as elsewhere. The pseudo-Marxist Nikolai Marr, who was also a pseudo-linguist, nearly led Soviet scholars into a kind of linguistic 'Lysenko affair': he had undertaken to *reconstruct languages*, which he identified as ideological superstructures, with the result that grammar became the stake in a 'class struggle' (cf. Stalin 1951; Balibar, E. 1966; and Vinogradov 1969).

The idealism of this conception lies both in a philosophical and political error (the idea that materialist philosophy can provide a science with its results – or impose them on it; in some sense do the work of a science for it), *and* in a theoretical error (regarding a language as part of the ideological superstructure of a social formation). In this double sense it can in fact be said that it was idealism and not materialism that was 'exploiting' linguistics by simulating-repressing that science itself.

As for the idea that one might distinguish by *linguistic criteria* between 'scientific utterances' and non-scientific utterances, it has, I think, been fairly clearly demonstrated in the first chapter of this book that this is just a matter of a theoretical fantasy peculiar to neo-positivism (see pp. 38–9 above).

How then should one conceive of the 'intervention' of materialist philosophy in the domain of linguistic science? I shall try to demonstrate that, far from providing results, this intervention consists above all in *opening new fields of questions*, providing work for linguistics in its own domain, on its own objects, this by bringing it into relation with the objects of another scientific domain, the science of social formations: the problems so revealed do thus concern linguistics, and at the same time they bear on the articulation between linguistics and the scientific theory of processes which are spontaneously represented-distorted, made quite un-knowable by idealist philosophy in general and the 'philosophy of language' in particular. Let me now be more precise as to the nature of this articulation.

In the course of his reading of this book, the linguist will have gradually recognised, perhaps in a form not completely familiar to him, allusions to linguistic phenomena well known to him, belonging to the domain of general linguistics as a theory of linguistic systems.

Let me list these pointers to linguistic phenomena:

On the one hand, the opposition between *explication* and *determination*, to which the linguist will have attached a number of morphological and syntactic properties, linked to the operation of relative clauses and nominal complements, to adjectivisation, nominalisation, etc.;

On the other, the opposition between *situational property* and *permanent property*, to which the linguist will similarly have related certain morpho-syntactic characteristics of the verb system, of the system of determiners (articles, demonstrative pronouns, etc.) and of 'shifters'.

To be brief, I shall say that these mechanisms belong to the *linguistic system*, or if you prefer, that they concern the operation of the language in relation to itself.

What the linguist may have learnt from a reading of Part I of this book (unless it has merely confirmed his suspicions) is that these linguistic mechanisms also formed the backdrop to a 'philosophical' reflection whose development he has been able to follow through the questions of reference, determination and enunciation. I say that these two elements (both linguistic phenomena and sites of philosophical questions) belong to the zone of articulation between linguistics and the historical theory of ideological and scientific processes, itself part of the science of social formations: the system of a language is indeed the same for the materialist and the idealist, for the revolutionary and the reactionary, for someone with access to a certain knowledge and for someone without that access. But it does not follow that these various people will hold the same *discourse*: the language thus appears to be the common *basis* of differentiated discursive *processes*, which are included within it to the extent that, as we saw above, ideological processes simulate scientific processes. Let me stop here a moment to consider this distinction between language (*langue*) and discourse and to bring out its significance.

In counterposing *linguistic basis* and *discursive process*, I want first of all to stress, as Paul Henry has recently reminded us (1977),[1] that every linguistic system, as a set of phonological, morphological and syntactic structures, is endowed with a *relative autonomy* that makes it subject to internal laws which constitute, precisely, the object of linguistics.[2]

Hence it is *on the basis of these internal laws that the discursive processes develop*, and not as the expression of a pure thought, of a pure cognitive activity, etc., which 'accidentally' makes use of linguistic systems.

It follows that the concrete/abstract couple cannot be super-imposed on the discourse/language opposition: *discursivity is not parole*, i.e., it is not a 'concrete' individual way of inhabiting the 'abstraction' of the *langue*; it is not a matter of a use, of a utilisation or of the realisation of a function. On the contrary, the expression *discursive process* is explicitly intended to put in their proper (idealist) places the notion of *parole* and the psychologistic anthropologism which goes with it; the formula Étienne Balibar uses to summarise

1. This book is a version, more thoroughgoing and correct, of part of the cyclostyled but unpublished text Henry (1974), to which I shall refer frequently.
2. In using the term 'basis' I do not mean to imply that *langue* is part of the economic infrastructure, but only that it is the indispensable prerequisite of any discursive process.

Stalin's thesis on the relation between language (*langue*) and class struggle is therefore correct, on condition that the terms '*indifference*', '*non-indifference*' and '*use*' are understood to refer to class practices and not to the subjective behaviours which these terms spontaneously evoke. Balibar writes: 'If language is "indifferent" to the division of classes and their struggle it does not follow that classes are "indifferent" to language. On the contrary, they *use* it in determinate ways in the field of their antagonism and especially of their political struggle' (Balibar, E. 1966, pp. 21f.).

In the terminology used above, the 'indifference' of language with respect to the class struggle characterises *the relative autonomy of the linguistic system* and, *asymmetrically*, the fact that classes are not 'indifferent' to language is conveyed by the fact that *every discursive process is inscribed in an ideological class relationship*. I shall return to this fundamental point. For the moment, remember that 'language is not a superstructure' and that it is not divided along the lines of class structures into 'class languages', each with its own 'class grammar'. Having said this, the 'solution' proposed by Stalin – the language is *at the service of society taken as a whole* – demands a critical examination, one which Balibar initiated in his discussion of the term 'society' used by Stalin: in fact Stalin's thesis according to which a language is 'the language of the whole people, as a society's single language, common to all members of the society' (1951, p. 70) corrects Marr's 'ultra-left' error, but at the same time it threatens to fall into another, 'rightist' error, of a *sociologistic* kind. To be brief, it can be said that this error is supported by the definition given by Marx and Engels in *The German Ideology* of language as a 'means of communication with other men' (cf. Marx and Engels 1976b, p. 44). Pierre Raymond has recently drawn our attention to the fact that this 'means' or this 'instrument' is not 'a technical or scientific instrument', and that this 'communication' is not 'identifiable a priori with the material communications provided by various means studied elsewhere', which suggests that the expression 'instrument of communication' be taken in a figurative sense and not literally, in so far as this 'instrument' allows both communication and *non-communication*, i.e., authorises division behind the appearance of unity, and does so because what is at stake is not *first* the *communication* of a meaning.[3] As I noted at the beginning of this

3. 'It is idealism which inverts the historical order when it begins by seeking meaning everywhere', says Pierre Raymond in an analysis to which I refer the reader (1973, pp. 208ff.).

book, Renée Balibar and her colleagues have approached the same question, from another angle, that of *the common language with a national character*, emphasising its links with compulsory education and the differentiation of ideological practices (in this case educational practices) achieved in the unitary school and the unitary common language which is one of its 'subjects' since 'the unitary form is the essential means of the division and contradiction' (Balibar, E. and Macherey 1974, p. 27).

I shall argue that the ideological contradictions which develop through the unity of *langue* are constituted by the contradictory relations which necessarily exist between what I have called the 'discursive processes', in so far as these are inscribed in ideological class relations. This being so, I find the expression 'codification of linguistic exchanges' used by Étienne Balibar and Pierre Macherey inadequate (ambiguity of the play on legal code and linguistic 'code') to characterise the relationship, historically determined in its evolution, between the relative autonomy of the linguistic system and the contradictory set of discursive processes; frankly, taken out of context, this expression would seem to me to constitute either a lapsus or a theoretical regression to the philosophical epoch of *The German Ideology* and the anthropologism restrospectively legible therein from the standpoint of the text of *Capital*.

For all the reasons set out in Part I, I have taken as reference point the explication/determination relationship, my intention being to study the common basis on which notional-ideological processes on the one hand and conceptual-scientific processes on the other are constituted as discursive processes. From this logico-linguistic point, I shall gradually proceed, via the question of the material nature of meaning, to the foundations of a *materialist theory of discourse*. The discussion which follows will thus be marked by an *unevenness* (necessarily affecting conceptual work in an under-explored domain) due to the *co-existence* of *local scientific elements*, whose definition and conceptual operation are still in many respects embryonic, *and materialist philosophical categories* which act as guides in this exploration.

4 Determination, Name Formation and Embedding

Consider the example proposed by Frege in his article 'On Sense and Reference': 'He who discovered the elliptic form of the planetary orbits died in misery.'

First, here is a large extract from Frege on which I shall then comment:

> If the sense [meaning] of the subordinate clause were here a thought, it would have to be possible to express it also in a separate sentence. But this does not work, because the grammatical subject 'he who' has no independent sense [meaning] and only mediates the relation with the consequent clause 'died in misery'. For this reason the sense [meaning] of the subordinate clause is not a complete thought, and its reference is Kepler, not a truth value. One might object that the sense [meaning] of the whole does contain a thought as part, viz. that there was somebody who first discovered the elliptic form of the planetary orbits; for whoever takes the whole to be true cannot deny this part. This is undoubtedly so; but only because otherwise the dependent clause 'he who discovered the elliptic form of the planetary orbits' would have no reference. If anything is asserted there is always an obvious presupposition that the simple or compound proper names used have reference. If one therefore asserts 'Kepler died in misery', there is a presupposition that the name 'Kepler' designates something; but it does not follow that the sense [meaning] of the sentence 'Kepler died in misery' contains the thought that the name 'Kepler' designates something. If this were the case the negation would have to run not 'Kepler did not die in misery' but 'Kepler did not die in misery, or the name "Kepler" has no reference'. That the name 'Kepler' designates something is just as much a presupposition for

the assertion 'Kepler died in misery' as for the contrary assertion (Frege 1952e, pp. 68f.).

This passage calls for a number of comments.

First of all, we observe that in his analysis Frege uses not only terms taken from the vocabulary of *logic*, but also expressions which belong to the *linguistics* of his time, such as 'sentence', 'subordinate clause', 'grammatical subject'. Without discussing here how, given the progress of linguistic science, Frege's work could be brought up to date in this respect, I shall simply take it as indicating that, for Frege, the operation of *language* has 'something to do with' what he here calls *thought*: what he *believes* he has discerned is the fact that the operation of *language* (the relationship between main clause and relative subordinate clause in this case) induces in 'thought' an *illusion* (posits an existence) that I shall examine in a moment. Not being a linguist by profession, he obviously does not ask if the linguistic operation he is interrogating in his example is or is not *linguistically* linked to other linguistic operations; he does not investigate whether he is dealing with a *systematic linguistic effect* or a special case; he settles the question *as a logician*, for he declares a few lines after the passage I have cited: 'This [illusion] arises from an imperfection of language, from which even the symbolic language of mathematical analysis is not altogether free' (p. 70). Thus Frege implies that if illusions can appear in language that is because 'natural' language is imperfect, because it contains traps and ambiguities which would disappear in a 'well-made' artifical language. Undoubtedly, logic, as a theory of artificial languages, did in fact develop by taking 'natural' language as its raw material, but it must immediately be added that this work was always aimed exclusively at the liberation of *mathematics* from the effects of 'natural' language (so that logic gradually became a part of the domain of mathematics), and not at all at the liberation of 'natural' language itself from its 'illusions' *in general*. Otherwise logic would contain all the sciences within it, to reappropriate one of Frege's own remarks about psychology.[1]

I wanted to make this clear straight away in order to guard against the logicist conception according to which ideological (and in some respects political) oppositions result 'in reality' from

1. 'Not everything is a representation. Otherwise psychology would contain all the sciences within it' (1977c, p. 25).

imperfections of language, which is more or less to reduce them to misunderstandings, 'pseudo-problems', which everyone could avoid if only they took a little trouble. Frege's 'blind spot', once again. Using his own example and the 'illusion' he discerns in it, I shall try to show that this is quite wrong.

In his example, as we have seen, Frege distinguishes between two elements: the designation of something on the one hand, and an assertion about that 'something' on the other. The 'something' designated in the sentence is in fact 'someone', namely 'he who discovered . . . etc.', i.e., Kepler. The assertion on the other hand concerns the material conditions in which the said Kepler died, in other words a reality which has little to do with the discovery of the laws of planetary motion, *except of course* in a religious or moral perspective for which misery is the counterpart of genius, and a punishment for knowledge seen as transgression (note in passing that in this latter case the 'explicative' transform of Frege's example: 'Kepler, who discovered . . . etc., died in misery' would be perfectly meaningful).

But Frege patently has no intention of alluding to the existence of *any relation of meaning* between the two parts of the sentence he is considering. He is only interested in the *formal relationship* between the 'whole sentence' (the 'thought') and the subordinate clause inscribed in it, as an object of thought. The 'illusion' to which he refers is the illusion by which this object of thought necessarily induces in thought *the existence of someone, not in general, but as an absolutely unique subject*: Johannes Kepler, the German astronomer who was born in 1571 and died in 1630 (the reader will have noticed, by the way, that to avoid the – logically tragic – eventuality that two astronomers independently discovered the elliptic form of the planetary orbits, Frege took care to specify 'who *first* discovered . . . etc.'). This being so, must the necessity of this 'illusion', by which an object of thought presupposes the existence of a real object which it designates, be said to lie in an 'imperfection of language', the irritating habit, in other words, which insists, as Frege says, that 'if anything is asserted there is always an obvious presupposition that the simple or compound proper names used have reference' (p. 69)?

Should one then declare absurd and totally meaningless a sentence such as: 'He who saved the world by dying on the cross never existed', in which the discourse of militant atheism denies in the 'whole sentence' the existence of the person it presupposes to exist in the subordinate clause?[2] Or should not one rather consider that there is a *separation, distance or discrepancy* in the sentence between *what is thought before, elsewhere or independently and what is contained in the global assertion of the sentence?*

This is what has lead Paul Henry to propose the term '*preconstructed*' to designate what relates to a previous, external or at any rate independent construction in opposition to what is 'constructed' by the utterance.[3] In other words, we are dealing with a discursive effect linked to syntactic *embedding*.

In this perspective, the 'illusion' which Frege discusses is not just the effect of a syntactic phenomenon constituting an 'imperfection of language': the syntactic phenomenon of the determinative relative clause is, on the contrary, the formal precondition of an effect of meaning whose material cause really resides in the asymmetrically discrepant relationship between two 'domains of thought', such that one element from one irrupts in an element of the other in the form of what we have called the 'preconstructed', i.e., *as if that element were already there*. Let me be clear that in speaking of 'domains of thought' I do not mean to designate *thought contents outside language* which meet other thought contents in language: really all 'thought contents' exist in language in the form of the *discursive*.

I shall return to this problem later; for the moment I will just say that in broaching the question of the preconstructed I have come to *one of the fundamental points of articulation between the theory of discourse and linguistics.*

One point remains to be examined, concerning the nature of the *proper name*: this point, whose examination will enable me to extend my elaboration of what I mean by 'preconstructed', consists of the fact that no determination can be applied to a proper name, for the excellent reason that the proper name (in its paraphrastic form: 'he who . . . etc.') is precisely the result of the operation of determination 'taken to its limits'. Of course I am aware of the possibility of forming expressions like 'the Jesus Christ of the Christians' (as

2. Cf. the anecdote recounted by Freud: 'Is this the place where the Duke of Wellington spoke those words? – Yes, it is the place; but he never spoke the words' (1960, p. 60n.).

3. I refer here to the work of Paul Henry, from whom I have borrowed the elaboration of this decisive question. For a critique of the notion of presupposition, see especially Henry (1977) Section 1: 'Le Sujet dans la linguistique'.

opposed to 'the Jesus Christ of Renan', for example) or 'the de Gaulle of the Resistance' (as opposed to 'the de Gaulle of the Fifth Republic'), and in Chapter 1 I mentioned the use Leibniz made of this possibility to counterpose an infinite number of possible destinies to the real destiny of Sextus Tarquinius. Yet the reference of such expressions raises a problem to which I shall return (p. 120). This problem apart, it remains true that if no determination can be applied to a proper name, there must necessarily exist *terms which are not proper names*, from which precisely proper names, or rather the paraphrastic expressions which correspond to them, can be constructed by determination. Consider, indeed, disciplines such as Astronomy, Geography or History such as are envisaged and used with special predilection by Frege (and in general by logicians who treat the problem of the proper name). These disciplines can be said to play the parts, respectively, of a register of Celestial Bodies, a catalogue of Remarkable Points on the Surface of the Earth, and a list of Great Men and Events who have lived and which have happened on the latter up to the present. The characteristic of these 'descriptive sciences' is to provide a kind of Record Office of the Universe, treating 'reality' as if it were the set of 'things', each being designated by its *proper name*: hence *Kepler, Berlin, Venus*, to take the examples used by Frege. Now, and this is the decisive point, this designation by a proper name correlatively implies the possibility of designating 'the same thing' by a periphrasis like 'he who discovered . . . etc.', 'the city which is the capital of Germany', 'the second of the planets orbiting around the sun': in other words, to 'simple' proper names there *necessarily* correspond 'compound' proper names which are not lexicalised but constructed by various syntactic operations, ranging from 'the N that VN' (where N represents a 'common noun' such as *city, planet, man*, etc.) to 'he who VN' or 'that which VN', in which all initial *lexical support* has disappeared.

It is now clear why the demonstrative (this or that)[4] can appear both as the first proper name and as a 'tool' for the construction of proper names: the planet Venus is thus

  that thing, of which I am speaking (that of which I am speaking)

---

4. Cf. Frege: 'Places, instants, stretches of time, are, logically considered, objects; hence the linguistic designation of a definite place, a definite instant, or a stretch of time is to be regarded as a proper name' (1952e, p. 71).

that thing, which I have been told is called the planet Venus
(that which I have been told . . .)
that thing, which is the second closest planet to the sun
(that which is the second closest planet to the sun . . .).[5]

This also explains the predilection of logicians for the domains of
astronomy, geography and history: it arises from the fact that these
domains particularly 'evidently' exhibit the mechanism of the
identification of an object, which is both a perceptual identification (I
see *that*, which I see = I see what I see) and an intelligible
identification (one knows that *this* is the X that . . ., which
corresponds to 'one knows what one knows').[6] This double
tautology – I see what I see/one knows what one knows – is, so to
speak, the apparent basis for the identification of the 'thing' and also
of the subject who sees it, speaks about it or thinks about it – the real
as a set of things and the subject unique in his proper name: literally
speaking, this 'evident fact' is quite literally repeated in the
empiricist myth of the construction of language from a starting-
point in what Russell called 'egocentric particulars' (*I, this, now*, for
example, in '*I see this now*'), the construction being performed by the
matching of *what I have seen* with *what I am seeing* that constitutes
'generalisation'.[7]

I shall return later to the basic characteristics of the *scene* (cf. pp.

5. In English, this is only possible with non-human nouns. In French, this 'tool' is
   more universal: *celui* can also enter constructions of the type
      celui-ci, qui a découvert la forme elliptique des orbites planétaires (*celui* qui a
      découvert . . .),
   which in English would have to be rendered
      that man, who discovered the elliptic form of the planetary orbits (*he* who
      discovered . . .).
   This example with a human noun was the one given in *Les Vérités de la Palice* at
   this point [Translator's Note].
6. Thus the effect of the preconstructed appears in its pure form where the positing
   of a *singular existence* is linked to the *universal truth* which affects assertions bearing
   on that singularity: this, I believe, is how we should understand the Port-Royal
   logicians' conception that a *singular proposition* such as 'Lewis the 13th. hath
   taken Rochel', although it is 'different from the Universal in this, that the
   Subject of it is not common', should nevertheless be compared to the *universal
   proposition* rather than to the *particular proposition*, 'because the Subject, for the
   very Reason that it is singular, is necessarily taken in its full Extent, which is the
   Essential Propriety of an Universal Proposition, and distinguishes it from the
   particular. . . . And this is the Reason that singular Propositions supply the
   place of Universals in Argumentation' (Arnauld and Nicole 1685, pp. 138f.).
7. And Frege criticises precisely this generalisation (cf. 1967, p. 181, for example).

86f. and 105f.) in which the subject 'sees what he sees with his own eyes' and 'knows what he has to think about it'. For the moment I shall just emphasise the fact that the identification of the subject, his capacity to say 'I, So-and-so', is offered here as something immediately evident: it is 'evident' that only *I* can say '*I*' in speaking of *myself*. But what is concealed in this 'evident truth' coeval with the identification of the thing? We will not learn this from Russell, who, when speaking of someone named Smith, says: 'In each case it is an arbitrary convention that the man has that name' (Russell 1940, p. 110).

Moreover, as if to endorse his acceptance of the evident truth I have just been discussing, Russell adds: 'A man's name is legally anything by which he publicly announces that he wishes to be called' (p. 110), which, *precisely from a legal point of view*, is a total absurdity, whatever type of law one decides to refer to. A name (surname) is in fact identified administratively by reference to (legitimate or natural) descent and its peculiarly *inalienable* character makes any change of name a matter of legal discussion. A central point has been uncovered here, characterised for the moment by a suspiciously 'evident' proposition. Later (p. 106) we shall see what is at stake in it.

I shall close this first approach to the problem of the *preconstructed* by underlining as its essential characteristic the fundamental separation between *thought* and *object of thought*, with the latter pre-existing and its pre-existence marked by what I have called a discrepancy between two domains of thought, such that the subject meets one of these domains as the unthought of his thought, necessarily pre-existing it. This is what Frege meant when he said that 'a name of an object, a proper name, is quite incapable of being used as a grammatical predicate' (1952d, p. 43).

We shall now see that this separation is at the same time, and paradoxically, the motor of the process by which *the object of thought* is thought, i.e., the process by which thought operates in the modality of the *concept*: at the same time it will become clear how the existential uniqueness of the object (designated by the proper name and based on the identification of the subject with himself) disappears in the 'common noun', which is the grammatical form of the concept, a fact characterised by Frege as follows:

In the sentence 'The morning star is Venus', we have two proper names, 'morning star' and 'Venus', for the same object. In the sentence 'the morning star is a planet' we have a proper name, 'the morning star', and a concept-word, 'planet'. So far as language goes, no more has happened than that 'Venus' has been replaced by 'a planet'; but really the relation has become wholly different (1952d, p. 44).

5 Articulation of Utterances, Implication of Properties, Sustaining Effect

Discussing what should be understood by *object* in his article 'Function and Concept' (Frege 1952a), Frege wrote:

> I regard a regular definition as impossible, since we have here something too simple to admit of logical analysis. It is only possible to indicate what is meant. Here I can only say briefly: An object is anything that is not a function, so that an expression for it does not contain any empty place (p. 32).

Thus according to Frege, it is as if there were a dual operation corresponding to the following table:

object (reference)	thought (meaning)
proper name ↓ object	predicate, function ↓ concept
'saturation' (no 'empty place')	'non-saturation' (empty place)

in which the two vertical arrows express respectively the fact that the reference of a proper name is a determinate object, and the fact that that of a predicate is a concept. As for the way relations are established between the two columns of the table, it is governed by Frege's assertion that *objects* should be regarded as *functional values*, i.e., as the result of the saturation of a function by an argument entering the 'empty place' in that function.

Clearly this takes us back to the problem, already touched on in the previous section, of the *formation of names*, but in a completely different perspective, one in which *thought* (in Frege's sense of the term) *seizes the object*: the formation of a name is indeed now envisaged as the 'mode of presentation of the object', which enables Frege to write:

> "2^4" and "4^2" certainly have the same reference, i.e., they are proper names of the same number; but they have not the same sense [meaning]; consequently, "$2^4 = 4^2$" and "$4.4 = 4^2$" have the same reference, but not the same sense [meaning] (which means, in this case: they do not contain the same thought) (1952a, p. 29).

I have already commented on the anti-subjectivism which always prevented Frege from confusing 'mode of presentation of the object' and 'creation of the object', and I shall have to return to this point vis-à-vis the problem of *fiction* (cf. pp. 118f.). For the moment I shall simply analyse the consequences of what has just been introduced concerning the question of the *proper name* by an examination of the grammatical forms by which saturation and non-saturation are realised: I have already observed that proper names (Kepler, Berlin, Venus . . .) operate in much the same way as the demonstratives (this, that) in so far as in both cases the *uniqueness of the object identified* is the common precondition for their correct operation. Consider now the forms 'that which . . ., he who . . .', which we have already met with (cf. p. 66n.5), for example in the designation of Kepler:

that one = Kepler = he who discovered the elliptic form of the planetary orbits

It is easy to see that, by contrast with the two grammatical phenomena considered above (Kepler/that one), *this construction does not in itself guarantee the uniqueness of the object identified*, quite the contrary, that uniqueness can be affected by syntactic and/or lexical variations and its degree of assignation can vary to the point of disappearing altogether: compare for example the cases 'he who will discover . . .', 'he who were to discover. . .', etc. Besides, one only has to replace the term 'discover' with 'admit' or 'recognise' for the uniqueness of the object identified to disappear completely: indeed, the sentence beginning 'he who admits the elliptic form of the planetary orbits . . .' is rather unlikely as a designation procedure, and would fit much better as the beginning of an argument or a polemic, of the type 'he who admits the elliptic form of the planetary orbits *must also admit that . . .*' or '. *. . does not take it into account that . . .*' etc. In other words, it is proper to the syntactic structure 'he who . . ./that which . . .' that under certain lexical and grammatical conditions (moods, tenses, articles, etc.) it allows a kind of *emptying of the object from the function*, with the result that the syntactic form of construction of the proper name ('he who *VN*', 'that which *VN*'), which might seem generative of determination *by its very nature*, appears in reality to be equally capable of referring to an indeterminate, in which case *he who* becomes the equivalent of *whoever* and *that which* the equivalent of *everything which* or *anything which*.

Now, and what has already been said about simulation should obviate the reader's surprise, we observe characteristically that this phenomenon of indetermination (or non-saturation) is encountered not only in the discourse of the legal apparatus: '*He who* does some damage to *someone* is bound to make it good'[1] but also in the 'everyday' operation of general notions (such as the example cited by Frege: 'Who touches pitch, defiles himself' (1952e, p. 73) or 'what is well conceived can be clearly stated', 'the labourer is worthy of his hire', etc.), and finally in the (scientific) operation of the concept such as 'all mammals have red blood', an expression which Frege points out is equivalent to '*whatever* is a mammal has red blood' (1952d, p. 47). The role of non-saturation, and the indeterminacy linked to it in the different types of statements I have just listed, did not of course escape Frege, although he only drew conclusions from it for 'scientific' statements: 'It is by means of this very indeterminacy that the sense [meaning] acquires the generality expected of a law' (1952e, p. 72). I should just like to remark here that the term 'law' can be understood in its different senses, including the *legal sense* in which someone 'falls within the provisions of the law' which has a penalty ready for him: this means, I believe, that the legal is not purely and simply a 'domain of application' for logic, as is held by the theoreticians of legal formalism (Kelsen, etc.), but that there is a constitutive *relationship of simulation*[2] between legal operators and the mechanisms of conceptual deduction, and

1. This example, used by Lenin in 'Explanation of the Law on Fines Imposed on Factory Workers' (Lenin 1963), has recently been cited and discussed by Bernard Edelman (1979, p. 21). My reliance on Edelman's work will be clear on many further occasions.
2. In the sense I gave to this term on pp. 44f and 50. I shall return to this point again.

especially between legal penalty and logical consequence.[3] This relationship is endorsed by the *apparently homogeneous* operation of the hypothesis (and the conditional connection) which sanctions the following paraphrases of the statements introduced above:

'He who does some damage to someone is bound to make it good.'
→ 'If somebody does ("someone else") some damage, he is bound to make it good.'
'Who touches pitch, defiles himself.'
→ 'If one touches pitch, one defiles oneself.'
'Whatever is a mammal has red blood.'
→ 'If anything is a mammal, then it has red blood.'[4]

This being so, it seems permissible to write the general form of the phenomenon under examination in the following way:

What(ever) is α is β with the following $\alpha_i \beta_i$ couples

$\alpha_1 =$ do some damage $\beta_1 =$ be bound to make it good
$\alpha_2 =$ touch pitch $\beta_2 =$ defile oneself
$\alpha_3 =$ be a mammal $\beta_3 =$ have red blood.

Note that the classical form of the above expression is none other than that of the implication:

$$\forall x, \alpha(x) \supset \beta(x)$$

The predicative and conceptual character of the 'common noun' stands out here, since, to adapt an example of Frege's vis-à-vis the term 'man', the expression 'men' corresponds in fact to 'the x which are men', such that the proposition 'a man is an animal' is equivalent to 'what is man is animal', i.e.:

$$\forall x, \text{be man } (x) \supset \text{be animal } (x).[5]$$

Consider now the following expression, derived from one of Frege's examples (1952e, p. 76):

'Ice, which is less dense than water, floats on water.'
Frege distinguishes the following three 'thoughts':

(1) Ice is less dense than water.

---

3. Further evidence of this promiscuity, which is worthy of study in itself: the terms *judgement, proof, indices, evidence*, etc.
4. This last paraphrase is Frege's (1952d, p. 47).
5. Note straight away that, from a linguistic point of view, the determiners which introduce the concept are first of all the indefinite article singular *a/an* and the indefinite adjectives *every/any*, though the definite article singular (*the* horse, *l'homme*) is also possible. I shall examine Frege's remarks on this point, the difficulties they raise and the consequences I myself think can be drawn later on (pp. 78f.).

(2) If anything is less dense than water, if floats on water.
(3) Ice floats on water.

It is clear straight away that these three 'thoughts' constitute in fact respectively (1) the minor premiss, (2) the major premiss and (3) the conclusion of a syllogism which could be stated as:

If anything is less dense than water, it floats on water.

But: Ice is less dense than water.

Hence: Ice floats on water.

Using the algebra introduced above, and taking

α = be ice
β = be less dense than water
γ = float on water,

we can write:

$\forall x, \beta(x) \supset \gamma(x)$ corresponds to (2)
$\forall x, \alpha(x) \supset \beta(x)$ corresponds to (1)

hence $\forall x, \alpha(x) \supset \beta(x) \supset \gamma(x)$

and, deleting the intermediary element $\beta(x)$:

$\forall x, \alpha(x) \supset \gamma(x)$

which can be paraphrased: 'Ice floats on water.'

The reader will have noticed that I have just reconstituted the mechanism of the 'explicative' relative clause whose essential characteristic is that it constitutes in itself what Frege calls a *thought*, that is a saturated element, as opposed to the 'determinative' relative clause and the corresponding effect of the preconstructed that we studied above. One can go further and remark that the explicative proposition (which, as Frege remarks, can, *among other possibilities*, be paraphrased by a subordinate clause introduced by 'because') intervenes as support for a thought contained in another proposition, and this by means of a relation of *implication* between two properties, α and β, a relation I have stated in the form 'what is α is β'. I shall call this the *sustaining effect*, to mark the fact that it is this relation that realises the *articulation* between the constituent propositions. The fact that the deletion of the explicative clause does not destroy the meaning of the basic proposition (here: 'Ice . . . floats on water') clearly marks its *accessary* character: it might be said to constitute a *lateral reminder* of something that is already known from elsewhere and helps to think the object of the basic proposition. I shall return (p. 116) to the ambiguous character of this 'reminder', which may be a simulated reminder surreptitiously introducing a new 'thought'. At any rate, for the moment let me say that, by contrast with the operation of the preconstructed, which presents its object to thought in the modality of externality and pre-existence, the articulation of assertions, based on what I have called the 'sustaining process', constitutes a kind of *return of the known in thought*. This seems to be what Leibniz was expressing in his own way when he said:

> Some one in danger needs a pistol-ball, and lacks the lead to found it in the form he has; a friend says to him: remember that the *silver* you have in your purse is *fusible*; this friend will not teach him a quality of the silver, but will make him think of a use he may make of it, in order to have pistol-balls in this pressing need. A large part of moral truths and of the most beautiful sentences of authors is of this nature: they very often teach us nothing, but they make us think at the right time of what we know (Leibniz 1896, p. 492).

The articulation of assertions in this example corresponds to a sentence of the kind: 'this silver, which is fusible, can be used to make pistol-balls.' I pointed out in Chapter 4 (p. 63) that the sentence used by Frege ('Kepler . . . died in misery') was susceptible to an explicative transformation of the type 'Kepler, who discovered the elliptic form of the planetary orbits, died in misery', *on condition* that a link be recognised between the fact of violating celestial secrets and the retribution constituted by the fact of dying in misery, a possibility that Frege, as I observed, does not evoke. It is all the more illuminating to compare this sentence with another, also used as an example by Frege:

> 'Napoleon, who recognised the danger to his right flank, himself led his guards against the enemy position.'

Frege says (1952e, pp. 73–6) that there are two thoughts expressed in this example, namely:

(1) Napoleon recognised the danger to his right flank;
(2) Napoleon himself led his guards against the enemy position.

And Frege adds:

> If the entire sentence is uttered as an assertion, we thereby simultaneously assert both component sentences . . . We can therefore expect that [the subordinate clause] may be replaced,

without harm to the truth value of the whole, by a sentence having the same truth value. This is indeed the case.

However, having developed this point and said that the substitution can be made without harm to the truth value of the whole sentence 'provided there are no grammatical obstacles', Frege is led to formulate a restriction vis-à-vis certain subordinate clauses:

These subordinate clauses have no such simple sense [meaning]. Almost always, it seems, we connect with the main thought expressed by us subsidiary thoughts which, although not expressed, are associated with our words, in accordance with *psychological laws*,[6] by the hearer . . . One might perhaps find that the sentence [above] . . . expresses not only the two thoughts shown above, but also the thought that the knowledge of the danger was the reason why he led the guards against the enemy position. One may in fact doubt whether this thought is merely slightly suggested or really expressed. Let the question be considered whether our sentence be false if Napoleon's decision had already been made before he recognised the danger.

Here Frege hesitates and seems even a little embarrassed:

If our sentence could be true in spite of this, the subsidiary thought should not be understood as part of the sense [meaning]. The alternative would make for quite a complicated situation: We would have more simple thoughts than clauses. If the sentence 'Napoleon recognised the danger to his right flank' were now to be replaced by another having the same truth value, e.g. 'Napoleon was already more than 45 years old' not only would our first thought be changed, but also our third one. Hence the truth value of the latter might change – viz. if his age was not the reason for the decision to lead the guards against the enemy.

Frege concludes with what I think is an extremely important remark:

This shows why clauses of equal truth value cannot always be substituted for one another in such cases. The clause expresses

6. My emphasis. See p. 77.

more through its connexion with another than it does in isolation.

In other words, Frege seems to be hesitating between two possible interpretations:

A 'contingent' interpretation of the type: 'It happens that Napoleon (of whom I say in another connection that he recognised the danger to his right flank) himself led his guards against the enemy position';

A 'necessary' interpretation of the type: 'Napoleon, because he recognised the danger to his right flank, himself led his guards against the enemy position.'

Note that we have here entered the psychological circle in which 'pure historical narrative' alternates with the analysis of the 'motives' and 'intentions'[7] which danger may provoke in *somebody*, to be precise in *a general*, and *not just any general*, but *Napoleon*: the question then is, can we think of some connection of precondition and consequence, of the form:

'If (being a general, or being Napoleon) one recognises a danger threatening, one must oneself lead the attack to ward it off,'

and if not, the questions arises, what is this allusion to a danger threatening the right flank of Napoleon's army doing in the 'pure narrative' of the latter's deeds? So we see the emergence of a kind of *complicity* between the speaker and his addressee as a condition of existence of a *meaning* for the sentence. This complicity in fact presupposes an *identification with the speaker*, in other words the possibility of thinking what he is thinking in his place. I shall return to examine this question more closely later (pp. 105f.), as I believe it is decisive for an understanding of ideological processes; for the moment it is enough to note that the question of the existence of a link between two predicates in fact involves the question of the domain of application of those predicates.

Now, precisely, it is as if the implicit ideal of logical reflection were to arrive at that 'system of perfect signs' (ideography) discussed by Frege, a system cleared of the blemishes of vulgar languages and in which *the emptying of the argument places attached to the predicates* would be carried right through, that is, to the point of the final 'disappearance' of objects. As is well known, Frege always hesitated to commit himself completely to this path (later followed

7. Cf. Benveniste's distinction between '*histoire*' (story or history) and '*discours*' (discourse).

by Russell and Wittgenstein for example),[8] thanks to a kind of spontaneous materialism which prevented him from confusing the object with the 'mode of presentation' of the object, i.e., reference with meaning. His discussion of what he called 'compound thoughts' of the type:

'If someone is a murderer, then he is a criminal'

seems nevertheless to tend towards the notion of a thought constituted by the connection of predicates emptied of all objects:

> Without some further clue, we cannot determine whether what is expressed in the sentence 'He is a criminal' is true or false when detached from this compound; for the word 'he' is not a proper name . . . This holds of the antecedent-clause as well, for it likewise has a non-designating component, namely 'someone'. Yet the compound sentence can none the less express a thought. The 'someone' and the 'he' refer to each other. Hence, and in virtue of the 'If—, then—,' the two clauses are so connected with one another that they together express a thought (1977, p. 71).

In some sense Frege seems here to suppose that, every 'thought' being for him by nature 'complete and saturated', *saturation in the example above is realised by the relationship between several empty places*: this conception of saturation, joined to the use of the hypothetical and a logicist apprehension of the 'composition of thought' (Frege 1977a), might be described as the element in Frege's reflection that constituted the theoretical obstacle hindering him (and almost preventing him) from developing the point I noted above about the restrictions which in reality affect the substitution for one another of clauses with the same truth value, and the reasons why 'the clause expresses more through its connection with another than it does in isolation' (1952e, p. 76). Thus he was condemned to a separation of the domain of his reflection into two spaces, dividing the 'composition of thoughts' (the domain of logic and of the syllogism) from what he is designating here in speaking of 'connection' and could not conceive henceforth *except* as an extra-logical adjunction of a *psychological* kind, producing in thought *the subjective impression of richness and depth* bound up with the concatenation-connection of 'thoughts' to one another.

8. 'I wish to suggest . . . that what would commonly be called a "thing" is nothing but a bundle of coexisting qualities such as redness, hardness, etc.'(Russell 1940, p. 97).

The example of 'common nouns' and conceptual terms will perhaps allow me to clarify what determined the form of this division in Frege's reflection; let me begin by noting that, as is quite obvious, the problem of the 'emptying' of the places attached to a predicate arises particularly acutely in the case of 'common nouns': to the ambiguity I discussed above corresponds that of statements such as '(the) man who is rational is free'[9] in which the 'determinative' interpretation presupposes an underlying 'relation' of the type:

'If (being a man), one is rational, one is (also, by that very fact) free',

which corresponds to the general form (with N designating the 'common noun', α and β two predicates):

$$\left\{ \begin{array}{c} \text{an } N \\ \text{any } N \end{array} \right\}, \text{ if it is } \alpha, \text{ is } \beta = \text{the } [N \left\{ \begin{array}{c} \text{who} \\ \text{which} \end{array} \right\} \text{ is } \alpha] \text{ is } \beta.$$

So, as I have already pointed out, the rule by which 'the indefinite article accompanies a concept-word' is not always borne out 'in surface structure' because, as Frege himself remarks:

The matter is not so simple for the definite article, especially in the plural . . . In the singular, so far as I can see, the matter is doubtful only when a singular takes the place of a plural, as in the sentence 'the Turk besieged Vienna', 'the horse is a four-legged animal'. These cases are so easily recognisable as special ones that the value of our rule is hardly impaired by their occurrence. It is clear that in the first sentence 'the Turk' is the proper name of a people. The second sentence is probably best regarded as expressing a universal judgement, say 'all horses are four-legged animals' or 'all properly constituted horses are four-legged animals' (1952d, p. 45).

Let us transpose the examples above à propos the concept man: what is the meaning of the sentence 'the man who is rational is free'? Can we arrive at it by answering the question as to whether 'all properly constituted men' are rational, or whether only some among men are rational, as opposed to others who, though not

9. Cf. p. 12 n. 6 above [Translator's Note].

rational, are still men for all that? Or again, can one say that *Man* (for example in a proposition such as 'Man has walked on the Moon') is the proper name of a people, i.e., the inhabitants of the Earth?[10]

One would anticipate here that the question cannot in fact be reduced to the analysis of the 'extension' and 'comprehension' of the concept *Man*, but that on the contrary, *something fundamental takes place first, on which that analysis is based.* I shall propose the idea that what takes place is the *identification* by which every subject 'recognises himself' as a man, and also as a worker, a technician, an executive, a manager, etc., and again as a Turk, a Frenchman, a German, etc., and how his relationship to *what represents him* is organised:[11] a first spark, the gleam of a solution. In Frege's example, 'the Turk besieged Vienna', the question seems to have been answered even before it has been asked: 'the Turk', i.e., 'the Turkish people', 'the Turks' and 'Turkey' all at once. If this is so, why would one not say 'the American bombs North Vietnam' but only, at a stretch, 'the Americans bomb North Vietnam' and more easily 'the United States', even 'the American government', or 'Nixon'?

In this connection, let me reproduce here a remark whose objective irony with respect to neo-positivism will perhaps help us locate the fundamental 'oversight' of logical idealism: in his study *L'Empirisme logique*, Professor Louis Vax remarks that in the theoretical perspective in which the universe is populated by distinct and observable realities, 'it is impossible to discover outside Hodge, Tibbles, Grimalkin, . . . some *reality* that is the class of cats, which leads to the consideration that the class of cats is a carnivorous logical construction' ('Every cat is carnivorous'). But, he adds:

> There is worse to come. As no one would dream of considering 'Marianne' as a being existing and subsisting in herself, I am licensed to consider France as a logical construction composed of concrete elements such as Dupont, Duval, Dubois, . . . Now a logical construction that declares war on another logical construction is even more embarrassing than a ratticidal and carnivorous logical construction. Because neither Dupont, nor

10. Once again, the French here has definite articles – 'l'Homme' and 'l'Homme a marché sur la lune' [Translator's Note].
11. 'It really is me, I am here, a worker, a boss or a soldier!' (Althusser 1971b, p. 166).

Duval, nor I declared war on Müller, Wagner, . . . in September 1939. In other words a political or legal entity is not the same thing as a class of individuals. Clear as day to everyone, the proposition 'France declared war on Germany in 1939' has become inscrutably obscure thanks to a logical analysis that was supposed to clarify it (Vax 1970, p. 25).

I can now propose a hypothesis about the origins of the positivist 'oversight' which invincibly leads to its arguments 'missing the point' as soon as politics enters the scene in one way or another: in this case it is as if the 'anti-metaphysical' vigilance had become a blindness to the seriousness of metaphors and their effectiveness; not for one moment is there the suspicion that for Dupont to belong to the 'class of Frenchmen' he must be produced *as French*, which presupposes the effective existence not of 'Marianne' but of 'France' and its political and legal institutions. In other words, the oversight blocks an appreciation of the constitutive, and not derivatory, inferred or constructed function of metaphor (and of metonymy = France/the King of France/the French), and correlatively fosters an ignorance of the *material effectivity of the imaginary*. The imaginary is then posited as equivalent to the unreal and reduced to an individual psychological effect of a 'poetic' kind. Reflecting on the proposition:
'Odysseus was set ashore at Ithaca while sound asleep'
Frege declares that:

the sentence . . . obviously has a sense [meaning]. But . . . it is doubtful whether the name 'Odysseus', occurring therein, has reference (1952e, p. 62).

And he adds:

In hearing an epic poem, for instance, apart from the euphony of the language we are interested only in the sense [meaning] of the sentences and the images and feelings thereby aroused. The question of truth would cause us to abandon aesthetic delight for an attitude of scientific investigation. Hence it is a matter of no concern to us whether the name 'Odysseus', for instance, has reference, so long as we accept the poem as a work of art (p. 63).

Now, it is striking to find that a few pages later Frege returns to this question of expressions devoid of any reference and the 'false pretences' they give rise to, and this time he develops another example:

> This lends itself to demagogic abuse as easily as ambiguity – perhaps more easily. 'The will of the people' can serve as an example; for it is easy to establish that there is at any rate no generally accepted reference for this expression. It is therefore by no means unimportant to eliminate the source of these mistakes, at least in science, once and for all (p. 70).

In my opinion this reveals the 'blind spot' in Frege's thought, what I have called *the limits of his materialism*: what Frege is proposing here is clearly that political expressions like 'the people', 'the will of the people', etc., *should be taken with a pinch of salt*, as he says elsewhere, i.e., they are marked, like 'Odysseus', with an index of unreality which denies them the referential stability of objects and makes them matters of individual appreciation, a thesis which is the hallmark of the bourgeois apprehension of politics. For bourgeois ideology, politics, like poetry, belongs to the register of fiction and game.[12]

But, it will no doubt be said, is this interpretation not incompatible with the other aspect of Frege's reflections, evoked above, in which he tries on the contrary to confer on 'historical science' and law (cf. in particular his remarks on the operation of juries, pp. 43 and 47) the character of scientific objectivity? Is this not also the sense of his final remark in the quotation above, that he wants 'to eliminate the source of these mistakes . . . once and for all'?

My position is quite simply that these two perspectives (politics as an objective formal science in which the source of errors will be rooted out 'once and for all *and* politics as fiction and game) are not in the slightest incompatible, but on the contrary essentially complementary: they derive in fact from *the two faces of idealism*, respectively *metaphysical realism* (the myth of universal science) and *logical empiricism* (the generalised use of fiction), that I discussed in Part I of this book (cf. p. 47). I can now say that it is indeed a

12. This is an essential point and the object of an important recent study by Michel Plon (1976). See also Plon (1972) and Plon and Prèteceille (1972). The cyclostyled text Plon (1975), to which I refer below, remains unpublished. A version of part of it, corrected (especially as to the notion of subjective appropriation), forms Plon (1976).

question of two 'theoretical detachments' of bourgeois ideology, aiming at the occultation of the political register, in two specialised forms, corresponding on the theoretical plane to different ideological and political dominances in the class struggle: metaphysical realism corresponds to *the bourgeois phantasy of the reabsorption of political struggle* in the pure operation of the legal-political apparatus[13] and characterises the conditions in which the question of state power is not directly posed, so the bourgeoisie can pretend to forsake political struggle and declare itself apolitical, treating problems 'solely in their technical aspect'; the empiricist fiction (and the sceptical cynicism that goes with it) corresponds on the contrary to the *bourgeois form of political practice*, when the bourgeoisie is obliged to 'go in for politics' by manoeuvring, stacking the cards, etc., i.e., when it conducts the political struggle in the form of a *game*.

It would be by no means useless to study in detail (as I cannot do here) how, from Frege to Russell and Wittgenstein (not to speak of ideologists like Karl Popper), the 'blind spot' I have designated in Frege has gradually become the central core of militant idealism, inspiring contemporary bourgeois ideology in the combined (and alternating) forms of the two 'theoretical detachments' I have just examined. I could go on. However, I shall restrict myself to an attempt to draw out the consequences of what precedes in the perspective of a materialist theory of discourse.

13. Cf. the latest invention in this domain, which goes by the name of 'administrative science'. It should be compared with the notion of the 'administration of things', understood as a form of apolitical social organisation. I shall refer later on to the recent discussion of this point raised by Étienne Balibar (Balibar, E. 1974).

6 Subject, Centre, Meaning

In what way has the examination just completed helped me to advance in the project I have undertaken?

I have of course located a certain number of relationships between *logic* on the one hand (universal/existential quantifier, function, predicate/arguments, implication and syllogism, inter-propositional composition, etc.) and *linguistics* on the other (proper name/common noun, demonstrative, definite/indefinite articles, lexical properties, etc.), and this vis-à-vis two 'operations', one ultimately concerned with the modalities of the 'filling' of the places of arguments in a predicate, as conditions of formation of the statement, the other bearing on the articulation between statements, i.e., in fact on the passage to discursivity, to the generation of 'text'.

This being so, can we consider that this description of the two mechanisms embedding/articulation fulfills the requirements I set at the end of the first chapter of this book with respect to the relationship between (linguistic) basis and (discursive-ideological) process? In other words, is it sufficient to have formally indicated the existence of these two mechanisms (linguistically realisáble and susceptible to a logical interpretation) to settle the question raised earlier of the simulation of scientific knowledges in ideological miscognition and hence the key problem of a theory of discourse? Should one regard the two operations as 'neutral' with respect to the discontinuity sciences/ideologies and hold that their logico-linguistic character makes them *base structures* capable of 'serving' *indifferently* both sciences and ideologies?

My answer demands extended treatment, by reason of the dialectical character of its content, i.e., by reason of the contradiction that constitutes it: if, indeed, 'non-neutrality' or 'non-indifference' with respect to the discontinuity sciences/ideologies is understood as a kind of specialisation such that one of the two mechanisms would be assigned to the 'domain of miscognition' while the other would characterise 'scientific discourse', then, I believe, the answer must clearly be that such a *specialisation*, breaking the neutrality and the indifference, *is a myth*. But, precisely, this myth cannot but *involve an ideological conception of the discontinuity sciences/ideologies*, one which I shall show in a moment consists of the substitution for this discontinuity of the opposition between 'science' (logic) on the one hand and 'metaphysics' on the other; and in this sense precisely the double logico-linguistic operation I am discussing is not 'neutral' or 'indifferent' with respect to ideology: it can be said to realise spontaneously the ideological covering up of the discontinuity by simulating it ideologically. Furthermore, this simulation depends in fact on the masking of a third element, neither logical nor linguistic, which has been glimpsed several times in the analyses developed above: indeed, I have emphasised that these two 'mechanisms' necessarily brought into play relationships between 'domains of thought', relationships of discrepancy taking the form

(1) of *externality-anteriority* (preconstructed) or that
(2) of the 'return of the known in thought' producing a *reminder* which provides the support for the subject's adoption of a position.

It is these relationships, within which *the thinkable* is constituted, that form the third element, which I said a moment ago was masked by the (exclusively) logico-linguistic conception of those mechanisms. This third element constitutes strictly speaking the object of the present study, in the form of a materialist theoretical approach to *the operation of representations and 'thought' in discursive processes*. As we shall see, this presupposes an examination of the relationship between the subject and what represents him, i.e., a theory of identification and of the material effectivity of the imaginary.

But I shall begin by a complete exposition of the *spontaneously idealist* character taken by the operation of the *embedding/articulation* couple as it is developed in logical neo-positivism, before attempting to show the transformations and displacements that are necessary for its materialist use. It is clear, indeed, that this opposition, left to itself, operates quite naturally as the current extension of the oppositions whose fate I have traced above, as pairs of philosophical categories: the couple *necessary/contingent* is, as we have seen, both taken over and concealed by the couple *object/subject*, which in logical empiricism takes the form of the coupled opposition 'logical construction'/'observables', in which one of the terms is constituted by the corpus of the observations of a subject described in 'concrete', 'situational' language, using what Russell calls egocentric particulars (I, here, now, etc.), and in which the other term corresponds to hypothetico-deductive relations conceived as the very basis of scientific abstraction. It is not difficult to predict, as a function of what has already been said, that in this perspective, which, I repeat, is of directly idealist descent, the dual operation *articulation of statements/embedding* will be spontaneously arranged so that *embedding* is the base mechanism providing the 'description of observables' and the *articulation of assertions* is that of scientific abstraction linking 'logical constructions' together. In this connection it should be noted that the determinative 'that which is α is β' corresponds to a pure 'universal' link between properties $(\alpha \supset \beta)$, and takes the form of the explicative when one returns to the world of 'things' conceived as bundles of properties: 'x, which is α, is β', which constitutes the logicist 'solution' to the problem of the determination/apposition relationship.

The inevitable result is thus the idea of a 'science of any object' for which only *thought relations* exist, emptied of all 'being': this is that 'logically perfect language' or ideography which, Frege says, 'should satisfy the conditions that every expression grammatically well constructed as a proper name out of signs already introduced shall in fact designate an object, and that no new sign shall be introduced as a proper name without being secured a reference' (1952e, p.70); an expression typical of Frege in its ambiguity, its 'natural' idealist interpretation emphasising the first part to the detriment of the second, forgetting the modality 'should satisfy the conditions', so that its spontaneous paraphrase runs: 'It is sufficient that an expression be grammatically well constructed as a proper name out of signs already introduced for it in fact to designate an object.' 'Logic' thus becomes the core of 'science', with, at the same time, the inevitable idealist oversight positing *the independence of thought with respect to being*, in so far as any syntactically correct designation constructs an 'object' . . . of thought, in other words a logical fiction, recognised as such. This explains how neo-positivist philosophy, otherwise so careful to get rid of 'metaphysical entities', can co-exist so happily with fiction as a 'manner of speaking': the ultimate secret of this paradox is explained by the rule of the 'suspension of existential judgement' which maintains that 'in a rigorous language, descriptions imply no belief in any existence' (Vax 1970, p. 19).

This being so, it is clearly apparent that the relationship

'concrete/abstract', or, to use Carnap's terminology, the relationship between observation language and theoretical language, is quite naturally superimposed onto the situational-property/permanent-property relationship, as this has traditionally been understood – and still is at the present time – by the majority of grammarians and linguists.[1]

Furthermore, it may be observed that the situational-property/permanent-property relationship is ineluctably conceived by the philosophy of language (which is, as I have said, the 'spontaneous philosophy' of linguistic science) along the lines of the *empirico-subjectivist myth of continuity* which holds that a gradual elimination of the situational leads steadily from the concrete individual subject 'in situ' (linked to his percepts and his notions) to a universal subject situated everywhere and nowhere and thinking in concepts. This movement can be summarised in the following table, taken from Catherine Fuchs, which reads from left to right:

	1 origin	*2* discrepancy	*3* general- isation	*4* universal- isation
logico-grammatical reference categories	I	you/I	he, x/I	any subject (everyone, anyone what- soever)
	see present here	say past elsewhere/ here	say past elsewhere/ here	think always everywhere
basic form of the utterance	(I say that) I see this	you have told me that . . .	I have been told that . . . it has been observed that . . .	it is true that . . .

It is in fact on the idealist basis of this continuous movement 'from the concrete to the abstract' that the explicative/determinative

---

1. Cf. Husserl's remark, already mentioned, about 'there are cakes, there are regular solids'.

distinction is most commonly understood,[2] not necessarily by conflating determination with 'concrete' on the one hand and explication with 'abstract' on the other, but by marrying the two oppositions without inquiring why in some cases the opposition is overdetermined, blurred or obliterated; for example in utterances like 'Long live communism which has nothing to do with Brezhnev!' (Lutte Ouvrière poster), or 'Consider an inclined plane which makes an angle of 15 degrees to the horizontal'. I shall return later to the various problems raised by these examples which relate in different ways to the question of *simulation*. For the moment, let me just say that the continuism underlying the situational-property/ permanent-property opposition depends, as I shall try to show, on the process of *identification* ('If I were where you/he/x are/is, I would see and think what you/he/x see(s) and think(s)'), adding that the imaginary of the identification radically masks any epistemological discontinuity, as is naively revealed by the commentator already quoted vis-à-vis Carnap's distinction between 'observation language' and 'theoretical language':

Within L, he [Carnap] distinguishes two languages: L_o whose predicates designate realities or relations that are directly observable (hot, blue, larger than . . .); and L_t containing theoretical terms designating entities or properties which escape direct observation (electrons, super-ego . . .). It is easy to appreciate the difference between an *observation concept* and a *theoretical concept*. Suppose a group of adolescents revolts because it does not enjoy the same advantages as another group. The broken windows, the graffiti on the walls, the insults are observable data to which the terms 'broken windows', 'graffiti',

2. I should point out, however, that linguistic research is beginning to question the simplicity of the opposition which associates the hypothetical with the determinative, and explanation with the explicative. Marie-Claire Barbault and Jean-Pierre Desclés have recently pointed out (1972, p. 82) that the latter can have different values, of mere conjunction, adversative conjunction or even temporal succession. The problem of the relative autonomy characterising the statement inserted in the explicative clause is considered in Fuchs and Milner (1979). Finally, at a more general level, the latter authors insist on the need to investigate the links between *linguistic phenomena* (pertaining to the system of the values involved in the operations of topicalisation – e.g., the differences induced by the nature of the 'relative clause' (determinative or explicative) and by the status (N_1 or N_2) of its antecedent – of determination, and of the verb system, etc.) and *lexical characteristics*.

etc., can correspond in language L_o. A social psychologist appointed to study the facts might refer to the term 'reference group', which does not correspond to any directly observable reality, but constitutes a theoretical concept, belonging to language L_t, capable of explaining the adolescents' behaviour (Vax 1970, p. 49).

This revealing example demonstrates with exceptional clarity the masking of the discontinuity (and the relationship of simulation) between scientific knowledge and ideological miscognition, in so far as the epistemological romance erected by neo-positivism as a description of the operation of a science is here taken seriously and realised in that other romance that the 'science of social psychology' in reality is.[3] Note, by the way, the complicity between the conceptions of logical empiricism and the ideology of the 'experimental method', a complicity dependent, as we shall see, on the process of identification, represented ideologically in the forms of 'inter-subjectivity' and 'consensus'.

All this should lead the reader who has followed me this far straightforwardly enough to the observation that neo-positivist idealism *makes no mistakes* in its pursuit of 'metaphysical entities', in so far as it 'turns a blind eye' too regularly for it to be an accident: it unhesitatingly falls into the trap of the social psychology of groups as a stock of explanatory hypotheses, but turns up its nose at 'demagogic fictions' like *the people*, *the masses* or *the working class*. Confronted with these 'entities', logical empiricism suddenly rediscovers all its critical vigour and tirelessly repeats that, unlike the 'physical world', which is stable and coherent, the 'mental world' does not allow of a secure reference, except by virtue of the illusions which capture all subjects in the form of 'consensus', conformism, etc. *The two faces of a single central error*, consisting on the one hand in the consideration of ideologies as *ideas* and not as *material forces*,[4] and on the other in the conception of these ideas as having their sources *in subjects*, whereas in reality they '*constitute*

3. For the reader who is shocked by the bluntness of this assertion, allow me to refer to Bruno, Pêcheux, Plon and Poitou (1973).
4. Clausewitz gives a very clear explanation of how, faced by the armies of the French Revolution, the strategic calculations of the Prussian generals always went astray, because *they were unable to conceive* the material force constituted by 'the will of the people'. The defeat of American strategy in Vietnam stems from the same 'error'.

individuals as subjects', in Althusser's words. I shall return to this point. The Port-Royal logicians, who also reflected on terms like body, community, people, etc., fell into the same error, but in a different way which it is interesting to stress: discussing expressions like 'The Romans vanquish'd the Carthaginians' or 'The Venetians make war against the Turk', they recognised that these propositions were neither universal nor particular, but singular:

'For the People *is consider'd morally as one Man*, living several Ages, and so long subsisting, as long as the Common-wealth endures: And ceases not to act by those People of which it is compos'd, *as a Man acts by his members*' (Arnauld and Nicole 1685, p. 228 – [my emphasis, M. P.]).

In other words, the idealist 'solution' consists on this point in starting from the 'concrete' individual subject both as element of a set (community, people, etc.) and as source of the metaphor constituted by the personification of this set operating 'as one man': I have already implied several times that the fundamental idealist obstacle lay in the *ideological notion of the subject* as the point of departure and point of application of operations. It is now possible to draw the materialist conclusions from this discovery in the area that concerns us, which will necessitate a transformation of the metaphor, so that it appears for what it is, namely a non-subjective process in which the subject is constituted. In his recent *Reply to John Lewis*, Althusser is designating just this point when he explains that *the masses are not a subject*, and he goes on:

Can we still talk about a 'subject', identifiable by the *unity* of its 'personality'? Compared with John Lewis's subject, 'man', as simple and neat as you can imagine, the masses, considered as a subject, pose very exacting problems of identity and identification. You cannot hold such a 'subject' in your hand, you cannot point to it. A subject is a being about which we can say: 'that's it!' How do we do that when the masses are supposed to be the 'subject'; how can we say: 'that's it'? (Althusser 1976b, p. 48).

I have tried to draw out in all its consequences the idealist conception that menaces the 'theory of discourse' at a number of points of attack which can be summarised as follows: the first of these points lies in a formalist interpretation of the two linguisticodiscursive mechanisms *embedding* (determination) and the *articulation of statements*, an interpretation that leads to the second point, consisting in an occlusion of the *sciences/ideologies* distinction by the idealist couple logic (= science)/metaphysics. And, as we have just seen, these idealist interpretations and occlusions find a basis in a third point, namely the ideological 'subject' effect, whereby subjectivity appears as source, origin, point of departure or point of application. I can now assert that it does not suffice for the constitution of a materialist theory of discursive processes for it to reproduce as one of its theoretical objects the ideological 'subject' as 'always-already-given';[5] in fact, and for crucial reasons connected with the imbrication of the different elements I have just stated, such a theory, if it genuinely intends to fulfill its claims, cannot do without a *(non-subjectivist) theory of subjectivity*. With the result that the theoretical domain of this work is ultimately defined by three inter-linked zones which can be designated respectively as *subjectivity, discursivity* and the *sciences/ideologies discontinuity*. If these inter-linkings are not adequately appreciated, a number of points will become utterly obscure and incomprehensible, as in fact happens with *all* idealist attempts at a theory of the (ideological/or scientific) 'subject in discourse'; or to be precise: what idealism makes incomprehensible is above all *political practice* and also *the practice of the production of knowledges* (as well as *educational practice*), in other words precisely the different forms in which 'blind necessity' (Engels) becomes *necessity thought and mastered as necessity*.

In this respect, a text which is already quite old (Herbert 1968) provides a revealing example of the difficulties to be confronted in such an investigation, and it seems appropriate in the present connection to emphasise both the materialist elements I believe it contains and the idealist mistakes that it stumbles into. In fact this text proposes an opposition between *'empirical' ideology, metaphor and semantics* on the one hand and *'speculative' ideology, metonymy and syntax* on the other, which now appears to be an attempt to designate (somewhat confusedly, because caught in the object it is designating) the existence and the effects in ideology of the joint system of the two mechanisms *embedding/articulation*. To start with

5. In other words, a pure *logico-linguistic* theory of discourse is perfectly possible (cf. some aspects of the work of Austin, Ducrot, etc.), but such a theory must remain blind to the question of the subject as 'always-already-given'. That is why it is a matter of idealism.

the stumbling points, one of the most obvious is a kind of identification of Ideology with 'the general form of discourse', which leads to a use of the disjunction empirical/speculative that is too easily superimposable on the opposition situational-property/ permanent-property already examined. But the real roots of this error lie elsewhere, namely in a miscognition of the class struggle: the term and concept of contradiction, and that of class struggle, are absent as such from the description of the empirical and speculative ideological processes. All we find are *oppositions*, *differences* expressing the *two-sided* complexity of the relationship productive forces/ relations of production. In my opinion, this is the reason why none of the effects (and none of the forms of realisation) of the class struggle are really taken into account; there is nothing about political practice, only a substitute for it about 'variation and mutation', and, finally, very little about the production of knowledges (and even less about educational practice). Thus it is this stumbling-point that renders useless as such the materialist elements I believe can be located in this article today, namely:

(1) the conception of the process of *metaphor* as a socio-historical process providing a basis for the *'presentation' of objects for subjects*, and not just as a *manner of speaking* that develops secondarily on the basis of an original non-metaphorical meaning, for which the object is something 'naturally' given, literally *pre*-social and *pre*-historical;

(2) the distinction between the two articulated figures of the *ideological subject*, in the form on the one hand of the *identification-unification of the subject with himself* (the 'I see what I see' of the 'empirical guarantee') and on the other of the *identification of the subject with the universal*, through the support of the other as reflected discourse, providing the 'speculative guarantee' ('everyone knows that . . .', 'it is clear that . . .', etc.), which introduces the idea of the *speculative simulation of scientific knowledge by ideology*;

(3) finally, and above all, a first (no doubt uncertain and incomplete) sketch of a non-subjectivist theory of subjectivity, designating the processes of 'imposition-concealment' that constitute the subject by 'putting him into place' (by signifying to him *what he is*) *and* by concealing from him at the same time that 'putting into place' (that *subjection*) thanks to the illusion of autonomy constitutive of the subject, such that the subject 'works by himself' in the words of Althusser who, in 'Ideology and Ideological State Apparatuses', has laid *the real foundations* for such a non-subjectivist

theory of the subject, as a theory of the ideological conditions of the reproduction/transformation of the relations of production: the relationship between the *unconscious* (in Freud's sense) and *ideology* (in Marx's sense), which inevitably remained a mystery in the structuralist pseudo-solution of Herbert's article,[6] thus *begins* to be clarified, as we shall see, by the fundamental thesis that '*Ideology interpellates individuals as subjects*':

> The individual is interpellated as a (free) subject in order that he shall submit freely to the commandments of the Subject, i.e., in order that he shall (freely) accept his subjection (Althusser 1971b, p. 169).

If I add, first, that this subject with a capital S – the absolute and universal subject – is precisely what Jacques Lacan calls the Other, with a capital O, and second, that, in Lacan's formulation again, 'the unconscious is the discourse of the Other', one can begin to see how *unconscious repression* and *ideological subjection* are materially linked, without being confounded, inside what could be called *the*

6. Thus I now consider absolutely unacceptable the objection that only 'physically observable', concrete individuals exist, an objection that claims to settle the question by *unpacking* the metaphor as follows: 'France is nothing but 50 million concrete individuals who . . .'. In fact, this 'materialism' is quite indistinguishable from the physicalist empiricism whose constant propensity to 'go astray' I have demonstrated above, which is not to say, indeed quite the contrary, that it does not 'find its way home' to a place in the ideological and political interests of the ruling class. Let me stress here that the (theoretical and *practical*) inadequacy of any interpretation of ideology *either* as pure illusion and non-being ('devoid of meaning') which one only has to cease to mention to deprive of any effect, *or* as pure fable, deliberately invented by Priests and Despots (I shall return to this question vis-à-vis the complex rhetoric-persuasion-inculcation).

In other words, when I speak of a Subject with a capital S which 'interpellates' individuals as subjects, etc., it is not because I 'believe in it', in the sense in which one 'believes in God': God does not exist, but religion – and more generally ideologies – do, with their own materiality and corresponding operation. This is what is at stake here. Hence in the use I am making here of concepts elaborated by Lacan, I am severing them from the idealist inscription of that elaboration, by Lacan himself among others, an aspect which Paul Henry's text already referred to (Henry 1974) seems to me to make crystal clear. Let me just say that formulations such as 'the subject of the unconscious', 'the subject of science', etc., partake of this idealist inscription. As for the question of *the absolute supremacy of the Symbolic*, it carries with it a Lacanian philosophy and epistemology whose interests need to be confronted with those of materialism.

process of the Signifier in interpellation and identification, a process by which are realised what I have called the ideological preconditions of the reproduction/transformation of the relations of production.

Here, I believe, I have reached a decisive point in my project: up to now this work has been marked by a *conditional* progress, constantly having to double back on itself and thereby indicating that the effects of idealism in the field of the philosophy of language and of the theory of discourse had not yet really been dealt with. This oblique, advancing and retreating movement is responsible for the really rather 'involved' appearance of the arguments hitherto, i.e., for the interweaving of often disparate and ambiguous elements, of notations constituting so many toothing stones, disjointed suggestions, the whole forming a kind of theoretical 'climate' (with its clouds and its bright intervals) in which the reader runs ahead or trails behind on several intersecting paths, several intertwining threads. But the ground we have reached (that of a non-subjective theory of subjectivity) should now allow me to lay the bases for *a (materialist) theory of discursive processes*, and by that very fact to register the relative positions of the paths we have travelled or, to use the other metaphor, to tie the threads together.

This does not mean, of course, that the development I am now going to attempt to make is definitively guaranteed in all its materialist import, idealism having disappeared (!), but just that it contains 'at the outset' the means to correct the idealist oversights, errors and slides that may arise in it.

PART III

DISCOURSE AND IDEOLOGY(IES)

7 On the Ideological Conditions of the Reproduction/ Transformation of the Relations of Production

I shall start by explicating the expression that I have just introduced, i.e., '*ideological conditions of the reproduction/transformation of the relations of production*'. This explication will be carried out within the limits of my objective, which is to lay the foundations of a materialist theory of discourse.

To avoid certain misunderstandings, however, I must also specify a number of points of more general import, concerning the theory of ideologies, the practice of the production of knowledges and political practice, without which everything that follows would be quite 'out of place'.

(a) If I stress '*ideological* conditions of the reproduction/transformation of the relations of production', this is because the region of ideology is by no means the *sole element* in which the reproduction/transformation of the relations of production of a social formation takes place; that would be to ignore the economic determinations which condition that reproduction/transformation 'in the last instance', even within economic production itself, as Althusser recalls at the beginning of his article on the ideological state apparatuses.

(b) In writing 'reproduction/transformation', I mean to designate the nodally contradictory character of *any mode of production which is based on a division into classes, i.e., whose 'principle' is the class struggle*. This means, in particular, that I consider it mistaken to locate at different points on the one hand what contributes to the reproduction of the relations of production and on the other what contributes to their transformation: the class struggle traverses the mode of production as a whole, which, in the region of ideology, means that the class struggle 'passes through' what Althusser has called the ideological state apparatuses.

In adopting the term *ideological state apparatus*, I intend to underline certain aspects which I believe to be crucial (apart of course from the reminder that ideologies are not made up of 'ideas' but of practices):

(1) Ideology does not reproduce itself in the general form of a *Zeitgeist* (i.e., the spirit of the age, the 'mentality' of an epoch, 'habits of thought', etc.) imposed in an even and homogeneous way on 'society' as a kind of space pre-existing class struggle: 'The ideological state apparatuses are not the realisation of ideology *in general* . . .'

(2) '. . . nor even the conflict-free realisation of the ideology of the ruling class', which means that it is impossible to attribute *to each class its own ideology*, as if each existed 'before the class struggle' in its own camp, with its own conditions of existence and its specific institutions, such that the ideological class struggle would be the meeting point of two distinct and pre-existing worlds, each with its own practices and its 'world outlook', this encounter being followed by the victory of the 'stronger' class, which would then impose its ideology on the other. In the end this would only multiply the conception of Ideology as *Zeitgeist* by two.[1]

(3) 'The ideology of the ruling class does not become the ruling ideology by the grace of God . . .', which means that the ideological state apparatuses are not the *expression* of the domination of the ruling ideology, i.e., the ideology of the ruling class (God knows how the ruling ideology would achieve its supremacy if that were so!), but are the *site* and the *means* of realisation of that domination: '. . . it is by the installation of the ideological state apparatuses in which this ideology [the ideology of the ruling class] is realised and realises itself, that it becomes the ruling ideology . . .'

(4) But even so, the ideological state apparatuses are not pure instruments of the ruling class, ideological machines simply reproducing the existing relations of production: '. . . this installation [of the ideological state apparatuses] is not achieved all by itself; on the contrary it is the stake in a very bitter and continuous class

---

1. On this point, see the analysis of reformism in Althusser (1976b, pp. 49f.).

struggle . . .' (Althusser 1971b, p. 172), which means that the ideological state apparatuses constitute simultaneously and contradictorily the site and the ideological conditions of the transformation of the relations of production (i.e., of revolution in the Marxist-Leninist sense). *Hence the expression 'reproduction/ transformation'.*

I can now take one more step in the study of the ideological conditions of the reproduction/transformation of the relations of production, by stating that these contradictory conditions are constituted, at a given historical moment and for a given social formation, *by the complex set of ideological state apparatuses* contained in that social formation. I say *complex* set, i.e., a set with relations of contradiction-unevenness-subordination between its 'elements', and not a mere list of elements: indeed, it would be absurd to think that in a given conjuncture *all the ideological state apparatuses* contribute *equally* to the reproduction of the relations of production *and* to their transformation. In fact, their 'regional' properties – their 'obvious' specialisation into religion, knowledge, politics, etc. – condition their relative importance (the unevenness of their relationships) inside the set of ideological state apparatuses, and that as a function of the state of the class struggle in the given social formation.

This explains why the ideological instance in its concrete materiality exists in the form of 'ideological formations' (referred to ideological state apparatuses) which both have a 'regional' character *and* involve class positions: the ideological 'objects' are always supplied together with 'the way to use them' – their 'meaning', i.e., their orientation, i.e., the class interests which they serve – which allows the commentary that practical ideologies are class practices (practices of class struggle) in Ideology. Which is to say that, in the ideological struggle (no less than in the other forms of class struggle) there are no 'class positions' which *exist abstractly* and *are then applied* to the different regional ideological 'objects' of concrete situations, in the School, the Family, etc. In fact, this is where the contradictory connection between the reproduction and the transformation of the relations of production is joined at the ideological level, in so far as it is not the regional ideological 'objects' taken one by one but the very division into regions (God, Ethics, Law, Justice, Family, Knowledge, etc.) and the relationships of *unevenness-subordination* between those regions that constitute what is at stake in the *ideological class struggle*.

The domination of the ruling ideology (the ideology of the ruling class), which is characterised, at the ideological level, by the fact that the reproduction of the relations of production 'wins out' over their transformation (obstructs it, slows it down or suppresses it in different cases) thus corresponds less to keeping each ideological 'region' considered by itself *the same* than to the reproduction of the relationships of unevenness-subordination between those regions (with their 'objects' and the practices in which they are inscribed):[2] this is what entitled Althusser to propose the apparently scandalous thesis that the set of ideological state apparatuses in a capitalist social formation includes also the *trade unions* and the *political parties* (without further specification; in fact all he meant to designate was the function *attributed* to political parties and trade unions within the complex of the ideological state apparatuses *under the domination of the ruling ideology (the ideology of the ruling class)*, i.e., the subordinate but unavoidable and so quite necessary function whereby the ruling class is assured of 'contact' and 'dialogue' with its class adversary, i.e., the proletariat and its allies, a function to which a proletarian organisation cannot of course simply *conform*).

This example helps explain how the relationships of unevenness-subordination between different ideological state apparatuses (and the regions, objects and practices which correspond to them) constitute, as I have been saying, the stake in the ideological class struggle. The ideological aspect of the struggle for the transformation of the relations of production lies therefore, above all, in the struggle to impose, inside the complex of ideological state apparatuses, *new relationships of unevenness-subordination*[3] (this is what is expressed, for example, in the slogan 'Put politics in command!'), resulting in a transformation of the *set* of the 'complex of ideological state apparatuses' in its relationship with the state apparatus and a transformation of the state apparatus itself.[4]

2. 'The unity of the different ideological state apparatuses is secured, usually in contradictory forms, by the ruling ideology, the ideology of the ruling class' (Althusser 1971b, p. 142).
3. By a transformation of the subordinations in the class struggle: for example by a transformation of the relationship between the *school* and *politics*, which in the capitalist mode of production is a *relationship of disjunction* (denegation or simulation) based on the 'natural' place of the school between the family and economic production.
4. Étienne Balibar (1974) reminds us that it is a matter of replacing the bourgeois state apparatus *both* with another state apparatus *and* with *something other than* a state apparatus.

To sum up: the material objectivity of the ideological instance is characterised by the structure of unevenness-subordination of the 'complex whole in dominance' of the ideological formations of a given social formation, a structure which is nothing but that of the reproduction/transformation contradiction constituting the ideological class struggle.

At the same time, where the form of this contradiction is concerned, it should be specified that, given what I have just said, it cannot be thought of as the opposition between two forces acting against one another *in a single space*. The form of the contradiction inherent to the ideological struggle between the two antagonistic classes is not *symmetrical* in the sense of each class trying to achieve to its own advantage *the same thing* as the other: if I insist on this point it is because many conceptions of the ideological struggle, as we have seen (cf. p. 98), take it as an *evident fact* before the struggle that *'society' exists (with the 'State' over it) as a space, as the terrain of that struggle*. This is so because, as Étienne Balibar points out, the class relation is concealed in the operation of the state apparatus by the very mechanism that realises it, such that society, the state and subjects in law (free and equal in principle in the capitalist mode of production) are produced-reproduced as 'naturally evident notions'. This flushes out a second error, the first one's twin, concerning the nature of this contradiction and opposing reproduction to transformation as *inertia* is opposed to *movement*: the idea that the reproduction of the relations of production needs no explanation because they 'go of their own accord' *so long as they are left alone*, the *flaws* and *failures* of the 'system' apart, is an eternalist and anti-dialectical illusion. In reality the reproduction, just as much as the transformation, of the relations of production is an *objective process* whose mystery must be penetrated, and not just a state of fact needing only to be observed.

I have already alluded several times to Althusser's central thesis: *'Ideology interpellates individuals as subjects'*. The time has come to examine how this thesis 'penetrates the mystery' in question, and, specifically, how the way it penetrates this mystery leads directly to the problematic of a materialist theory of discursive processes, articulated into the problematic of the ideological conditions of the reproduction/transformation of the relations of production.

But first a remark on terminology: in the development that has brought us to this point a certain number of terms have appeared such as ideological state apparatuses, ideological formation, dominant or ruling ideology, etc., but *neither the term 'ideology'* (except negatively in the sentence 'the ideological state apparatuses are not the realisation of Ideology in general') *nor the term 'subject'* has appeared (and even less the term 'individual'). Why is it that as a result of the preceding development, and precisely *in order to be able to strengthen it in its conclusions*, I am obliged to change my terminology and introduce new words (Ideology in the singular, individual, subject, interpellate)? The answer lies in the following two inter-mediary propositions:

(1) there is no practice except by and in *an* ideology;
(2) there is no Ideology except by the subject and for subjects,

that Althusser states before presenting his 'central thesis': in transcribing these two intermediary propositions, I have empha-sised the two ways the term 'ideology' is determined: in the first, the indefinite article suggests the differentiated multiplicity of the ideological instance in the form of a combination (complex whole in dominance) of elements each of which is *an ideological formation* (in the sense defined above), in short, *an ideology*. In the second proposition, the determination of the term 'Ideology' operates 'in -general', as when one says 'there is no square root except of a positive number', implying that *every* square root is the square root of a positive number: in the same way, the signification of this second proposition, which in fact prefigures the 'central thesis',[5] is that 'the category of the subject . . . is the constitutive category of every ideology'. In other words, *the emergence of the term 'subject'* in the theoretical exposition (an emergence which, as we shall see, is characterised grammatically by the fact that the term is neither subject nor object but an attribute of the object) is strictly contemporaneous with *the use of the term 'Ideology' in the singular*, in the sense of 'every ideology'.

Naturally, this makes me distinguish carefully between *ideological formation, dominant ideology* and *Ideology*.

5. 'This thesis [Ideology interpellates individuals as subjects] is simply a matter of making my last proposition explicit' (Althusser 1971b, p. 160).

8 Ideology, Interpellation, 'Munchausen Effect'

Ideology in general, which as we have seen is *not* realised in the ideological state apparatuses – so it cannot coincide with a historically concrete *ideological formation* – is also not the same thing as the *dominant ideology,* as the overall result, the historically concrete form resulting from the relationships of uneveness-contradiction-subordination characterising in a historically given social formation the 'complex whole in dominance' of the ideological formations operating in it. In other words, whereas 'ideologies have a history of their own' because they have a concrete historical existence, 'Ideology in general has no history' in so far as it is 'endowed with a structure and an operation such as to make it a non-historical reality, i.e., an omni-historical reality, in the sense in which that structure and operation are immutable, present in the same form throughout what we can call history, in the sense in which the *Communist Manifesto* defines history as the history of class struggles, i.e., the history of class societies' (Althusser 1971b, pp. 151f.). The concept of *Ideology* in general thus appears very specifically as the way to designate, within Marxism-Leninism, the fact that the relations of production are relationships between 'men', *in the sense that they are not relationships between things, machines, non-human animals or angels; in this sense and in this sense only*: i.e., without introducing at the same time and surreptitiously, a certain notion of 'man' as anti-nature, transcendence, subject of history, negation of the negation, etc. As is well known, this is the central point of the *Reply to John Lewis* (Althusser 1976b).

Quite the contrary, the concept of *Ideology in general* makes it possible to think 'man' as an 'ideological animal', i.e., to think his specificity as *part of nature* in the Spinozist sense of the term: 'History is an immense "*natural-human*" system in movement, and the motor of history is class struggle' (Althusser 1976b, p. 51). Hence history once again, *that is* the history of the class struggle, i.e., the

reproduction/transformation of class relationships, with their corresponding infrastructural (economic) and superstructural (legal-
political and ideological) characteristics: it is within this 'natural-
human' process of history that 'Ideology is eternal' (omni-
historical) – a statement which recalls Freud's expression 'the
unconscious is eternal'; the reader will realise that these two
categories do not meet here *by accident*. But he will also realise that on
this question, and despite important recent studies, the *essential
theoretical work* remains to be done, and I want above all else to avoid
giving the impression, rather widespread today, that we already
have the answers. In fact, slogans will not fill the yawning absence of
a worked out conceptual articulation between *ideology* and the
unconscious: we are still at the stage of theoretical 'glimmers' in a
prevailing obscurity, and in the present study I shall restrict myself
to calling attention to certain connections whose importance may
have been underestimated, without really claiming to pose the true
question that governs the relationship between these two
categories.[1] Let me simply point out that the common feature of the
two structures called respectively *ideology* and the *unconscious* is the
fact that they conceal their own existence within their operation by
producing a web of *'subjective' evident truths*, 'subjective' here
meaning not 'affecting the subject' but 'in which the subject is
constituted':

> For you and for me, the category of the subject is a primary
> 'evident truth' (evident truths are always primary): it is clear that
> you and I are subjects (free, ethical, etc.) (Althusser 1971b,
> p. 161).

Now, and it is, I believe, at this precise point that the necessity for a
materialist theory of discourse begins, the evidentness of the
spontaneous existence of the subject (as origin or cause in itself) is
immediately compared by Althusser with another evidentness, all-
pervasive, as we have seen, in the idealist philosophy of language,

1. One of the merits of Elisabeth Roudinesco's work (1973) is that she shows why
   the 'Freudo-Marxist' juxtaposition cannot be a solution.
   It might be said that it is *this lack of a link between ideology and the unconscious* which
   today 'torments' psychoanalytic research, in diverse and often contradictory
   forms. There is no question of anticipating here what will result. Suffice it to say
   that the idealist reinscription of Lacan's work will have to be brought to book,
   and that this will above all be the business of those who are working today *inside*
   psychoanalysis.

the evidentness of meaning. Remember the terms of this comparison, which I evoked at the very beginning of this study:

> Like all evident facts, including *those that make a word 'name a thing'*
> *or 'have a meaning' (therefore including the evident fact of the*
> *'transparency' of language)*, the 'evident fact' that you and I are
> subjects – and that that does not cause any problems – is an
> ideological effect, the elementary ideological effect (1971b,
> p. 161).

It is I who have stressed this reference to the evidentness of *meaning* taken from a commentary on the evidentness of the *subject*, and I should add that in the text at this point there is a footnote which directly touches on the question I am examining here:

> Linguists and those who appeal to linguistics for various purposes
> often run up against difficulties which arise because they ignore
> the action of the ideological effects in all discourses – including
> even scientific discourses (p. 161n).

All my work finds its definition here, in this linking of the question of the *constitution of meaning* to that of the *constitution of the subject*, a linking which is not marginal (for example the special case of the ideological 'rituals' of reading and writing), but located inside the 'central thesis' itself, in the figure of *interpellation*.

I say in the *figure* of interpellation in order to designate the fact that, as Althusser suggests, 'interpellation' is an 'illustration', an example adapted to a particular mode of exposition, ' "concrete" enough to be recognised, but abstract enough to be thinkable and thought, giving rise to a knowledge' (1971b, p. 162). This figure, associated both with religion and with the police ('You, for whom I have shed this drop of my blood'/'Hey, you there!'), has the advantage first of all that, through this double meaning of the word 'interpellation', it makes palpable the superstructural link – determined by the economic infrastructure – between the *repressive* state apparatus (the legal-political apparatus which assigns-verifies-checks 'identities') *and* the *ideological* state apparatuses, i.e., the link between the 'subject in law' (he who enters into contractual relations with other subjects in law, his equals) *and* the ideological subject (he who says of himself: 'It's me!'). It has the second advantage that it presents this link in such a way that the theatre of consciousness (I see, I think, I speak, I see you, I speak to you, etc.) is observed from behind the scenes, from the place where one can grasp the fact that the subject is spoken *of*, the subject is spoken *to*, before the subject can say: 'I speak'. The consequences that follow directly from this point for the problem of enunciation will be examined later.

The last, but not the least, advantage of this 'little theoretical theatre' of interpellation, conceived as an illustrated critique of the theatre of consciousness, is that it designates, by the discrepancy in the formulation 'individual'/'subject', the paradox by which *the subject is called into existence*: indeed, the formulation carefully avoids presupposing the existence of the subject on whom the operation of interpellation is performed – it does not say: 'The subject is interpellated by Ideology.'

This cuts short any attempt simply to *invert* the metaphor linking the subject with the various 'legal entities' (*personnes morales*) which might seem at first sight to be subjects made up of a collectivity of subjects, and of which one could say, inverting the relationship, that it is this collectivity, as a pre-existing entity, that imposes its ideological stamp on each subject in the form of a 'socialisation' of the individual in 'social relations' conceived of as intersubjective relations. In fact, what the thesis 'Ideology interpellates individuals as subjects' designates is indeed that 'non-subject' is interpellated-constituted as subject by Ideology. Now, the paradox is precisely that interpellation has, as it were, a *retroactive effect*, with the result that every individual is 'always-already a subject'; as we examine the different aspects of this 'circle', we shall find, in condensed form, the different elements we met at the beginning of the second chapter of this book.

First the *evidentness of the subject* as unique, irreplaceable and identical with himself: the absurd and natural reply 'It's me!' to the question 'Who's there?' (Althusser's example – 1971b, p. 160) echoes the remark made on pp. 66f. – i.e., it is 'evident' that *I* am the only person who can say 'I' when speaking of myself; I also said that this evidentness conceals something, which escapes Russell and logical empiricism.

What it is that this evidentness conceals can now be seen; it is the fact that the subject has always been 'an individual interpellated as a subject', which, to remain in the ambience of Althusser's example, might be illustrated by the absurd injunction children address to one another as a superb joke: 'Mister So-and-so, remind me of your name!', an injunction whose playful character masks its affinity with the police operation of assigning and checking *identities*. Because this is indeed what is involved: the 'evidentness' of identity conceals the fact that it is the result of an identification-interpellation of the subject, whose alien origin is nevertheless 'strangely familiar' to him.[2]

We have already met this astonishing mixture of absurdity and evidentness, and this return of strangeness in the familiar, in connection with the notion of the *preconstructed* (cf. for example the joke quoted by Freud and to which I have already referred about the place where the Duke of Wellington did (not) speak his famous words, p. 64n.2 above), but at the time I could only say that this effect of the preconstructed consisted of a *discrepancy*, by which an element irrupted in the utterance as if it had been thought 'before, elsewhere, independently'.

Now, taking into account what I have just set out, it is possible to regard *the effect of the preconstructed as the discursive modality of the discrepancy by which the individual is interpellated as subject . . . while still being 'always-already a subject'*, stressing that this discrepancy (*between* the familiar strangeness of this outside located before, elsewhere and independently, *and* the identifiable, responsible subject, answerable for his actions) operates 'by contradiction', whether the latter be suffered in complete ignorance by the subject, or on the contrary he grasps it in the forefront of his mind, as 'wit': many jokes, turns of phrase, etc., are in fact governed by the contradiction inherent in this discrepancy; they constitute, as it were, the symptoms of it, and are sustained by the circle connecting the contradiction suffered (i.e. 'stupidity') with the contradiction grasped and displayed (i.e., 'irony'), as the reader can confirm using whatever example he finds especially 'eloquent'.[3]

---

2. Hence the well-known children's utterances of the type: 'I have three brothers, Paul, Michael and me', or 'Daddy was born in Manchester, Mummy in Bristol and I in London: strange that the three of us should have met!'

3. Such examples might be multiplied indefinitely:
   (1) *on the family-school relationship*: the story of the lazy pupil who telephoned his headmaster to excuse himself from school, and when asked 'Who am I speaking to?' replied 'It's my father!';
   (2) *on ideological repetition*: 'There are no cannibals left in our area, we ate the last one last week';
   (3) *on the cultural apparatus and the cult of Great Men*: Freud's joke cited above; and also 'Shakespeare's works were not written by him but by an unknown contemporary of the same name';

The role of symptom I have discerned in the operation of a certain type of joke (in which what is ultimately involved is the *identity* of a subject, a thing or an event) with respect to the question of ideological interpellation-identification leads me to posit, in connection with this symptom, the existence of what I have called (p. 93) a *process of the signifier, in interpellation-identification*. Let me explain: it is not a matter here of evoking the 'role of language' in general or 'the power of words', leaving it uncertain whether what is invoked is the *sign, which designates something for someone*, as Lacan says, or the *signifier*, i.e., *what represents the subject for another signifier* (Lacan again). It is clear that, for my purposes, it is the second hypothesis which is correct, because it treats of *the subject as process (of representation) inside the non-subject constituted by the network of signifiers, in Lacan's sense: the subject is 'caught' in this network* – 'common nouns' and 'proper names', 'shifting' effects, syntactic constructions, etc. – *such that he results as 'cause of himself'*, in Spinoza's sense of the phrase. And it is precisely the existence of this contradiction (the production as a *result of a 'cause of itself'*), and its motor role for the process of the signifier in interpellation-identification, which justifies me in saying that it is indeed a matter of a *process*, in so far as the 'objects' which appear in it duplicate and divide to act on themselves as other than themselves.[4]

One of the consequences, I believe, of the necessary obliteration within the subject as 'cause of himself' of the fact that he is the result of a process, is a series of what one might call *metaphysical phantasies*, all of which touch on the question of causality: for example the phantasy of the *two hands* each holding a pencil and *each drawing the other on the same sheet of paper*, and also that of the perpetual leap in which *one leaps up again with a great kick before having touched the ground*; one could extend the list at length. I shall leave it at that, with the proposal to call this phantasy effect – by which the individual is interpellated as subject – the 'Munchausen effect', in memory of the immortal baron who *lifted himself into the air by pulling on his own hair*.

If it is true that ideology 'recruits' subjects from amongst individuals (in the way soldiers are recruited from amongst

---

(4) *on metaphysics and the religious apparatus*: 'God is perfect in every way except one: he doesn't exist'; 'X didn't believe in ghosts, he wasn't even afraid of them', etc.

4. On this duplication and division in contradiction, and in the manner of a joke: 'What a shame they did not build the cities in the country – the air is so much cleaner there!'

civilians) and that it recruits them *all*, we need to know how 'volunteers' are designated in this recruitment, i.e., in what concerns us, how all individuals *accept as evident* the meaning of what they hear and say, read and write (of what they *intend* to say and of what it is *intended* be said to them) as 'speaking subjects': really to understand this is the only way to avoid repeating, in the form of a theoretical analysis, the 'Munchausen effect', by positing the subject as the origin of the subject, i.e., in what concerns us, by positing the subject of discourse as the origin of the subject of discourse.

9 The Subject-Form of Discourse

I can sum up what precedes by saying that behind the evident proposition that 'Of course I am myself' (with my name, my family, my friends, my memories, my 'ideas', my intentions and my obligations) there is the process of interpellation-identification that *produces* the subject in the place left empty: 'he who . . .', i.e., X, the quidam who *happens to be there*; and that in various forms imposed by 'legal-ideological social relations'.[1] The future perfect tense of juridical law, 'he who will have done some damage to . . .' (and the law *always* finds someone to bite on, a 'singularity' to which to apply its 'universality') produces the subject in the form of the *subject in law*.[2] As for the ideological subject who duplicates the subject in law, he is interpellated-constituted in the evident character of the observation that carries and masks the identificatory 'norm': 'a French soldier does not retreat' signifies in fact 'if *you* are a *true* French soldier, which is what you are, you *cannot/must not* retreat'.[3] Through 'habit' and 'usage', therefore, it is ideology that designates both *what is* and *what ought to be*, sometimes with linguistically marked 'deviations' between observation and norm which operate

1. These legal-ideological social relations are not atemporal: they have a history which is bound up with the gradual construction, at the end of the Middle Ages, of the legal ideology of the Subject, corresponding to new practices in which Law was detached from Religion, and then turned against it. But this is not at all to say that the ideological effect of interpellation only appeared with these new social relations: just that they constitute a new form of subjection, the *completely visible form of autonomy*.
2. Hence what the Port-Royal logicians called 'Moral Universality', which produces expressions such as 'the French are valiant; the Italians are jealous; the Germans are tall, the Orientals are voluptuous; though they be not true of all particulars, but only for the most part' (Arnauld and Nicole 1685, p. 227), emerges in fact as one of the conditions of the operation and realisation of ideology.
3. On this question as a whole, see Edelman (1979).

as a device for the 'taking up of slack'.[4] It is ideology that supplies the evidentness with which 'everyone knows' what a soldier is,[5] or a worker, a boss, a factory, a strike, etc., the evidentness that makes a word or an utterance 'mean what it says' and thereby masks in the 'transparency of language' what I shall call *the material character of the meaning* of words and utterances.

Let me explain what I mean by this. I shall say that the material character of meaning, masked by its transparent evidentness for the subject, lies in its constitutive dependence on what I have called the 'complex whole of the ideological formations', specifying this dependence with two 'theses':

(1) The first consists of the proposition that the *meaning* of a word, expression, proposition, etc., does not exist 'in itself' (i.e., in its transparent relation to the literal character of the signifier), but is determined by the ideological positions brought into play in the socio-historical process in which words, expressions and propositions are produced (i.e., reproduced). This thesis could be summed up in the statement: *words, expressions, propositions, etc., change their meaning according to the positions held by those who use them*, which signifies that they find their meaning by reference to those positions, i.e., by reference to the *ideological formations* (in the sense defined above) in which those positions are inscribed.[6] Henceforth I shall call a *discursive formation* that which in a given ideological formation, i.e., from a given position in a given conjuncture determined by the state of the class struggle, determines '*what can and should be said* (articulated in the form of a speech, a sermon, a pamphlet, a report, a programme, etc.)' (Haroche, Henry and Pêcheux 1971, p. 102).

This amounts to saying that words, expressions, propositions, etc., obtain their meaning from the discursive formation in which they are produced: returning to the terms I introduced above, and applying them to the specific point of the materiality of discourse

4. For example, the 'deviation' (and profound coherence) between the norm '*a* French soldier does not retreat' and the observation '*the* French soldier is stingy', helping, in the specificity of French conditions, to guarantee the interpellation-identification of the subject as a French soldier.

5. Cf. on this point Husserl's remarks already quoted (p. 43 n. 3) on the sentence 'a soldier must be brave', remarks which constitute a self-appreciation of evidentness.

6. For the moment I shall leave in suspense the case of 'scientific discourses'; I shall return to it later (pp. 133ff.).

and meaning, I shall say that individuals are 'interpellated' as speaking-subjects (as subjects of *their* discourse) by the discursive formations which represent 'in language' the ideological formations that correspond to them.[7]

At the same time this provides the starting-point for an answer to the question (posed on p. 58) of the relationship between (linguistic) *basis* and (discursive-ideological) *process*: if the same word, the same expression and the same proposition can have different meanings – all equally 'evident' – depending on which discursive formation they are referred to, it is because, I repeat, a word, expression or proposition does not have a meaning *'of its own'* attached to it in its literalness;[8] its meaning is constituted in each discursive formation, in the relationships into which one word, expression or proposition enters with other words, expressions or propositions of the same discursive formation. Correlatively, if it is admitted that the *same* words, expressions or propositions change their meanings as they pass from one discursive formation to another, it must also be admitted that words, expressions or propositions which are *different literally* can, in a given discursive formation, 'have the same meaning', which if you follow me, is in fact the condition for each element (word, expression or proposition) having a meaning at all. Henceforth I shall use the term *discursive process* to designate the system of relationships of substitution, paraphrases, synonymies, etc., which operate between linguistic elements – 'signifiers' – in a given discursive formation.[9]

It should now be clearer why what I have been calling 'domains of thought' (cf. p. 64 and 84) are socio-historically constituted in the form of points of stabilisation which produce the subject and simultaneously *along with him* what he is given to see, understand,

7. I shall not settle here the problem of the *nature* of this correspondence. Let me just say that it cannot be a matter of a pure equivalence (ideology = discourse), nor of a mere distribution of functions ('discursive practice'/'non-discursive practice'). It would be more appropriate to speak of an 'imbrication' of the discursive formations into the ideological formations, an imbrication whose principle lies precisely in 'interpellation'.

8. The very notion of 'literal meaning', which goes with those of 'figurative', derivatory, secondary meanings, etc., loses all significance here.

9. It follows that any *purely linguistic* criterion (i.e., any criterion of a morpho-syntactic kind) is strictly inadequate to characterise the discursive processes inherent in a discursive formation. On this point see Pêcheux and Fuchs (1975), in which these consequences are examined and discussed in greater detail, in the perspective of a non-subjective theory of reading as the basis for a theory of discourse.

do, fear and hope, etc. As we shall see, this is how every subject 'finds' himself (in himself and in other subjects), and this is the *condition* (and not the *effect*) of the notorious intersubjective 'consensus' with which idealism pretends to grasp being from a starting-point in thought. By so recognising that the discursive formation is the site of the constitution of meaning (its 'womb' so to speak), I am led directly to my second thesis, which can be stated as follows:

(2) *Every discursive formation, by the transparency of the meaning constituted in it, conceals its dependence on the 'complex whole in dominance' of discursive formations, itself imbricated with the complex of ideological formations defined above.*

Let me develop this: I propose to call this 'complex whole in dominance' of discursive formations 'interdiscourse', with the qualification that it too is subject to the law of unevenness-contradiction-subordination which I have described as characterising the complex of ideological formations.

Given this, I shall say that it is proper to every discursive formation[10] to conceal, in the transparency of the meaning formed in it, the contradictory material objectivity of interdiscourse, determining that discursive formation as such, a material objectivity that resides in the fact that 'it speaks' ('*ça parle*') always 'before, elsewhere and independently', i.e., under the domination of the complex of ideological formations. Thus we find that the two types of discrepancy, respectively the *embedding effect of the pre-constructed* and the effect I have called *articulation* – initially considered as psycho-logical laws of thought – are in reality materially determined in the very structure of interdiscourse.

I shall close on this point by saying that the operation of Ideology in general as the interpellation of individuals as subjects (and specifically as subjects of their discourse) is realised through the complex of ideological formations (and specifically through the interdiscourse imbricated in them) and supplies 'each subject' with his 'reality' as a system of evident truths and significations perceived-accepted-suffered. By saying that the *ego*, i.e., the imaginary in the subject (the place in which is constituted for the subject his imaginary relationship to reality), cannot recognise its subordination, its subjection to the *Other* or to the *Subject*, because

10. Leaving aside once again the case of 'scientific discourse', to which I shall return.

this subordination-subjection is realised precisely in the subject *in the form of autonomy*, I am thus not appealing to any 'transcendence' (a *real* Other or Subject), I am merely repeating the terms that Lacan[11] and Althusser respectively have given (deliberately adopting the travestied and 'phantasmagoric' forms inherent in subjectivity) to the natural and socio-historical process by which the subject-effect is constituted-reproduced as an *interior* without an *exterior, and that by the determination of the real* ('*exterior*'), and specifically, I would add, *of interdiscourse as real* ('*exterior*').

It is clear then that idealism is not first an epistemological position, but above all the spontaneous operation of the *subject form*,[12] by which what is an effect of the real represented for a subject is given as the essence of the real.

Thus we are led to examine the discursive properties of the subject-form, of the 'imaginary ego' as 'subject of discourse'. I have already mentioned the fact that the subject was constituted by his 'forgetting'[13] of what determines him. I can now specify that the interpellation of the individual as subject of his discourse is achieved by the identification (of the subject) with the discursive formation that dominates him (i.e., in which he is constituted as subject): this identification, which founds the (imaginary) unity of the subject, depends on the fact that the elements of interdiscourse (in their double form, described above as 'preconstructed' and 'sustaining process') that constitute, in the subject's discourse, *the traces of what determines him*, are re-inscribed in the discourse of the subject himself.

One point has been left in suspense here: it concerns the differential specificity of the two types of elements of interdiscourse ('preconstructed' and 'articulation') which, now that we have warded off the idealist illusions about them, appear to determine the subject by imposing-on-him-concealing-from-him his subjection behind the appearances of autonomy, i.e., through the discursive structure of the subject-form. I shall resort here to the distinction

11. 'The subject is subject only from being subjected to the field of the Other, the subject proceeds from his synchronic subjection in the field of the Other' (Lacan 1977b, p. 188).

12. The expression 'subject-form' was introduced by Althusser (1976b, p. 95): 'No human, i.e. social individual, can be the agent of a practice if he does not take *the form of a subject*. The "subject-form" is actually the historical form of existence of every individual, of every agent of social practices.'

13. The term 'forgetting' here does not mean the loss of something once known, as when one speaks of 'a loss of memory', but the occlusion of the cause of the subject inside its very effect.

domination/determination and propose that the discursive formation which conveys the subject-form is the *dominant* discursive
formation, and that the discursive formations which constitute what
I have called its interdiscourse *determine the domination of the dominant
discursive formation*. The distinction between preconstructed and
articulation will help us go further here.

Indeed, I shall say that the 'preconstructed' corresponds to the
'always-already there' of the ideological interpellation that supplies-
imposes 'reality' and its 'meaning' in the form of universality (the
'world of things'), whereas 'articulation' *constitutes the subject in his
relationship to meaning*, so that it represents, in interdiscourse, what
determines the domination of the subject-form. Let me specify what is at
issue here: I proposed above (p. 112) a conception of the meaning
effect as a relationship of substitutability between elements (words,
expressions, propositions) inside a given discursive formation. I
shall now add that this substitutability can take two basic forms:
that of *equivalence* or symmetrical substitutability, such that the two
substitutable elements *a* and *b* 'have the same meaning' in the
discursive formation considered, and that of *implication* or orientated
substitutability, such that the relation of substitution $a \rightarrow b$ is not the
same as the relation of substitution $b \rightarrow a$. Let me illustrate this with
some examples.

Consider the substitution
    triangle with one rightangle/rectangular triangle
It is clear that the relationship between the substitutables is a 'non-
orientated' relationship of identity, because the substitutables
cannot be syntagmatised[14] by any relation but the meta-relation of
identity.
Consider on the other hand a substitution such as
    passage of an electric current/deflection of the galvanometer
in the context of a sequence of the type
    'we observe a/b'
It is clear here that the relation between the substitutables results on
the contrary from a concatenation (or connection) which is not a

---

14. By the 'syntagmatisation' of two elements I mean their entry into the same
    'syntagmatic relationship' in the sense that Saussure gave this expression in
    part two, chapter five of the *Course in General Linguistics*: 'Words acquire
    relations based on the linear nature of language because they are chained
    together. This rules out the possibility of pronouncing two elements
    simultaneously' (1974, p. 123).

relation of identity: it is as if another sequence S_y had perpendicularly crossed the sequence S_x containing the substitutables, linking them together in a necessary concatenation:

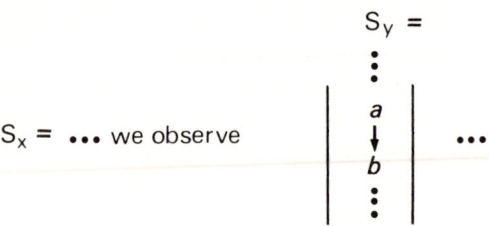

In my example, the sequence S_y, belonging to what I shall call the *'transverse-discourse'* of S_x and establishing a concatenation between *a* and *b* in S_x, could be

'The passage of an electric current *causes* the deflection of the galvanometer'

or

'The deflection of the galvanometer *indicates* the passage of an electric current'.

Note that the operation of the 'transverse-discourse' belongs to what is classically called *metonymy* as a relationship of part to whole, cause to effect, symptom to what it designates, etc.

At the same time, it is clear that what I have previously called 'articulation' (or 'sustaining process') is directly related to what I have just characterised as *transverse-discourse*, in so far as it can be said that articulation (the effect of the 'explicative' accessary clause that corresponds to it) derives from the linearisation (or syntagmatisation) of the transverse-discourse in the axis of what I shall call by the name *intradiscourse*, i.e., the operation of discourse with respect to itself (what I am saying now, in relation to what I have said *before* and what I shall say *afterwards*, i.e., the set of 'co-reference' phenomena that secure what can be called the 'thread of the discourse' as discourse of a subject).[15]

This example shows, in fact, that syntagmatisation of the

15. Note on this point that this articulation, although it does operate at the *conscious* level in the different forms of logical consistency (relations of 'cause', 'concession', 'temporal connection', etc.), cannot be reduced to them: the occurrence of certain appositions or interpolations may represent the irruption into the thread of the discourse of an *unconscious* process, as Freud pointed out in relation to *Verneinung*.

transverse-discourse yields an 'accessary' construction of the type:
  'We observe a deflection of the galvanometer, which indicates the
  passage of an electric current'
The development I have just carried out calls for a remark about the
domain of the examples used: it is a matter of an example drawn
from the domain of the science of physics, and hence appealing to
what I have called conceptual-scientific processes, which are not
supported by a 'subject' (such a subject would be the impossible
'subject of science'). Which, in the present case, is to say that the
'reminder' produced here is not the reminder, in the discourse of the
subject, of the thought of a subject (even if it appears as such to
the subject, by a spontaneous re-ideologisation of the process without a subject). In the case of a notional-ideological process, on the
contrary, the determining effect of the transverse-discourse on the
subject necessarily induces in the latter the relationship between
subject and (universal) Subject of Ideology, which thus 'recalls
itself' to the thought of the subject ('everyone knows that . . .', 'it is
clear that . . .').

I shall return later (p. 164 and in the Conclusion) to the
relationship between process without a subject and ideological
universality of the Subject, which is directly linked to what I have
already designated in speaking of *the simulation of the sciences by
ideology* (p. 50).

In another connection, let me point out that *interdiscourse as
transverse-discourse* crosses and connects together the discursive
elements constituted by *interdiscourse as preconstructed*, which supplies
as it were the raw material in which the subject is constituted as
'speaking-subject', with the discursive formation that subjects him.
In this sense it can indeed be said that intradiscourse, as the 'thread
of the discourse' of the subject, is strictly an effect of interdiscourse
on itself, an 'interiority' wholly determined as such 'from the
exterior'. The character of the subject-form,with the spontaneous
ideology it contains, will consist precisely in an inversion of this
determination: I shall say that the subject-form (by which the
'subject of discourse' identifies with the discursive formation that
constitutes him) tends to absorb-forget interdiscourse in
intradiscourse, i.e., *it simulates interdiscourse in intradiscourse*, such that
interdiscourse *appears* to be the pure 'already-said' of intradiscourse,
in which it is articulated by 'coreference'.[16] This being so, I think

16. Coreference designates the overall effect by which the stable identity of the
    'referents' – what is at issue – comes to be guaranteed in the thread of dis-

the subject-form can be characterised as realising the incorporation-concealment of the elements of interdiscourse: the (imaginary) unity of the subject, his present-past-future identity, finds *one of its foundations* here.

Now, this identification of the subject with himself is, as I have said, simultaneously an identification with the other (with a small o), as an other 'ego', discrepant origin, etc.: the subject-effect and the 'intersubjectivity-effect' are thus strictly coeval and co-extensive. In this perspective, the self-appraisal by which the *subject's discourse* develops and props itself up on itself (articulating itself with 'accessary clauses' which, as we have just seen, syntagmatise substitutable elements) is a special case of the phenomena of paraphrase and reformulation (as general form of the relationship between substitutables) which are constitutive of a given discursive formation in which the subjects it dominates recognise one another as mirrors for each other. This means that coincidence (which is also complicity, even collusion) between the subject and himself is established by the same movement between subjects, according to the modality 'as if' (as if I who speak were over there where I am being listened to), a modality in which the 'incorporation' of the elements of interdiscourse (preconstructed and articulation-sustaining) can go so far as to confound them, so that there is no longer a demarcation between what is said and what it is said about. This modality, which is that of *fiction*, represents as it were the pure idealist form of the subject-form in its various forms from 'journalism' to 'literature' and 'creative thought', which I shall examine briefly.

Take for example the following sentence from an article on Ireland published in the newspaper *Le Monde*:[17]

'The white cross which the demonstrators had tied to a lamp-post has not been touched by the police'.

It is clear that the demarcation between the accessary character of a reminder (you know: that white cross . . .) *and* the evident character of a pregiven element (you see that white cross that the demonstrators . . .) is strictly zero, since the two operations amount to the same phenomenon of simulation-presentification (Ireland *as*

---

course. *Anaphore* (see p. 39n. 9) is the most obvious of the linguistic mechanisms by which this effect is realised.

17. I have taken this example from Fuchs and Milner (1979), who mark it as a case of the suppression of the difference between 'explicative' and 'determinative' interpretations.

if you were there): 'If you had been there, you would have seen that white cross and you would know what I am talking about'. The power of *mise en scène*, the 'poetic' effect that takes you right to the scene,[18] thus depends on the implicit condition of a displacement (*décalage*) of origins (of the 'zero points' of subjectivities), a displacement from the present to the past, coupled with the displacement from one subject to other subjects, which constitutes identification. We can thus understand retrospectively that the real object encountered by Frege in his commentary on the sentence describing Napoleon's deeds was simply what I shall call the forms of identification of the subject, with the narrator and with the 'object' of his narrative (Napoleon, and his calculations, his intentions, etc.).

Given this one can predict that the novelistic effect of presence operates according to the same modality. Imagine, indeed, a sentence capable of appearing in a 'classical' novelistic sequence such as

'it was one of those pallid dawns that resemble a birth . . .'

in order to show what I mean: clearly, it would be quite incongruous to ask whether 'in reality' *all* pallid dawns resemble a birth or only *some* of them. Here, too, the difference in operation has vanished: the aesthetic theory of the classical novel speaks in this connection of the novelistic 'transmutation' of 'everyday' contents (dawn, pallid, birth) as a means by which the novelist creates 'his world', 'outside reality', with its own objects, their specific qualities and properties, etc., in complicity with the reader. Thus, the aesthetic ideology of 'creation'[19] and that of the recreation by reading which is its corollary also find their origin in what I have called the 'subject-form' and mask the materiality of aesthetic *production*.

Finally, it is easy to show that the conception of *thought as 'creative activity'* is a spontaneous extension (in the form of an aestheticising theory of knowledge) of the idealism inherent in the subject-form. Once 'the point of view creates the object',[20] all notions and also all

18. In a study of the ideological operation of the newspaper *Le Monde*, Aimé Guedj and Jacques Girault speak of the 'novelistic organisation of the news' (1970, p. 146).
19. On this point, see Macherey (1978), especially the chapter entitled 'Creation and Production'; Balibar, R. and Laporte (1974); Balibar, R. (1974); and Balibar, E. and Macherey (1974).
20. Which corresponds in fact to making the 'mode of presentation of the object' coincident with the 'object' itself (cf. p. 70).

concepts become convenient fictions, 'ways of speaking' which, by multiplying fictional entities and possible worlds, suspend *the independent existence of the real as external to the subject*. This is an effect that can be exemplified by expressions like 'the Berlin of the 1930s', 'Abel Gance's Napoleon', 'the World of the Ancients', etc., which signify indifferently 'Berlin during the 1930s' *and* 'Berlin-1930', 'Napoleon as "seen" by Abel Gance' *and* 'the character Abel Gance has "created" with the name Napoleon', 'the World such as the Ancients conceived it' *and* 'the World-for-the-Ancients', etc. This relation by which 'reality' becomes dependent on 'thought' is well and truly the mark of idealism as we have encountered it in Lenin's description in *Materialism and Empirio-criticism* and for which the distinction between thinking and imagining has been abolished. Let me stress once again here that the idealism does not lie in the formal (linguistic or logical) structure of the expression, i.e., a proper name with a determination, but in the positing of reality as reality-for-thought. In this sense, despite their formally analogous character, the operation I have just evoked is actually the strict opposite of that of polemical expressions such as 'Your Virgin Mary' or 'the fire-air of the alchemists', etc. (signifying 'the hallucination that *you* call the Virgin Mary', 'what the alchemists *meant when they spoke of* fire-air', etc.), which involve not a general reversal of the relationship between thought and the real, but quite the contrary, the tracing of a materialist line of demarcation between the real and illusion as miscognition of the real. I shall return to this point later on (cf. p. 157).

So we see that the effect of the real on itself, in so far as it produces what I have called the 'subject-form', supplies-imposes 'reality' for the subject in the general form of miscognition, of which *fiction*, as we have just examined it, represents the 'purest' modality.[21] Given all that has gone before, the reader will not be surprised to discover that this *miscognition* is based on a *recognition* which Althusser characterises as 'the mutual recognition of subjects and Subject, the subjects' recognition of each other, and finally the subject's recognition of himself' (1971b, p. 168). It is in this recognition that the subject 'forgets' the determinations that have put him in the place he occupies – by which I mean that, being 'always-already' a subject, he has 'always-already' forgotten these determinations that con-

21. In Balibar, R. (1974), the reader will find a series of concrete analyses of the relationship between *realism* and *fiction* as hallucinatory production of the real, concealing the work of fiction.

stitute him as such. This explains the not fortuitous but absolutely necessary character of the double form ('empirical' *and* 'speculative' in Herbert's terminology) of ideological subjection, which enables us to understand why the *preconstructed* as I have redefined it involves simultaneously 'what everyone knows', i.e., the thought contents of the 'universal subject', support of identification, and what everyone, in a given 'situation', can see and hear, in the form of the evident facts of the 'situational context'. In the same way, *articulation* (and the transverse-discourse which we now know is its basis) corresponds both to 'as I have said' (intradiscursive reminder), 'as everyone knows' (return of the Universal in the subject) and 'as everyone can see' (implicit universality of every 'human' situation). In short, every subject is subjected in the universal as an 'irreplaceable' singular, something Althusser has translated into the forms of religious ideology as follows:

> God . . . needs to 'make himself' a man, the Subject needs to become a subject, as if to show empirically, visibly to the eye, tangibly to the hands (see St. Thomas) of the subjects, that, if they are subjects, subjected to the Subject, that is solely in order that finally, on Judgement Day, they will re-enter the Lord's Bosom, like Christ, i.e. re-enter the Subject (1971b, pp. 167f.).[22]

I shall say that the mark of the unconscious as 'discourse of the Other' designates in the subject the effective presence of the 'Subject' which makes every subject 'work', i.e., take up positions 'in full awareness and full freedom', take initiatives for which he is 'responsible' as the author of his actions, etc., and the notions of *assertion* and *enunciation* are there to designate in the domain of 'language' the subject's actions in taking up positions as a speaking subject.

The preceding argument allows me to say that the notion of 'speech acts' in fact conveys a miscognition of the determination of the subject in discourse, and that *taking up a position* is really by no

---

22. The material conditions under which the human animal is reared and trained, including the specific materiality of the imaginary (the family apparatus as an ideological apparatus) thus represent the way, to use Althusser's words, in which the Subject becomes a subject, i.e., the way in which the determinations that subject the physiological individual as an ideological subject are necessarily realised in the body of an animal belonging to the 'human species' in the biological sense of the term.

means conceivable as an 'originary action' of the speaking-subject: on the contrary, it must be understood as an effect, in the subject-form, of its determination by interdiscourse as transverse-discourse, i.e., an effect of the 'exteriority' of the ideologico-discursive real, in so far as it 'returns upon itself' and crosses itself.[23] Taking up a position is therefore the result of a return of the 'Subject' in the subject, such that the subjective non-coincidence characterising the subject/object duality, by which the subject separates himself from what he is 'conscious' of and takes up a position towards, is fundamentally homogeneous with the coincidence-recognition by which the subject identifies with himself, with his 'like' and with the 'Subject'. The 'duplication' of the subject – as 'consciousness' and its 'objects' – is a duplication of identification, precisely in so far as it designates the lure of that impossible construction of exteriority *even within the interiority of the subject.*

Note in passing that Husserl's phenomenological project, the attempt to rediscover in the 'originary ground' of the subject's actions (as consciousness, activity, etc.) the source of what in reality determines the subject as such, is very precisely a repetition of this idealist myth of interiority, for which the 'un-asserted' can only be something *already-asserted* or *assertable* which the subject can re-discover by a reflection on himself. I shall say that the core of this myth lies in the notion of *consciousness* as a synthetic unificatory power, the centre and active point of organisation of representations determining their concatenation.[24]

I would add that the 'truth' of this idealist myth consists precisely of the operation (conceived as autonomous) of a *discursive formation* in the sense in which I have defined it, i.e., as a space of reformulation-paraphrase in which is constituted the necessary illusion of a 'speaking intersubjectivity' by which everyone knows in advance what the 'other' is going to think and say . . . and for good

23. Commenting on the topological properties of the *cross-cap* and the *Möbius surface*, whose 'recto continues its verso', Lacan is led to characterise the *intersection* as 'structurally definable . . . by a certain relation of the surface to itself, in so far as, returning upon itself, it crosses itself at a point no doubt to be determined. Well! This line of intersection is for us what may symbolise the function of identification' (1977b, p. 271).

24. 'We do not enact a mere sequence of representations, but a *judgement*, a peculiar "unity of consciousness", that binds these together. In this binding together the consciousness of the *state of affairs* is constituted: *to execute judgement, and to be "conscious" of a state of affairs, in this "synthetic" positing of "something as referred to something"*, *are one and the same thing*' (Husserl 1970b, vol. II, p. 632).

reason, since everyone's discourse reproduces that of another (since, as I have said – cf. pp. 87 and 118 – everyone is a mirror for everyone else).

Let me go further on the operation of this illusion in the space of reformulation-paraphrase that characterises a discursive formation: in employing the term 'speaking intersubjectivity' I am not leaving the closed circle of the subject-form, quite the contrary, I am inscribing in that subject-form the necessary reference of what *I* say to what *another* may think, in so far as what I say *is not outside the field of what I am determined not to say*. By using terms such as 'I might', 'I am determined to', I am designating the subjective sector of virtualities, goals, intentions, reluctances, refusals, etc., and what this sector occludes it is only possible to reveal with the help of Freud.

In an earlier work (Pêcheux and Fuchs 1975), basing ourselves on an interpetation of Freud's first topography, Catherine Fuchs and I used the opposition between 'preconscious-consciousness system' and 'unconscious system' to define two radically different types of 'forgetting' inherent in discourse.

We agreed to call *forgetting no. 2* the 'forgetting' by which every speaking subject 'selects', from the interior of the discursive formation which dominates him, i.e., from the system of utterances, forms and sequences to be found there in relations of paraphrase, *one utterance, form or sequence and not another, even though it is in the field of what may be reformulated in the discursive formation considered*.

On the other hand we appealed to the notion of the 'unconscious system' to characterise another kind of 'forgetting', *forgetting no. 1*, supposed to explain the fact that the speaking subject cannot, by definition, locate himself outside the discursive formation which dominates him. To that extent, *forgetting no. 1*, by analogy with unconscious repression, involved that exterior in so far as the latter, as we have seen, determines the discursive formation in question.

The advantage of this interpretation of the first topography was that it explained the fact that there is no frontier or break 'in the interior' of a discursive formation, with the result that access to the 'unsaid' as said 'in other words' (accepted or rejected) remains constitutively open. This interpretation also enabled us to explain the impression of reality the speaking subject has of his thought ('I know what I am saying', 'I know what I am talking about'), an impression triggered by this constitutive openness which he makes use of all the time, doubling the thread of his discourse back on itself, anticipating its effect and adjusting to the discrepancy produced in it by the discourse of another (as another himself), in order to make what he is saying clear to others and to himself and to 'deepen his thinking'.

Finally, the same interpretation found a justification in the association between preconscious and purposive idea (*Zielvorstellung*), in so far as the latter is accompanied by topicalisations, focusings of attention, etc. And indeed, in the particular context of the *Traumdeutung* (i.e., of the analysis of dreams, but also more generally), Freud described the preconscious process in these terms:

> Now it seems that the train of thought which has thus been initiated and dropped can continue to spin itself out without attention being turned to it again, unless at some point or other it reaches a specially high degree of intensity which forces attention to it. Thus, if a train of thought is initially rejected (consciously, perhaps) by a judgement that it is wrong or that it is useless for the immediate intellectual purpose in view, the result may be that the train of thought will proceed, unobserved by consciousness, until the onset of sleep. To sum up – we describe a train of thought such as this as 'preconscious': we regard it as completely rational (Freud 1953, pp. 593f.).

Today I find these formulations inadequate, in so far as their net result is to make the preconscious-consciousness an autonomous zone with respect to the unconscious, divided from it by the barrier of repression and censorship: hence, once again, the illusion of an empire within an empire, of the struggle of the empire of reason and consciousness against the empire of the unconscious. In fact this illusion was itself no more than a new form of the illusion of the autonomy of thought vis-à-vis the unconscious, i.e., of the secondary process with respect to the primary process.

But Freud himself, notably in the *Project for a Scientific Psychology* (Freud 1966), re-established the primacy of the primary processes over the secondary processes by re-affirming that thought is unconscious: the consequences of this re-establishment are taken to their conclusion in the second topography, and I am therefore obliged to re-examine the problem of the preconscious, via Lacan's re-elaboration.

For our purposes here I shall therefore say that the preconscious characterises the reappropriation of a (conscious) verbal representation by the (unconscious) primary process, resulting in the formation of a new representation which appears to be consciously linked to the first although its real articulation with the latter is unconscious. It is this link between the two verbal representations in question that is re-established in discursivity, in so far as these two verbal representations can be assigned to the same discursive formation (one being able to relate to the other by paraphrastic reformulation or by metonymy). This link between the two representations derives from *symbolic identification*[25] and as such it is represented through the 'laws of *langue*' (logic and grammar), so that here again it is clear that any discourse is an occulation of the unconscious.

This explains why what I shall continue to call *forgetting no. 2 precisely coincides with the operation of the subject of discourse in the discursive formation that dominates him*, and why *it is there precisely that his 'freedom' as a speaking subject lies*: I think this will help us understand that the notorious problematic of 'enunciation' found so frequently in linguistic research today, along with the subjectivism that usually accompanies it, arises in reality from the theoretical absence of *a linguistic corollary of the Freudian imaginary and ego*: it still remains to construct the theory of the 'verbal body' that finds a position in a time (tenses, moods, aspects, etc.) and a space (localisation, determiners, etc.) which are the imaginary time and space of the speaking subject. It is here, I believe, that one should look for the 'semantic effects bound up with syntax', in so far as, in Lacan's words, 'syntax, of course, is preconscious' (Lacan 1977b, p. 68).

Remember, in this connection, what Freud proposed in his article on 'Negation' (*Verneinung*) (Freud 1961), namely, that, by the action of negation in particular as a minimal syntactic effect, two representations are placed in a preconscious relationship.

That a verbal representation and its grammatical or logical 'contrary' can thus be linked marks the fact that the preconditions of a *detachment* (separating the verbal representation from the discursive formation which gives it a meaning and thus making that verbal

25. This symbolic identification dominates the imaginary identification through which each verbal representation, and hence each 'word', 'expression' or 'utterance' acquires a meaning of its own which 'absolutely evidently' belongs to it. I shall return later to this relationship between symbolic identification and imaginary identification. On this same point, too, and more generally on the relationship between discursivity and the unconscious, see Henry (1977), section II, chapter II: 'Le Sujet et le signifiant'.

representation a pure signifier) are inscribed as a universal feature in syntax. *Hence the signifiers appear* not as the pieces in an eternal symbolic game which determines them, *but as what has 'always-already' been detached from a meaning*: there is no naturalness about the signifier; what falls within the reach of the unconscious as a verbal signifier has 'always-already' been detached from a discursive formation which supplied it with a sense for it to lose in the non-sense of the signifier.

Note that this is by no means in contradiction with the supremacy of the signifier over the signified, so long as that supremacy is understood to act in the context of a discursive formation determined by its specific exterior, which, as has been seen, is radically occulted for the speaking subject that that discursive formation dominates (what I shall continue to call *forgetting no. 1*), and this in conditions such that any access to that exterior by reformulation is prohibited him for constitutive reasons connected with the relationships of division-contradiction which traverse-organise the 'complex whole of discursive formations' at a given historical moment.

The effect of the subject-form of discourse is thus above all to mask the object of what I am calling *forgetting no. 1* via the operation of *forgetting no. 2*. Thus the space of reformulation-paraphrase that characterises a given discursive formation becomes the site of the constitution of what I have called the *linguistic imaginary* (verbal body).

To this *linguistic imaginary* should no doubt also be attached the 'evident' lexical facts inscribed in the structure of the *langue*, taking it into account that the lexicalised equivalences between substitutables in fact result from the (type 1) forgetting of the transverse-discourse that links them together, so these equivalences appear, in what I call the linguistic imaginary, *as mere effects of lexical properties*, evident in their eternity. This marks, I believe, the ascendency of ideological-discursive processes over the system of the *langue* and the historically variable limit of the autonomy of that system.[26]

Without taking this point any further here, I shall concentrate on

26. I said above (p. 60) that the separation language/discourse was not fixed *ne varietur* but was subject to a historical transformation by a reaction of discursive processes on the *langue*. In this sense the 'theory of discourse', however embryonic, seems to me to open up 'new fields of questions' for linguists, if only with respect to the problem of the definition of the *bounds and limits of the linguistic object*.

the fact that the space of reformulation-paraphrase of a discursive formation – the space in which, as I have said, meaning is constituted – is where the unthought (exterior) that determines it is occulted; and also the fact that this occultation takes place in the reflexive sphere of consciousness and intersubjectivity, i.e., in the borderless and limitless sphere of the subject-form which, like ideology (and because it is the latter's kernel) 'has no outside' in Althusser's words.

Now – and this will be a decisive step forward in our examination – the formula 'ideology has no outside' is posited by Althusser immediately and paradoxically next to another formula which reverses it, saying ideology is 'nothing but outside'. More exactly, the two formulae are linked and discussed in two short parentheses: 'Ideology *has no outside* (for itself), but at the same time . . . *it is nothing but outside* (for science and reality)' (1971b, p. 164).

Hence the question which cannot fail to be asked, given everything that precedes, and which constitutes what might be called the *pons asinorum* of a materialist (Marxist-Leninist) theory of ideology, a question I shall set out in a deliberately 'naive' and provocative way, as follows:

Given that ideology has no outside *for itself*, i.e., if I have made myself clear, *for the subject* – which is more or less to say for 'any man', for 'all of us', etc. – *how, why, from what point of view*, etc., can one say that ideology is *nothing but outside*? An elementary question, the *pons asinorum* of Marxism-Leninism, which is not to say that it is easy to answer (in fact, as we shall see, this is relatively difficult and presupposes a transformation of the question itself), but does signify that *everything depends on it,* and first of all the conception of revolutionary theory and practice, with all the consequences that follow for questions such as 'what is it to struggle?' and 'what is it to produce (and "reproduce") scientific knowledges?'.

Let me very quickly evoke, *for memory's sake*, two 'solutions' which are no solutions but are constantly put forward to settle the question.

The first of these 'solutions' consists of imagining *the subject sallying forth from ideology* by an (individual or collective) act whereby one 'crosses the threshold' to 'pass over' *into science and the real,*[27] i.e., to 'reach things themselves' (cf. Husserl) beyond the subjectivity of

27. I shall use the term *real* here rather than that of *reality*, given the role I have hitherto attributed to the latter term in the description of the operation of ideologies.

discourse. In other words, the subject will 'see elsewhere' what is, 'piercing the appearances', 'breaking the mirror' of subjectivity, etc. There is no need to go on: this conception of the subjective desubjectification of the subject corresponds, as could easily be demonstrated, to a politically 'heroic' and epistemologically theological position in which the science/ideology discontinuity operates as an epistemological and political phantasy deriving from Plato ('science' pre-existing the actual historical production of knowledges, politics transcendent as the 'royal science'). In short, this first road is that of *metaphysical realism*, whose 'ins and outs' I think I have sufficiently demonstrated.

I can be even briefer with the second 'solution', which consists of imagining that 'science' is *the most convenient ideology* at a given moment and in given circumstances (the most 'practical' 'system of representations'), so that to take up 'the point of view of science and the real' amounts, in this road in which all the characteristics of empiricism are recognisable, to constructing that point of view pragmatically and subjectively *in ideology*, hence, epistemologically, a consecration of the continuity by which ideology itself conceives its relationship to 'science' and, politically, a benediction of the existing balance of forces, in so far as that balance determines the 'convenience' of any position at any given moment.

Finally, what is peculiar to these two pseudo-solutions (which could be shown to correspond respectively to the voluntarism of the Stalinist deviation in the Third International and the empiricist and opportunist quietism of the Second International) is that they seek to resolve the problem *precisely where its solution is radically impossible*, i.e., by taking as point of departure what I have called the 'subject-form', which, I think I have shown, is in fact an effect and a result, i.e., precisely *anything but a point of departure*.

To take the subject-form as point of departure is to consider that there is on one side 'the point of view of the sciences' on the real, and on the other 'the point of view of ideology', by a division into two camps confronting one another from their respective positions. In fact, every 'point of view' is the point of view of a subject; a science cannot therefore be a point of view on the real, a vision or a construction which represents the real (a 'model' of the real): a science is the real in the modality of its necessity-thought, so the real with which the sciences are concerned *is not anything different from* the real producing the figurative-concrete that is imposed on the subject in the 'blind' necessity of ideology. This is to say that the *true point of departure from which we can understand why 'ideology is nothing but outside' for science and the real is exactly the same point of departure as the one that has been our guide in developing our analysis of the subject-form in which ideology has no outside*: this true point of departure, as we know, is not man, the subject, human activity, etc.,[28] but, once again, *the ideological conditions of the reproduction/transformation of the relations of production.*

28. Cf. Marx: 'My analytical method does not start from man, but from the economically given social period . . . Society is not composed of individuals' (cit. Althusser 1976b, p. 52).

PART IV

DISCURSIVE PROCESSES IN THE SCIENCES AND IN POLITICAL PRACTICE

10 Epistemological Break and Subject-Form of Discourse: There is no Pure 'Scientific Discourse'

I shall therefore return to the 'true point of departure' to find out what the expression 'ideology is nothing but outside' means, but still with the aim of advancing as far as possible in the materialist theory of *discursive processes*. This immediately brings us back to the *double reference* I pointed out at the beginning: in the operation of the subject-form (and specifically of the subject-form of discourse) as it is realised in the conditions produced by the capitalist mode of production and beneath the general domination of the legal, a double system of reference is distinguishable, to *scientific* practice and to *political* practice, with a constant cross-reference between the signifiers of knowledge and those of politics. We shall see how Marxism-Leninism transforms the relationships between these two practices, with the consequences, some of them 'discursive', that follow.

Without it being necessary to see here a rational order of questions making it obligatory to start with one rather than the other, I shall approach first the question of the production of scientific knowledges as it impinges on the problem of discursive processes.

As I have just recalled, it is now quite impossible to sustain any longer the 'evident proposition' that it is *man*, the *subject*, *human activity*, etc., that produce scientific knowledges. Of course, the reader may be thinking, faced with the 'evident' idealism of this first solution, it is not Man who produces scientific knowledges, it is *men*, in society and in history, i.e., *social and historical human activity*. However I shall exclude this second formulation, too, by virtue of the lack of focus it brings with it and which swallows up the materialist reference to the relations of production and the mode of production that implies them. I exclude this formulation because it presupposes the existence of society and of history outside the relations of production and the class struggle.[1] Now the history of the production of knowledges is not *above* or *separate from* the history of the class struggle, as a 'good side' of history counterposed to its 'bad side'; this history is inscribed, with its specificity, in the history of the class struggle. This implies that the historical production of a given scientific knowledge cannot be thought as a 'change of mentalities', a 'creation of the human imagination', a 'revolution of habits of thought', etc. (cf. Thomas Kuhn), but rather as the effect (and a part) of a historical process determined in the last instance by economic production itself. In saying that the conditions of the production of scientific knowledges are inscribed in the conditions of the reproduction/transformation of the relations of production, I am only stating more explicitly my previous assertion. To be precise: the conditions of this reproduction/transformation are, as I have already pointed out, both economic and non-economic. This means, to take the example of the sciences of nature, that the conditions of the emergence of the latter were linked to the new forms of organisation of the labour process imposed by the installation of the capitalist mode of production and to the new conditions of reproduction of labour power corresponding to these forms of organisation; these conditions of emergence were by that very fact linked to the practical ideologies of the capitalist mode of production and to the relationship between these ideologies and the ideologies of previous modes of production, and, through them, with those sciences already 'initiated' (essentially the continent of mathematics). In other words, the 'scientific ideas', the general and particular (epistemologically regional) conceptions historically registrable for each given period – in short, the theoretical ideologies and the different forms of 'spontaneous philosophy' which accompany them – are not separate from history (the history of the class struggle): they constitute specialised 'detachments' of the practical ideologies on the terrain of the production of knowledges, with varying degrees of discrepancy and autonomy. In other words, to borrow Dominique Lecourt's excellent formulation, 'practical ideologies assign theoretical ideologies their forms and their limits'

---

1. Hence reformism once again, only too vulnerable to a certain ethno-socio-historicism which speaks so eloquently of the 'social evolution of mankind'.

(1975, p. 211), which is to say that the system of theoretical ideologies peculiar to a given historical period, with the discursive formations that correspond to them, is in the last instance determined by the complex whole in dominance of the ideological formations present (i.e., the set of ideological state apparatuses).

This signifies that the contradictions which constitute what I have called *the ideological conditions of the reproduction/transformation of the relations of production* have repercussions, with slippages, shifts, etc., in the complex whole of theoretical ideologies, in the form of *relationships of unevenness-subordination determining the theoretical 'interests' in struggle in a given conjuncture*,[2] and this as much in the period before the historical initiation of a science as during the endless development which that initiation inaugurates.

In the perspective that concerns us here, I shall say that the specific material objectivity of the complex of theoretical ideologies constituting a given epistemological field lies precisely in the relationships of unevenness-subordination which assign to each element (notions, representations, procedures, methods, etc.) of that field a determinate role in which are combined, each time in specific forms, the character of *epistemological obstacle* and that of *raw material* or *instrument*, in different 'doses', such that certain elements constitute, at a given moment, pure obstacles, and others *the focal points of a transformation of the field* (the points where 'things are moving' and those where 'they're stuck'). This leads me to posit that, for a given 'scientific continent', every epistemological event (the break inaugurating a science, the 'discovery' and production of knowledges, 'recastings', etc.) is inscribed in a conjuncture histori-cally determined by the state of the relationships of unevenness-

2. Remember that, even in *Reading Capital*, Althusser designated the historical materiality of the process of the production of knowledges as 'the historically constituted system of an *apparatus of thought*, founded on and articulated to natural and social reality . . . [Theoretical production] is constituted by a structure which combines (*"Verbindung"*) the type of object (raw material) on which it labours, the theoretical *means of production* available (its theory, its method and its technique, experimental or otherwise) and the historical relations (both theoretical, ideological and social) in which it produces. This definite system of conditions of theoretical practice is what assigns any given thinking subject (individual) its place and function in the production of knowledges. This system of theoretical production – a material as well as a "spiritual" system, whose practice is founded on and articulated to the existing economic, political and ideological practices which directly or indirectly provide it with the essentials of its "raw materials" – has a determinate objective reality' (1970, pp. 41f.).

subordination I have just evoked: there was no pre-epistemological 'stage' in which 'men' confronted the world in a state of complete ignorance, there was no epistemological 'state of nature' – or innocence. The forms of 'empirical knowledge' and the 'descriptive theories' which are so many 'spontaneous' materialist embryos thus 'always-already' bring *objects of knowledge* into play, theoretical 'raw materials' with their own history and uneven development, up to the cumulative point which constitutes the conditions of possibility of the epistemological break in which the *founding concepts* of a science are produced and which thus marks the historical initiation of the latter. As I have already emphasised, this is to say that *all theoretical ideologies are not equally valuable* and that their historically determinate combination is by no means to be identified as a fog of pre-scientific ignorance which will be cleared by who knows what 'revelation'.

This being so, why continue to speak of epistemological break and epistemological discontinuity? For one crucial reason which could not have been explained until the analysis of the subject-form had been presented: basing myself on what precedes, I shall say that what is peculiar to the knowledges (empirical, descriptive, etc.) *prior to the break* in a given epistemological field is the fact that they *remain inscribed in the subject-form*, i.e., they exist in the form of a *meaning evident* to the subjects who are its historical supports, through the historical transformations that affect that meaning. The result of this for discursivity (cf. pp. 111f. above) is that, this being so, the knowledge effect coincides with a meaning effect inscribed in the operation of a discursive formation, i.e., as we have seen the system of reformulations, paraphrases and synonymies that constitutes it.

The historical process which opens the conjuncture of the break can be characterised, then, as the gradual formation of a 'block' inside the complex whole of theoretical ideologies, such that the state of the relationships of unevenness-subordination that traverse the latter will no longer 'work' and are forced to *repeat themselves circularly* through various re-labellings, adjustments, etc., such that the very structure of the subject-form (with the circular relation subject/object) becomes the visible 'limit' of the process.

This is straightaway to say that the historical moment of the break inaugurating a given science is necessarily accompanied by a challenge to the subject-form and the *evident character of meaning* which is a part of it. In other words, what is specific to every break is, I believe, that it inaugurates, in a particular epistemological field, a relationship between 'thought' and the real *in which what is thought is not as such supported by a subject*.[3] When, a moment ago, I mentioned the *founding concepts* of a science, produced in the very work of the break which inaugurates it, I was in fact pointing to the 'paradox' (which, we shall see, is only a paradox from the point of view of idealism) of *a thought from which any subject is absent as such*, so that the concepts of a science as such do not strictly speaking have a *meaning*, but rather a function in a process.[4] 'Paradox' of a discourse and a *construction* (experimental devices) without a subject which, from the point of view that concerns us, and taking into account what has already been put forward, results in the realisation that in the conceptual process of knowledge, the determination of the real (the 'exterior') and its necessity, a necessity independent of thought, is materialised in the form of an articulated body of concepts which at once *exhibits* and *suspends* the 'blind' action of this same determination as subject-effect (centring-origin-meaning), i.e., as interior without exterior – or to which the exterior is subordinate – produced by the determination of the real ('exterior') and specifically by the determination of interdiscourse as real ('exterior'). Hence it is not surprising to observe that the discursive elements I have assigned to interdiscourse, namely the operations of the *preconstructed* and of the *transverse-discourse*, come by nature to play a specific and essential part in the process of the constitution of the 'discourse' of a science. What I am referring to here is that work of the unthought in thought whereby the very terms of a question, with the answer it presupposes, disappear, so that the question literally loses its meaning while new 'answers' form to questions which had not been asked – that process in which certain names and expressions vanish, with the 'evident' reference to their objects, while other names and expressions appear as a result of certain shifts of the field, certain 'incongruous' intrusions of 'random' elements, detached-fallen from elsewhere, shifts and intrusions which constitute precisely the *work of the philosophical*, in the sense in which, according to Althusser, philosophy acts 'by modifying the way problems are

---

3. I say every break inaugurates such a relationship; I do not say that such a relationship in itself constitutes the 'epistemological condition of possibility' of a science. In reality it is a question of the analysis of an effect on the subjective position inside scientific practice.

4. This (essential) point of the foreclosure of meaning in the concept I shall return to in the Conclusion to this book.

posed, by modifying the relation between the practices and their object' (1976, p. 58n.).

A shift, then, in the space of questions,[5] a 'change of terrain' by which what the nascent science has broken from, i.e., emerged from, can be discerned retrospectively, and it is in this hindsight (the discovery that up to now one had not really *begun*, that one had remained 'beside the question') that ideology can be discerned as *nothing but outside* for knowledge, and for the real.

It is in this hindsight that, in relation to a given science, the possibility is born of *taking up a materialist position* (i.e. recognising the objectivity which is being installed in the discourse and the experimental practice of that science), and of taking up an *idealist* position which disavows and represses that objectivity, constantly repeating the block that preceded the break, and thereby impeding the development of the new scientific continent thus opened, exploiting-distorting-obliterating its first results in order to return to the past. It has been shown elsewhere (Fichant and Pêcheux 1969) that complex alliances are established in this connection in which the already existing scientific continents provide, *as such*, a support and a guarantee to the materialism of the new discipline (through inter-scientific articulations and props), but can also provide pretexts for the anti-materialist struggle against this new discipline, *not in themselves* (i.e., as scientific continents) but through the theoretical ideologies and conceptions of the world that accompany them and 'interpret' their results. One of the clearest symptoms of this exploitation is the accumulation of *word plays* involving the terms *matter* and *materialism*:

for example, Cartesian mechanistic 'materialism' providing the pretext for the repression of the materialist objectivity of electro-magnetism in the scientific continent of physics (then, during the so-called 'crisis of physics', this same 'materialism' sanctioning the notorious idealist slogan of 'the disappearance of matter');

for example, the same imaginary 'materialism' in the face of the materialist objectivity of physiology;[6]

for example, pseudo-physiological 'materialism' exploiting-mis-appropriating the results of physiology against the materialist objectivity of Freud's discovery, etc.

5. I refer the reader to Althusser (1970), sections 5 to 17, which are very directly relevant to this point, vis-à-vis the scientific revolution that bears Marx's name.
6. On this point, cf. the work of demystification carried out by the historians of biology, above all Georges Canguilhem.

One could multiply these examples of cases in which a 'reactive' theoretical ideology, representing determinate theoretical and practical 'interests' in the terrain of a science or a scientific continent, intervenes in the name of that science (and hence in a 'materialist' disguise) to obstruct the objective-materialist development of knowledges, in a scientific field of some 'strategic' importance within a given theoretical and ideological conjuncture, whose characteristics are ultimately determined by the state of the ideological conditions of the reproduction/transformation of the relations of production, i.e., by the state of the ideological class struggle. We shall see shortly why historical materialism represents, in this regard, a new case.

But first I should like to stress the fact that every epistemological break provides the opportunity for a 'shake-up', a specific redistribution of the relationship between materialism and idealism, to the extent that, as I have said, every break exhibits and challenges, in its own field, the effects of the subject-form. *On the one hand*, then, and on each occasion in specific conditions, the *idealist* repetition of the subject-form characterised by the coincidence of the subject with himself (I/see/here/now) in the 'seen-ness' of a scene, in the evidentness of the *experience* of a situation, in the sense of the German *Erfahrung*, i.e., of an experience which can be transferred by identification-generalisation to every subject; a coincidence, then, which guarantees continuity in the evidentness of meaning between empirical lived experience and speculative abstraction,[7] continuity between the concrete subject and the universal subject, supposed to be the subject of science (notional-ideological operation).[8]

7. Thus, in the hindsight opened up by the beginning of a scientific discipline, the *descriptive theories* which preceded it as its 'spontaneous' materialist embryos change their status and become brakes and obstacles, shifting into empirico-speculative idealism.

8. This continuity, regarded as perfectly evident, in fact constitutes the basis of evolutionism, in its various psychological, sociological and historical forms, including in works written in the name of Marxism. The reader will not be surprised to find that, for example, this position is held, in the domain we are considering here, by Adam Schaff, who thinks that Marr's theory 'included, beyond doubt, many interesting and valuable ideas of general theoretical significance', in particular 'the concept of the "manual" language as the protolanguage, and the related hypothesis of the development of human speech from the pictorial concrete to the abstract' (1962, p. 18). This evolutionist conception rests on what Schaff calls 'the process of *human* social life', inside which the notion of communication plays a primordial part: 'The process of labour and the process of using signs, i.e. *human communication* – are intercon-

On the other hand, in quite as specific conditions, the *materialist* process of knowledge, as a process without a subject, in which experimentation (in the sense of the German *Experiment*) realises the body of concepts in devices which contain the objectivity of the science considered, without any foreign admixture (conceptual-scientific operation). The paradox, which is not really a paradox, is that every 'scientist', as the practitioner of a given science, *necessarily takes up a position for objectivity, i. e., for materialism.* In speaking of the spontaneous materialism of scientists, one is simply describing the effects, in the subject-form, of their being 'in the truth' even if they are unable to 'speak that truth'. But it must immediately be added that *the struggle between materialism and idealism never stops,* so that at each stage in the history of a science, throughout its endless development, that struggle is realised via theoretical confrontations which characterise the scientific *front* of questions, i.e., the front of the struggle for the production of knowledges. These confrontations involve *positions* and *problematics* (marked, among other things, by the use of 'shifters': 'As proponents of thesis X, *we* hold that . . .') whose distribution can be identified retrospectively by the history of the sciences.

The notion that the production of knowledges consists of the mere (empirico-deductive) unravelling of the properties of objects[9] is

nected genetically and functionally. If that connection is understood, one can well introduce communication as an element in the definition of man and human society' (1962, p. 122). In short, Schaff has advanced no further than the Marxism of *The 1844 Manuscripts,* the *Theses on Feuerbach* and *The German Ideology,* the last being anyway the text from which he draws nearly all his references to Marx: he cannot advance any further, bècause to do so he would have to look again at what I have called his 'ethno-socio-historicism'. He prefers to display it with disarming frankness: 'As a "human individual" man is "the ensemble of human relations" in the sense that this origin and spiritual development can be understood only in the social and historical context, as a specimen of a "species", but this time not only a natural, but also a social species. *This means historicism and sociologism in the definite sense of these terms.*' (It doesn't have to be said for him! The emphasis on the last sentence is mine.) Schaff goes on: 'Thus historical materialism has introduced a sociological, scientific point of view to the study of man's spiritual life in general, and the study of culture in particular' (1962, p. 145). After which Schaff has cleared the decks for a 'Marxist' rehabilitation of semantics . . .

9. 'Imagine as small a world as possible, one with only two inhabitants, my cat and my dog; and that they have no other characteristics than their respective colours: grey and black. Such a world has two elements, my grey cat and my black dog. *The elementary science of this world* is reduced to two atomic propositions: "my cat is grey" and "my dog is black". It is clear that there is a strict

therefore an idealist myth which identifies science and logic, and by making the latter the *principle* of every science ineluctably conceives scientific practice as the sorting out of the true statements from the false ones,[10] repressing everything that concerns the very conditions of the emergence of those statements, i.e., the *questions* which correspond to them within a historically given problematic. The process of the production of knowledges is thus indissociably linked to *a struggle vis-à-vis names and expressions* for *what they designate* (electricity/positive and negative electricity/animal electricity; limit velocity in relativist mechanics; dephlogisticated air; the most slowly converging series, etc.) and *vis-à-vis the formulation of the questions*: the myth of 'scientific neutrality', of the supposed indifference to words and of the intertranslatability of questions over and above confrontations (reduced to polemics or controversies) masks the fact that in reality scientific objectivity is inseparable from *the taking up of a materialist position*, for which there is *never* equivalence among a number of formulations, and which *never* waits for the verdict of 'experience' to reveal the 'right' problematic. This is at the same time to recognise the confusion involved in the distinction evoked above (cf. p. 40) between 'practical language', supposedly characterised by the fact that it is linked by 'shifters' to the 'situation', implying the joint existence of 'presuppositions' and subjective positions, *and* 'theoretical or formulation language', whose closure excludes any reference to 'situations', presuppositions or the taking of positions: a confusion between mirror-situation, seat of *Erfahrung*, *and* theoretical-concrete situation characterising the front of the production of knowledges in a given discipline at a given

---

correspondence between the realities of the world and the statements of language' (Vax 1970, p. 12 – [my emphasis]).

10. Cf. the rules of division proposed by the Port-Royal *Logic* (Arnauld and Nicole 1685, p. 230):

'1. When the *Genus* is divided by its Species. Thus, *All substance is either Body or Spirit. All Creatures are Man or Beast.*

'2. When the *Genus* is divided by differences: *Every Creature is either rational or irrational. All numbers are even or odd. All Propositions are true or false. All Lines are streight or crooked.*

'3. When a common Subject is divided by the opposite Accidents, of which it is capable; or according to the diversity of Accidents and Times. *As every Star gives light of itself, or by reflection. All bodies either move, or stand still. All the* French *are either Gentlemen, or* Plebians. *All men are sick, or well. All People to express their minds, make use of words or of writing.*

'4. When the Accident is divided into various Subjects. *As when happiness is divided into that of the Mind or Body.*'

moment in its development; a confusion between the 'emptying' of any reference, leaving only a pure, 'consistent' system of logical properties, *and* deconstruction (of the cores of evidentness referred to certain names and expressions) sustaining itself only by reference to other (theoretical) constructions, through other names and expressions.

The roots of this confusion lie finally in the idea that there is a *discourse of science*, i.e. a *discourse of the subject of science*, of which it is characteristic that that subject is obliterated in it, i.e., 'present by its absence', just like God on this earth in religious discourse!

The only way to clear up this confusion is to recognise that there is no 'discourse of science' (nor even, strictly speaking, a 'discourse of *a* science') because every discourse is the discourse of a subject – not of course in the behaviourist sense of the 'discursive behaviour of a concrete individual', but on the understanding that every discourse operates with respect to the subject-form, while the knowledge process is a 'process without a subject'.

To sum up, I shall state the three points whose reunion constitutes an incomprehensible paradox from the idealist point of view, because they form the basis of a materialist position:

(1) the process of the production of knowledges is a process without a subject, i.e., a process from which every subject is absent as such;

(2) the process of the production of knowledges operates through the taking of positions ('demarcations', etc.) *for* scientific objectivity;

(3) the process of the production of knowledges is a 'continuing break'; it is as such co-extensive with the theoretical ideologies from which *it never ceases to separate itself*, such that it is absolutely impossible ever to have a pure 'scientific discourse' unconnected with any ideology.

11 Marxism-Leninism Transforms the Relationship between the Subject-Form of Discourse and Political Practice

To say that *every* science is *always* invested (surrounded and threatened) by 'ideological matter' is to recognise, I repeat, that the struggle between materialism and idealism is an endless struggle, such that an unassailable position is *never* reached which would of itself and for ever constitute a certificate and guarantee of materialism.[1] In other words, the sciences can in no way make philosophy 'redundant' since *every science* presupposes in its concrete development the *taking up of a position for objectivity*.[2] But this, true even for the 'natural sciences', is all the more true in the case of the (Marxist) science of history: like every other science, the (Marxist) science of history began with an 'epistemological break' constituting a *point of no return*. As Althusser says, following Lenin:

> Something begins which will have no end, a 'continuing break' . . ., the beginning of a long period of work, as in every other science. And although the way ahead is open, it is difficult and sometimes even dramatic, marked by events – theoretical events (additions, rectifications, corrections) – which concern the scientific knowledge of a particular object: the conditions, the

1. This, it would seem, was the illusion of Zhdanovism.
2. This does not mean that every science depends on the postulate of objectivity as an 'ethics of scientific knowledge'. Taking up a position for objectivity is not the prior condition but the form of realisation taken by scientific practice.

mechanisms and the forms of the class struggle. In simpler terms, the science of history (1976b, pp. 66f.).

Hence: the Marxist-Leninist science of history is indeed *a science* (and *not* a 'point of view', a 'wager', an 'interpretation' or a 'gospel', in short a *political myth*), and, 'like any science', the work of producing Marxist-Leninist knowledges is a struggle and not that harmonious development (the 'Nevsky Prospekt' of scientific progress) that rationalism classically attributes to every science, progressing 'in a simple straight line . . . without problems or internal conflicts, and under its own power, from the moment of the "point of no return" – the "epistemological break"'.

There certainly is a 'point of no return', *but* in order not to be forced to retreat, it is necessary to advance – and to advance, how many difficulties and struggles there are! For if it is true that Marx had to pass to proletarian class positions in theory in order to found the science of history, he did not make that leap all at once, once and for all, for ever. It was necessary to *work out* these positions, to take them up over and against the enemy. The philosophical battle continued within Marx himself, in his work: around the principles and concepts of the new revolutionary science, which was one of the stakes of the battle (Althusser 1976b, p. 71).

Thus, 'like any science' it has to advance, in order not to be forced to retreat, but *this is where the epistemologically novel character of historical materialism is revealed*: this specificity lies in the nature of the *object* of this new and revolutionary science; in the 'natural sciences', indeed, the struggle for the production of knowledges (the struggle *in theory* between materialism and idealism) unfolds mainly in the arena of 'theoretical ideologies', even if, of course, the 'forms and limits' of that arena and the struggle unfolding in it are *in reality* determined, as we have been reminded, by 'practical ideologies', which are themselves influenced to some extent by these struggles. In other words, the domination of the ruling ideology (in the sense I defined above, inside the contradictory process of the reproduction/ transformation of the relations of production) is only *indirectly* affected by the production of knowledges in the 'continent' of the natural sciences: what the exploration of this continent does have direct links with – in a relationship of mutual determination – is essentially the historical forms of development and organisation of the productive forces, within the determination, unrecognised as such (i.e., 'eternalised'), of the relations of production, i.e., with *indirect and blind* effects on the structure of the mode of production (the link between the development of capitalism and the initiation of the natural sciences, with the contradictions, discrepancies, non-correspondences, etc., that resulted) and *repercussions* on the terrain of the ideological class struggle, in 'practical ideologies' (for example, the repercussions of Galileo's work on the religious apparatus in the seventeenth century, and more generally the ideological role of 'science' and 'enlightenment' in the class struggle of the bourgeoisie against the religious ideology dominant in the feudal mode of production).

I shall sum up by saying that the specificity of the process of the production of knowledges in the continent of the 'natural sciences' is that it is *as such blind* to the way its effects are inscribed in the process of the reproduction/transformation of the relations of production, such that the 'forms and limits' which practical ideologies assign to theoretical ideologies (detachments of the practical ideologies) are here quite ungraspable in it, which can be reformulated by saying that the production of knowledges in the domain of the natural sciences occurs, by and large,[3] in a complete miscognition of history, i.e., of the class struggle, so that *its results are spontaneously re-inscribed in the forms of the dominant ideology without the process of the production of knowledges in this sector being directly impeded thereby.*

In other words, the specificity of the 'natural sciences' continent is that the ideological recuperation that accompanies it as its shadow *does not in itself constitute a 'retreat' in the production of knowledges,* at least so long as the struggle of the bourgeois class does not withdraw, as is at present happening in this domain, to the terrain of precapitalist ideologies (irrationalism, mysticism, etc.). Thus it is clear how the 'natural sciences' have, until the appearance of socialism, been able to develop in the gradually formed framework of the bourgeois university.

Now, and this is the point where the nature of the 'history

3. By and large, i.e., until the historical formation of a Marxist-Leninist position on the production of knowledges in the natural sciences (Marx, Engels, then Lenin), and within the effective limits of that position, with the 'deformations' to which it may be subject (for example the Zhdanovism of the Stalin period, and also the neutralist reaction after 'de-Stalinisation').

continent' endorses its specificity as an *epistemologically novel case*, the very object of the (Marxist-Leninist) science of history ('conditions, mechanisms and forms of the class struggle') is such that any *ideological recuperation of this object* (re-inscription in the forms of the dominant ideology) *constitutes simultaneously a 'retreat' in the class struggle in theory*, and *in the class struggle in general, i.e., in the struggle for the transformation of the relations of production.*

The immediate consequence is that, given the specificity of its object, historical materialism is even less dissociable than any other science from the philosophy which sustains it (i.e., from the class position in the theoretical struggle which governs that philosophy). That is why speculative-academic Marxism, giving credence to unthinkable 'Marxist human sciences',[4] i.e., to a recuperation of Marxism in a new academicism, constitutes a *political* deviation, the deviation called theoreticism. This deviation consists essentially of the refusal to recognise that in the specific case of Marxism-Leninism, *the scientific break is subordinate to a philosophical revolution*, such that a 'general theory (of the history) of the sciences' is impossible, in so far as such a theory would imply the projection onto historical materialism of epistemological characteristics linked to the emergence of the natural sciences, incorrectly confused with 'the sciences' in general. It goes without saying that this rectification of the theoreticist deviation is by no means the same thing as to invalidate the analysis of historicism and voluntarism carried out in *For Marx* (Althusser 1969) and *Reading Capital* (Althusser and Balibar, E. 1970): the attempt to *counterpose* Marxism-Leninism and the natural sciences, making the (Marxist) science of history a 'critical' science, based on a humanist conception of history as 'anti-nature', is another academic variant of the same political deviation.

In this way we reach the second point, on which everything under discussion here has a bearing: this point is, as I have said, that of a revolutionary political practice, in *the union of the Workers' Movement and Marxist theory*. Indeed, this – and this alone – gives the (Marxist) science of history its epistemologically novel character: as we have seen, like every other science, this science depends, for the conditions of its appearance and development, on the infra- and superstructural conditions of the reproduction/transformation of the relations of production, but its specificity – its radical 'novelty' –

4. In saying that the idea of 'Marxist human sciences' is literally *unthinkable*, I do not mean to say that the academic effect it conveys *cannot be realised*, quite the contrary, unfortunately.

lies in the fact that its *object* (the object of the theory and practice of this science) is precisely nothing but *the very same reproduction/ transformation of the relations of production*, so that the *theoretical* interests of historical materialism and the *practical* (political) interests of the Workers' Movement are absolutely inseparable. In other words, the theoretical practice of historical materialism presupposes and implies proletarian political practice and the bond that links the one to the other: in short, at issue is the historical formation of a *scientific politics* coeval with the historical constitution of the Workers' Movement, and inwardly linked to a scientific knowledge of the class struggle.

So there is not and cannot be a 'bourgeois science' of history, which is not, of course, to make the rather unlikely statement that the bourgeoisie is not politically active (!), but rather to argue that the bourgeois forms of political practice – essentially the *denegation* of politics and politics as a *game* (cf. pp. 81f.) – are 'spontaneous' forms in which are *blindly*[5] expressed the class interests of the bourgeoisie.

A science, then, whose conditions of emergence are determined by an uneven, contradictory and overdetermined complex of theoretical ideologies, which *depend* in their 'forms and limits' on practical ideologies, themselves inscribed in the class struggle peculiar to the capitalist mode of production, such that *the recognition of this dependence constitutes one of the first things at stake in this 'science of a new type'*: the unevenness-contradiction-overdetermination is therefore not *only* nor *in the first instance* that of a new theoretical field (the 'history continent'), but above all a characteristic and an effect of the class divisions peculiar to the capitalist mode of production, and appears as such at the level of the practical ideologies in which is *'represented the imaginary relation* of individuals to their real conditions of existence' (Althusser 1971b, p. 152). This characteristic may be summarised by speaking of a differential effect of ideological subjection, imposed by the capitalist form of class division, such that the real conditions of existence assigned by the capitalist mode of production to the proletariat constitute for the latter a constant 'reminder' of the *place* prepared for it, whereas the bourgeoisie *forgets its own place* – and that of the proletariat – in the imaginary of economic, legal, ethical and other universalities. Thus the

5. Nevertheless, I do not want to suggest that the bourgeoisie is politically *blind* (!): quite the contrary, its (economic and political) representatives are all the time calculating, computing, predicting, as if politics were a *problem to solve*. I shall return to this in a moment.

'proletarian spontaneity' which results from the representation of the (imaginary) relationship of the proletariat to its real conditions of existence, characterises the way the latter can be 'in the truth' (recognise that *this* cannot go on, that something has to be done about *it*,[6] etc.) even if it is not always able to 'speak that truth'. But the possibility of 'speaking the truth' about history and the class struggle, i.e., the historical emergence of the (Marxist) science of history – the opening up of the 'forbidden continent'[7] – was in fact only possible because that continent was already 'inhabited':

> It was not thanks only to his theoretical intelligence that Karl Marx was able to cross the frontier of the new continent. To set out on his voyage of discovery, he needed guides, he needed the help of those already *living* on that continent, those whose objective situation meant the secret could not quite be a secret – the members of the proletariat (Karsz 1974, p. 271).

Moreover, this is why, as Étienne Balibar points out, 'Marxist theory has not been mummified or gradually rejected by the Workers' Movement, but transformed by it at the same time as the theory in turn transformed the movement' (1974, p. 70). In other words, historical materialism can be called quite literally *the experimental science of history*, using the distinction between *Erfahrung* and *Experiment* I introduced above. Indeed, it can be said that, compared with the empirical and spontaneous political practice which forms under the domination of bourgeois ideology as *political Erfahrung*, the Marxist-Leninist practice of politics constitutes a true 'historical experimentation' (Balibar, E. 1974, p. 86); *Experiment*, simultaneously knowledge and transformation, knowledge *in order to* transform, in the specific conditions of the process 'history'. It therefore contains, like every other science, *both concepts and devices* (*dispositifs*) through which their effects are realised, in new epistemological and practical conditions (which exclude, for example, the miniaturisation of this experimentation in the shelter of a

6. The real conditions of existence of the proletariat cannot be *obliterated* by the dominant ideology. As Plon and Prèteceille write (1972, p. 67): 'One can be a worker and vote Conservative, read only the most insipid bourgeois newspapers, or not read at all, but the exploitation of labour power will still exist and produce its effects, which in the worst case one may try to justify: "That's life!" "Nothing can be done about it", but the "it" is there, witness to something.'

7. Althusser's expression (1974b, p. 321).

'laboratory' . . .): to be brief, the *concepts* are those of Marxism-Leninism, and the *devices* (not to be confused with 'instruments', 'systems' or 'erections') are the organisations of the Workers' Movement, and, above all, 'parties of a new type', in the Leninist sense of the term.

Let me explain, beginning with the *Erfahrung/Experiment* distinction as applied to political practice. The term *Erfahrung* has already been applied above to the effect of miscognition linked to the *identification* of the subject with the Subject, the other subject and himself. To say that the empirical and spontaneous form of political practice, before the emergence of Marxism-Leninism, is *Erfahrung*, is to say that the form of this practice is none other than the subject-form with the series of its effects, including in the sphere of 'discourse' the responsibility and imputability associated with *the freedom of the subject* ('Caesar crossed the Rubicon . . .'), which invincibly invokes the category of the possible (the 'possible worlds') as the counterpart to that freedom (the Caesar out of all possible Caesars who crossed the Rubicon, i.e., the world out of all possible worlds in which Caesar, etc.). On this point I would draw the reader's attention once again to Clausewitz on the oversight of the Prussian generals and their strategy towards the people's war of the French Revolution: the characteristics of the inscription of political practice in the 'subject-form' lies in the undefined character of the identification of the 'other' and of the calculation which is coextensive with it – 'if I were you, he, the government, the police, etc.'. Remembering the incongruity of the 'masses-subject', one might go on in pre-emptive irony: 'If I were the people, the masses, the working class, the Party . . .!' It can be demonstrated (I shall not do this here, but simply refer the reader to Michel Plon's study (1976) which deals centrally with this question) that the identification process inherent in the subject-form carries with it (and through the representation of the possible and the obliteration of the place of the subject which characterises them both) a symmetrification-dichotomisation of the political field which confers on the latter all the appearances of a *logical* construction in which one can advance step by step answering *yes or no* to each question.[8] The bourgeois art of the politico-dramatic dilemma,[9] the phantasy of a

8. On the same grounds this is the law of operation of the administrative or judicial inquiry.
9. The way this is staged has been brilliantly analysed by Jacques Frémontier (1971).

'formalisation of politics', the notion that calculation is sufficient to bring about agreement (Leibniz), in short, the project to apply '*the experimental method*' in politics (Kissinger) are all only formal counterparts to the empirical effect inscribed in the subject-form.[10] This explains why the emergence of Marxism-Leninism (both scientific theory of historical processes *and* proletarian political practice) constitutes a practical break in the region of politics, a break which 'continues' today; one of the essential characteristics of this break has been recently pointed out by Étienne Balibar in the article already referred to:

> The proletarian revolution is not conceived as an *act*, the act of the proletariat realising its own programme or project, even though it is indeed the proletariat's political practice that accomplishes the revolution . . . The revolution is not conceived simply as an act, but as an objective *process* (1974, p. 79).

In other words, proletarian political practice is not *the act of a subject* (supposedly the proletariat); this practice breaks with the spontaneous political operation of the subject-form, and that is what makes it *Experiment*, scientific experimentation, and not *Erfahrung*. This is not to say, as we shall see, that the effect of the subject-form simply disappears, but that it is transformed and displaced – and it is here, strictly speaking, that the point I have been developing impinges on the question of proletarian politics: as with every break, the configuration in which the latter occurs is reorganised by it into elements operating differentially as *obstacles* and/or as *raw materials* in relation to it. In other words, the empirical and spontaneous – subjective – forms of political practice operate differentially as a function of the class positions to which they correspond, and constitute the point of application of a political practice of a new type (non-subjective practice of experimentation-transformation of history developed by the masses through their organisations). The transformation of the relations of production, in its various stages – from the seizure of political power by the workers to the oc-

10. In the study already mentioned, Étienne Balibar quotes from an interview (*Le Monde*, 18 May 1972), in which Pham Van Dong was asked why the USA, although it makes war 'with all the scientific means at its disposal' can still be defeated. The answer is given in these words: 'We make war scientifically . . ., we fight on our own ground, for our own objectives and with our own methods' (cit. Balibar, E. 1974, p. 99n.).

cupation-transformation-destruction of the 'state machine' in the socialist transition to the communist mode of production – is the object of this new type of practice characterised by a 'transformation of the struggle into non-struggle by the development of a new struggle' (Balibar, E. 1974, p. 82) which is the strict political correlate of the scientific work of the production of knowledges as a transformation of ideological 'raw materials' into materialist objectivities through the development of new ideologies (cf. p. 135). Thus, just as scientific discoveries do not help to bring about an 'end of ideologies', proletarian politics cannot consist purely and simply of a 'disappearance of politics'.[11]

To proceed, with the emphasis on the aspect that specifically concerns us here, I shall say that this 'practice of a new type' includes in a necessary imbrication both political work on the state apparatus (on this point see Étienne Balibar's arguments about the relationship between state apparatus and state power)[12] *and* politico-ideological work on the 'ideological state apparatuses'. More exactly, work on the dominant ideology which is realised in them, as the 'ideological conditions of the reproduction of the relations of production', in other words (cf. pp. 97f) in fact work on the contradictory-uneven-overdetermined complex of ideological state apparatuses. This aspect of the 'political' practice of a new type constituted by Marxism-Leninism aims to transform the configuration of the 'complex of ideological state apparatuses' such that *in the contradictory relationship of the reproduction/transformation of the relations of production, transformation predominates over reproduction*, by a 'reversal-rearrangement' of the relationships of unevenness-subordination which characterise the 'complex whole in dominance' of the ideological state apparatuses and ideological formations inherent in capitalist relations of production. (*For example*, the transformation of the relationship between *education* and *politics* evoked above, a transformation that involves *both* the relationships of subordination between different ISAs – the school, the family,

11. To be replaced, for example, by the economy alone as the administration of 'things' and psycho-pedagogy as the training of 'men'.
12. 'The bourgeoisie "organises itself as the ruling class" *only* by developing the state apparatus . . . The proletariat "organises itself as the ruling class" *only* by bringing into being alongside the state apparatus and against it forms of political practice and organisation which are radically different: in fact, therefore, by destroying the existing state apparatus and replacing it not just with another apparatus, but with *the ensemble constituted by a new state apparatus plus something other than a state apparatus*' (1974, p. 97).

trades-union organisations, political parties – *and* the relationships which these apparatuses have with forms of practice and organisation not inscribed in the state apparatus.

Hence it is in the context of this politico-ideological work on the complex of ideological state apparatuses and hence on the ideological formations and the *discursive formations* which are coextensive with it that the emergence of a new 'discursive practice', to use Michel Foucault's expression, can be understood. In this context, and only in this context, as Lecourt points out in a commentary on the discussion of discursivity in *The Archaeology of Knowledge* (Foucault 1972): 'In fact, it is because Marx took up the point of view of the proletariat that he inaugurated a "new discursive practice" ' (1975, p. 213).

Once again this brings us to the link between *taking up a position* and *materialist objectivity* as the taking up of a position in relation to 'what is': the 'point of view of the proletariat' is neither one particular point of view that can be compared with others in the disinterested search for truth (to everyone his own point of view, with inaccessible truth beyond!) nor a point of view that is 'universal' *de jure* while remaining *de facto* the point of view of a class. It is as a class point of view that it is objective, and this throughout history. I must insist on this decisive point – it is what I called above the *pons asinorum* of Marxism-Leninism – and apply it to my own theses: it must be understood both that the dominant ideology (the ideology of the ruling class) dominates the whole of the social formation (including the dominated class) *and* that 'the class struggle is the motor of history'. To do so it is first necessary to root out completely the idea of a *disjunction* between history and the class struggle, according to which one can *first* think history in its 'objectivity' (for example as technical and social progress, 'humanisation', etc.) and *then* the class struggle as an *effect in history*, implying the taking up of positions with respect to that 'objectivity'. One cannot fail to see that this disjunction would lead, in the particular case of the question of discourse, to the opposition between an 'ideological language' (referred to concrete situations implying the taking up of positions) and a 'scientific language' (the pure deployment of 'abstract' properties, i.e., properties that are 'true' over and above any position taken), such that in any discourse, including 'political discourse', it would be possible to register and distinguish between 'what is ideological' (as linked to the taking up of a position) and 'what is not ideological' (as located beyond the taking up of any position).

I think I have already established the theoretical methods which allow me to assert that the materialist objectivity of the proletarian point of view is characterised discursively by the taking up of positions *for* certain words, formulations, expressions, etc., *against* other words, formulations or expressions, exactly as in the struggle for the production of knowledges.

In 1968, in an interview in the newspaper *l'Unità* entitled 'Philosophy as a Revolutionary Weapon', Althusser summed up this point in the following way:

> Why does philosophy fight over words? The realities of the class struggle are 'represented' by 'ideas' which are 'represented' by words. In scientific and philosophical reasoning, the words (concepts, categories) are 'instruments' of knowledge. But in political, ideological and philosophical struggle, the words are also weapons, explosives or tranquillisers and poisons. Occasionally, the whole class struggle may be summed up in the struggle for one word against another word. Certain words struggle amongst themselves as enemies. Other words are the site of an *ambiguity*: the stake in a decisive but undecided battle . . . The philosophical fight over words is a part of the political fight. Marxist-Leninist philosophy can only complete its abstract, rigorous and systematic theoretical work on condition that it fights both about very 'scholarly' words (concept, theory, dialectic, alienation, etc.) and about very simple words (man, masses, people, class struggle) (1971c, pp. 24f.).[13]

Everything that has been argued hitherto justifies me in considering that what Althusser says here about 'words' in fact concerns the region of discursive processes as a whole,[14] and is applicable *ipso facto* to the more general case of those expressions, formulations, etc., which, in conjunctures of varying historical importance, come to

13. Remember in this connection the position taken by Frege on 'the will of the people'.
14. Moreover, this is what he implies in a note on the word 'man' in the 'Reply to John Lewis' (1976b, p. 52n.): 'The word "man" is not simply a word. It is the place which it occupies and the function which it performs in bourgeois ideology and philosophy that give it its *meaning*' (Althusser's emphasis).

represent different *politico-ideological stakes* (by expressions like 'the oil crisis', 'the dictatorship of the proletariat', 'the end of history' . . ., or statements like 'man makes history', 'the class struggle is the motor of history' . . .). I shall say that as a function of the 'complex whole in dominance' of the ideological state apparatuses and their corresponding discursive formations, with their specific relationships of contradiction-unevenness-subordination, certain discursive 'lines of demarcation' are drawn, lines gained through struggles over *ambiguous formulations* emerging originally on the terrain of the dominant ideology and then more or less 'worked over', 'turned about', etc., by politico-theoretical work on the 'preconstructeds' and 'transverse-effects' that have produced them. Political formulations, expressions and slogans, political questions and problematics, are thus worked out in a given conjuncture, with varying degrees of autonomy (sometimes *weapons*, for example 'dictatorship of the proletariat', sometimes formulations which retain an *ambiguous* status, for example, 'the end of history'), the degree of autonomy being directly dependent on the degree of political autonomy that, on a given question, the Workers' Movement and its organisations enjoy within the set of political forces present, for a given phase of the class struggle.

12 The Subject-Form of Discourse in the Subjective Appropriation of Scientific Knowledges and Political Practice

At this point I can return to the expression *discursive practices*, in so far as we now have the necessary conceptual bearings, both in the domain of the sciences *and* in that of politics (domains which are not juxtaposed or counterposed but articulated, as we have seen). We now know that every discursive practice is inscribed in the contradictory-uneven-overdetermined complex of the *discursive formations* which characterise the ideological instance in given historical conditions. These discursive formations are asymmetrically related to one another (by the 'effects of the preconstructed' and 'transverse-effects' or 'articulation effects' that I have expounded above) in such a way that they are the sites of a *work of reconfiguration* which constitutes in different cases either a work of recuperation-reproduction-reinscription or a politically and/or scientifically productive work.

Here, after a long but indispensable re-construction, we come once again to the problem of *discourse in the subject-form*: if there is no practice without a subject (and, in particular, no discursive practice without a subject), if 'agent-individuals thus always act in the subject-form, as subjects' (Althusser 1976b, p. 95), the problem of discursive practice necessarily leads on to the problem of the effect of the complex of discursive formations on the subject-form. At the same time we must beware of any suggestion that a practice (discursive or otherwise) is *the practice of subjects* (in the sense of being a subject's acts, actions, activities – that would be to fall into the trap of what I have called the 'Munchausen effect'!), and note rather that every subject is constitutively *held to be* the responsible author of his acts (of his 'behaviour' and of his 'utterances') in each practice in which he is inscribed as a subject, and this by virtue of the determination of the complex of ideological formations (and, in particular, of discursive formations) in which he is interpellated as 'responsible-subject'.

I said earlier that 'individuals are "interpellated" as speaking subjects (as subjects of *their* discourse) by the discursive formations which represent "in language" the ideological formations that correspond to them', and I specified that 'the interpellation of the individual as subject of his discourse is achieved by the identification (of the subject) with the discursive formation that dominates him'. I shall now add, taking up Paul Henry's recent formulations (1974 and 1977, esp. pp. 118–22), that this interpellation necessarily presupposes a *reduplication* constitutive of the subject of discourse, such that *one of the terms* represents the 'speaker' or what it is now customary to call the 'subject of enunciation' in so far as he is 'supposed to take responsibility for the contents posed' – i.e., the subject who 'takes up a position' in full awareness of the consequences, complete responsibility, total freedom, etc. – and the other term represents 'the so-called universal subject, the subject of science or of what passes as such' (Henry 1974, p. 37). Note that this *reduplication* corresponds exactly to the relationship also *made clear above* between the *preconstructed* (the 'always-already' there of the ideological interpellation that supplies-imposes 'reality' and its 'meaning' in the form of universality – the 'world of things') and *articulation* or *transverse-effect* (which, I said, constitutes the subject in his relationship to meaning, i.e., represents in interdiscourse what determines the domination of the subject-form). What can I add to this after the detour we have just made concerning the practice of the production of knowledges and proletarian political practice? One element, a crucial one, I believe, which concerns the 'paradoxical effects' which these two practices induce in the *subject-form as relationship of reduplication between 'subject of enunciation' and 'universal subject'*.

Let me explain, beginning with the observation that the reduplication can take different modalities, two of which are 'evident':

The *first modality* consists of a superimposition (a covering) of *the subject of enunciation and the universal subject* such that the subject's 'taking up a position' realises his subjection in the form of the 'freely consented to': this superimposition characterises the discourse of the 'good subject' who spontaneously reflects the Subject (in other words: interdiscourse determines the discursive formation with which the subject identifies in his discourse, and the subject suffers this determination blindly, i.e., he realises its effects 'in complete freedom').

The *second modality* characterises the discourse of the 'bad subject', in which the *subject of enunciation* 'turns against' *the universal subject* by 'taking up a position' which now consists of a *separation* (distantiation, doubt, interrogation, challenge, revolt . . .) *with respect to what the 'universal Subject' 'gives him to think'*: a struggle against ideological evidentness on the terrain of that evidentness, an evidentness with a negative sign, reversed in its own terrain. The reversal leaves linguistic traces: *'what you call* the oil crisis', *'your* social sciences', *'your* Virgin Mary' (as one might say 'your hang-up'!), etc. Compare the example given on p. 63: 'He who saved the world by dying on the cross never existed'. In short, the subject, a 'bad subject', a 'trouble-maker', *counteridentifies* with the discursive formation imposed on him by 'interdiscourse' as external determination of his subjective interiority, which produces the philosophical and political forms of *the discourse-against* (i.e., *counter-discourse*) which constitute the core of humanism (anti-nature, counter-nature, etc.) in its various theoretical and political forms, reformist *and* ultra-leftist.[1]

Having once grasped these two discursive modalities of subjective operation, I should be quite incapable of going any further were it not for the double reference (to the production of scientific knowledges on the one hand and to political practice on the other) that I have explored within the specific problem I am discussing here; and I might by the same token have fallen for the illusion that these two practices could be 'theorised' *on the basis of the discursive modalities of the subjective operation,* in other words that one could have a discursive 'theory' of the sciences and of politics! Nothing could be simpler than to counterpose freely consented acceptance (first modality) to rejection (second modality) and to see in this 'antagonism' the 'secret' of politics and scientific work. But my

1. Thus the 'second modality' appears as the symmetrical inversion of the first. A statement like 'socialist revolution is incompatible with democracy', *a statement that can be turned inside out like a glove,* constitutes a political example in which this symmetry is particularly clearly demonstrated. On this question of symmetry see the analyses in Guedj and Girault (1970).

detour enables me to see, precisely, that this 'antagonism' (which has the form of the Hegelian contradiction: negativity, *Aufhebung*, etc.) in fact unfolds *inside the subject-form* in so far as the effect of what I have defined as *interdiscourse continues to determine the subject's identification or counter-identification with a discursive formation in which he is supplied with the evidentness of meaning, whether he accepts it or rejects it.* What we have here is what Henry has recently characterised as the *occultation-rejection* couple, which must be distinguished from the process he calls 'integration':

> If constituted proletarian ideologies do exist, then in the last instance what distinguishes them from the ideologies of the ruling class in a social formation dominated by the capitalist mode of production is the knowledges which they *integrate* by the reproduction of certain signification effects, whereas the ideologies of the other class *reject* them or *occult* them (Henry 1974, p. 235).

This integration in fact designates the historically novel character of proletarian ideological practice, which consists, in my opinion at any rate, of working explicitly and consistently *on* the subject-form. But this is also to designate at the same time the crucial existence of a 'third modality' of the subject and discourse, one paradoxically characterised by the fact that it integrates *the effects of the sciences and of proletarian political practice on the subject-form,* effects which take the form of a *disidentification*, i.e., of the *taking up of a non-subjective position*: this disidentification is the corollary of the fact already mentioned that scientific concepts do not have 'a meaning' graspable in the operation of a discursive formation, which implies at the same time that, as concepts, they have no corresponding 'representations'.[2] I shall return to this point in the conclusion to this study. Let me add that this is equally true, and for reasons I have already explained, for the 'political organisations of a new type' which constitute what I have called historical devices of experimentation-transformation. Is this to say that the practice of the production of knowledges and the political practice of a new type that Marxism-Leninism constitutes realise (imply or determine) a *desubjectification of the subject*, i.e., a kind of abolition of the subject-form (dissubjection, rupture or fragmentation of the subject, as a certain formalist

2. 'Not only is every concept not representational, a concept cannot ever be so completely, its production as a concept is not the image of the real object that it subsumes' (Raymond 1973, p. 277).

conception of 'writing' suggests today)? *The answer is no*, unless one is to fall back precisely into the theoretical and political myth of the 'end of ideologies'. In reality, the operation of this 'third modality' constitutes a *working* (transformation-displacement) *of the subject-form* and not just its *abolition*. In other words, this disidentification effect is paradoxically realised by *a subjective process of appropriation of scientific concepts and identification with the political organisations 'of a new type'*. Ideology – 'eternal' as a category, i.e., as the process of interpellation of individuals as subjects – does not disappear, but operates as it were *in reverse*, i.e., *on and against itself*, through the 'overthrow-rearrangement' of the complex of ideological formations (and of the discursive formations which are imbricated with them). In my opinion, it is only on this condition that one can understand what constitutes *the subjective appropriation of knowledges* (specifically the operation of scientifico-educational discursive processes) *on the one hand*, and *the subjective appropriation of proletarian politics* (specifically the operation of proletarian political discursive processes) *on the other*.

A few remarks on these two points one by one.[3]

The intention behind this formulation *subjective appropriation of knowledges* is to fight both against the myth of a 'pure education', in the sense of a pure exhibition-transmission of knowledges[4] 'without any presuppositions'(!), and also against the myth of a reconstruction of knowledges in the subject's 'activity' (let me repeat, Piaget notwithstanding, 'activity' is not the same thing as 'practice', which cannot be the practice of a subject: strictly speaking there is no practice of a subject, there are only the subjects of different practices). In both these positions there is in fact a confusion between the practice of the production of knowledges *and* the

3. The expression 'subjective appropriation' (of knowledges, of proletarian politics) emerged, at the time this book was written, in the context of joint work with Michel Plon and Paul Henry. Since then the extent to which it is laden with political and theoretical ambiguities has become clear, and Plon and Henry have rightly been careful to avoid any 'positive' use of it in Plon (1976b) and Henry (1977). The reader will find, in Appendix 3 (written in 1978), my own attempt at a rectification of this point.

4. 'Science is communicated by instruction, in order that one man may profit by the experience of another and be spared the trouble of accumulating it for himself; and thus, to spare posterity, the experiences of whole generations are stored up in libraries' (Mach 1960, p. 577; cit. Lecourt 1973, p. 94).

practice of the transmission-reproduction of those knowledges,[5] evading what I believe is the crucial issue, that there is never an educational *starting-point* (an absence masked by such 'evident' facts as that children 'start' school). A recognition of this crucial point makes it possible to understand that every educational effect rests on some pre-existent 'meaning', produced in discursive formations which are 'always-already-there' and providing it with raw material:

> It would be absurd to attempt to introduce children to mathematical knowledge by starting with the axiomatised propositions of set theory, because one could not thereby produce the evidentness by which children recognise knowledges as knowledges, since it is never possible to get to the bottom of this axiomatised enunciation (Henry 1974, p. 219).

This means that all educational practice presupposes 'jumping in at the deep end', since one cannot talk about the beginning until after one has 'begun' – each subject having really always-already begun – with the result that this question of the beginning as it were occults itself: this 'jumping in at the deep end', which is the specific form of the 'Munchausen effect' in the domain of the subjective appropriation of knowledges, designates the place of politics in 'education'; using the arguments developed earlier (cf. pp. 81f.), I shall say that the bourgeois forms of politics in educational practice can be reduced in principle to two polar forms (combined in alternation), that of *metaphysical realism* (which passes off purely ideological effects as an object of knowledge) on the one hand, and that of *logical empiricism* (which presents the object of knowledge as a convenience, an arbitrary convention) on the other, such that, in either case, the transmission-reproduction of knowledges is in

5. One must distinguish between the way in which a 'classical' school question is organised, with the forms of identification from one place to the other in educational practice ('let us consider *this* triangle' on the blackboard which is in front of *you*, etc.), *and* the distribution of takings of positions demanded by a proposition which, at a given moment in the history of a science, has been neither proven nor refuted. One could make the same comment about *nonexistent preconstructeds* according to whether they are introduced for educational purposes (e.g. 'a triangle with two right angles' in Euclidian geometry, a 'regular decahedron', etc.) in connection with *reductio ad absurdum* proofs, or are at issue in a debate in a given scientific conjuncture (for example: in the theory of relativity, the concept of the 'limit velocity').

practice identified with an inculcation. Hence the explicitly 'rightist', scientist mystification of 'mathematical economics', 'rational sociology', 'scientific psychology', the 'formal theory of law', among others, alternating, according to circumstances, with obcurantism and regressive-liquidatory tendencies, often in an 'ultra-left' guise. In contrast with these two forms of the bourgeois practice of politics in education, it is possible to characterise the effect of proletarian politics in this domain by the drawing of a line of demarcation between scientific knowledges and processes of ideological inculcation, a line historically determined by the state of development of knowledges in different sectors of research, i.e., by the state of the theoretical and ideological class struggles, a line which varies as a function of the existing ideological formations and works on them to transform them, but a line which at the same time continues for ever, like Ideology itself. The fact that 'every epistemological break' is a 'continuing break', means, then, in the domain I am considering here, that the distinction between scientific training and ideological inculcation is a political distinction[6] and not a purely scientific distinction, which would presuppose that it were inscribed in the very materiality of the 'object' or in educational 'techniques' and 'discourse', etc. The uneven or discrepant relationship between scientific knowledges (as conceptual operation) and 'ignorance' (which, as we know, is not an emptiness but the over-fullness of the unthought) may take different forms depending on the nature of the educational apparatus in which it is realised, and, in the last instance, as a function of the mode of production which dominates the social formation considered (for example, in contrast to bourgeois ideology, proletarian ideology *distorts without mystifying*),[7] but this also signifies that nothing can simply abolish the discrepancy in question: this discrepancy can no more be abolished, i.e., disappear as what I have called 'jumping in at the deep end' than can Ideology (as the interpellation of individuals as subjects) itself.

And this is indeed what is at stake; discussing, as we saw above, the impossibility of teaching children mathematics in the form of the axiomatised propositions of set theory, Henry continues: 'It is therefore necessary to re-inscribe this enunciation in the form of a discourse about the physical world, to restore to it a subject in whose

6. Cf. the studies of Christian Baudelot and Roger Establet on the two educational networks in Baudelot and Establet (1971).
7. I have borrowed this expression from Karsz (1974, p. 215).

place the child can imaginarily locate himself by identification' (1974, p. 219). The subjective appropriation of the concept and the disidentification it demands are thus paradoxically achieved by an identification-presentification which inevitably involves complicities, perceptual and notional 'guarantees' ('I see what I see'/'one knows what one knows', cf. pp. 66, 91). This identification-presentification depends *both* on a *mise en scène* (*realisatory* fiction) of the concept or experimental device as *things* (figures, schemata, diagrams, etc.) on the blackboard – 'the diagram *shows* that point H is between B and C' (an example of Henry's, 1974, p. 219); 'let there be a sphere moving on a plane inclined at 15° to the horizontal', etc. – *and*, simultaneously, on the return of the 'known' (of the Universality of the concept) in the subject's thought in the form of a *reminder* – '*this* triangle, which is an isosceles one, has two equal angles at the base' – i.e., the sustaining effect produced by the accessary clause, i.e., the intervention of what I have called the 'transverse-discourse'.

Hence the appropriation of knowledges is never achieved in the form of a *deduction from first principles* (i.e. a discourse which is at the same time a logical machine) but rather (and this irrespective of what scientific field is in question) as an *ascent to first principles*, by a path which is, as it were, constructed retrospectively; for on this path it is a matter of something quite different from the promenade of a mirror: in the course of the appropriation of the knowledges their configuration is transformed so that statements which operated as definitions take on the status of theorems or *vice versa*, statements are rejected as false and replaced, marginal (lateral or accidental) results are universalised or *vice versa*, etc., this displacement overall producing the *disidentification effect* mentioned above,[8] i.e., exhibiting *the real as 'necessity-thought'*. An example drawn from a physics text-book in the shape of the following statement will clarify what I mean here: 'High-frequency currents produce at a distance induction currents whose intensity is greatest when the frequency of the induced current is equal to the frequency of the emitting circuit.'

8. As I have already emphasised, the historical process of the production of a set of knowledges is not at all superimposable on the process of appropriation of that same set. It should however be emphasised that one might find in the history of geometry, say, a historico-epistemological parallel to the subjective disidentification effect in the gradual process by which the place of the geometer (and correlatively of the diagram as 'context') disappears in the passage from *ostensive* demonstration to *axiomatic* demonstration.

Note that no 'grammatical' or 'logical' analysis of the statement itself can solve the (linguistically and/or logically inappropriate) question as to whether this is a determinative construction or on the contrary an explicative-appositional construction, and for good reason. Read as containing an *appositional clause*, the statement may in fact signify either:

'high-frequency currents produce induction currents, about which *it is found* that S'

one learns that it is so and not otherwise, but the latter is perfectly conceivable; or on the contrary:

'high-frequency currents produce induced currents, about which it is obviously necessary that S'

one is reminded that it cannot be otherwise if one knows the definition of 'induced currents'.

Exactly the same remarks could be made about the possibility of a determinative construction, in so far as it is compatible not only with the 'contingent' interpretation:

'induced currents that S'

as opposed to *other types of induced currents* with different properties; but also with the 'necessary' interpretation:

'currents that S, called induced currents'

as opposed to *other types of currents*.

What does this mean if not that the operation of the logico-linguistic elements of an utterance depends on the discursive formations in which each of these elements can find a 'meaning', with the result that it is in the end the configuration of the discursive formations in which a given subjectivity is inscribed that will determine *the* 'meaning' that that utterance will find, along with the necessary or contingent, disjunct or integrated character, etc., of the objects and properties that feature in it?

But this is immediately to recognise that the disidentification effect inherent in the subjective appropriation of knowledges is achieved in different ways (and may in the limit case not be achieved at all) according to the nature of the discursive formations which provide this effect with 'raw material'. The reader will have realised that this is *one* of the causes of 'educational inequality', an inequality which is by no means a psycho-biological fatality, nor even a sociological phenomenon: in fact it transcribes the effect of the ideological class struggle in the terrain of the social appropriation of knowledges, in its links with their subjective appropriation. This struggle is transcribed in education by the struggle over the 'mode of presentation of a question', the 'correct order of questions', etc., as a function of the ideologico-discursive effects any given presentation presupposes and reactivates: to be slightly provocative, one could half-jokingly say that, contrary to Frege's assertion, expressions like '*my* Pythagoras' theorem' (i.e., the presentation of Pythagoras' theorem that I support, given my position on the teaching of mathematics, as opposed to other presentations of which I disapprove) are perfectly comprehensible! Moreover – and now I am quite serious – one only has to attend a discussion between teachers on this problem to realise that the ideological class struggle traverses it through and through.

Lastly I must explain myself about *the subjective appropriation of politics*, in so far as it is affected by a theory of discursive processes. I shall start by remarking that this question is bound up with the one I have just been considering in the matter of *inculcation*:

> The school (but also other state institutions like the Church, or other apparatuses like the Army) teaches 'know-how', but in forms which ensure *subjection to the ruling ideology* or the mastery of its 'practice'. All the agents of production, exploitation and repression, not to speak of the 'professionals of ideology' (Marx), must in one way or another be 'penetrated by' this ideology in order to perform their tasks 'conscientiously' – the tasks of the exploited (the proletarians), of the exploiters (the capitalists), of the exploiters' auxiliaries (the managers), or of the high priests of the ruling ideology (its 'functionaries'), etc. (Althusser 1971b, p. 128).

A *penetration* that takes place 'by itself', and simultaneously an *inculcation* that works consciously on the result of that penetration, 'laying it on' so that *in toto* each subject knows and sees that that is how things are. Given what we have just seen, it can be said that the educational apparatus contributes to this penetration-inculcation in a specific way, which is to simulate the 'necessity-thought' of scientific knowledges in the form of various kinds of ideological evidentness,[9] in an imbrication such that the 'incomprehension' (the doubt, the resistance and the revolt) of those who undergo their schooling as an imposition, a bad period to be got over as soon as

9. Hence, as I said earlier: the ideological universality of the Subject – the legal, ethical, philosophical, etc., Subject – simulating the necessity of the process without a subject.

possible, etc. (i.e., the vast majority of the exploited in the capitalist mode of production) is a symptom transcribing *both* the objective separation between manual labour and intellectual labour in that mode of production *and also* their spontaneous resistance to that penetration-inculcation, the whole constituting what is sometimes called their 'trouble-making'. But two very important points should be emphasised here: first, that *this penetration does not start in the school*, which is only one of the sites of its realisation; second, that this spontaneous ideological resistance is *a reversal and a rejection*, in short, that the discursive processes which are linked to it are inscribed in what I have called the 'second modality' (in which the enunciating subject turns against the universal Subject of Ideology and counter-identifies with it). This counter-identification represents the 'raw material' of the work on the subject-form constituted by the subjective appropriation of proletarian politics, but it by no means realises that appropriation in itself, as I shall now try to show.

I have chosen as the domain for my example the period of the First World War, for various reasons, not the least of which is the hitherto unanswered question as to whether, ultimately, 'Marianne' is or is not 'a being existing and subsisting in herself'!

Note first of all that there is *no subjective appropriation* of *bourgeois* politics, simply because the dominant ideology that underlies the latter is 'always-already' there, in the form of a spontaneous ideological operation older than the bourgeoisie itself: France is in danger/we are *all* Frenchmen/we are at war! – a chain of evident propositions of the order of accomplished facts which will operate in the 'first modality' for most of the French people, minted and articulated as a variety of statements and injunctions pregnant with inculcated preconstructeds ('a French soldier never retreats', 'To the last man!' etc.). Identification of every French subject with the Subject-France: 'France goes to war', as the newspapers of the day headlined it and the history books still repeat it today; and in the same way 'Germany', 'Russia', etc., 'go to war'.

This by no means signifies that the operation of what I have called the 'second modality' (governed by counter-identification, rejection and reversal) was simply obliterated: on the contrary, it was very much present, as the spontaneous operation of *the ideology of the urban and rural proletariat*, in the form of the cruelly absurd but highly meaningful evident fact that 'it is always the same people who get killed', which forms the basis of *pacifism* in France, and also in Germany, in Russia, etc. The 'paradox' of this ideologically evident fact of pacifism ('Down with war! Long live peace!'), which traversed the German, French and Russian Socialist Parties' action *against war*, was, as we know, that it led each of these parties to join the 'Union Sacrée', the 'Burgfrieden', etc., by voting for war credits, in the name of the defence of peace and against annexationist policies, with the result that the spontaneous proletarian ideology (pacifism) was subordinated to the dominant bourgeois ideology (the fatally evident character of the war).

How did this come about, and what had to be done to get out of this situation? It was to this enormous task of explanation and organisation of the proletarian struggle that Lenin dedicated himself, in the context of a 'political practice of a new type', aiming to *work* the masses ideologically and politically while they were still under the influence by the 'social chauvinism of the Second International'. And this practice included, among other things, a 'political discourse of a new type', a discursive modality capable of drawing *lines of demarcation* with respect to the ideologico-discursive effects of identification and counter-identification, by destroying certain evident truths (for example, the evident truth that France was [also] the fatherland of French proletarians, Germany of German proletarians, etc.) and also by constructing certain comparisons, by re-establishing the relationships concealed in certain oppositions (for example, the opposition war/peace).

This (Marxist-Leninist) political practice implied both a theoretical effort to return to historical materialism, and an effort of struggle to organise the proletariat, and it was thereby inscribed in the line of the *Communist Manifesto*, in which Marx and Engels had already pre-emptively dealt with certain 'evident facts'. Thus for example: 'The working men have no country. We cannot take from them what they have not got', a tautological statement followed by a comment that might be said to be profoundly Leninist *ante diem*: 'Since the proletariat must first of all acquire political supremacy, must rise to be the leading class of the nation, must constitute itself *the* nation, it is so far, itself national, though not in the bourgeois sense of the word' (Marx and Engels 1976a, pp. 502f.).

Indeed, everything depends on the way the relationship between the proletariat and the nation is conceived. This is what is at stake in Lenin's struggle against Kautsky's positions, which recalls that of Marx and Engels against Lassallean 'socialism':

It is altogether self-evident that, to be able to fight at all, the working class must organise itself at home *as a class* and that its own country is the immediate arena of its struggle. In so far its class struggle is national, not in substance, but, as the *Communist Manifesto* says, 'in form'. But the 'framework of the present-day national state,' for instance, the German Empire, is itself in its turn economically 'within the framework' of the world market, politically 'within the framework' of the system of states. Every businessman knows that German trade is at the same time foreign trade, and the greatness of Herr Bismarck consists, to be sure, precisely in his pursuing a kind of *international* policy (Marx 1970, p. 21).

In short, the crux of the matter – and Lenin repeated this a thousand times – lies in the link between social chauvinism and opportunism, a link based on the 'evident' character of the opposition-disjunction between *war* and *peace*, and implying an opposition between *the struggle for socialism in the national context* (in times of peace) and *the struggle between nations* (the state of war forcing one to put the struggle for socialism 'on ice'). Lenin showed that the roots of this 'betrayal' lie in the very conception of the class struggle and of its relation to the 'context' of state and nation, leading to a confusion between what Marx and Engels called the *immediate arena* of the struggle and the *substance* of that struggle, a confusion (constitutive of opportunism) one of whose characteristics is to exhibit symptomatic formulations which, as a reminder of what has been argued above, can be called political 'Munchausen effects', in so far as they presuppose the solution at the very moment the question they evoke is posed, while concealing the fact that the basis of the solution is incompatible with that of the question. Hence the series of 'preconstructeds' and 'universal relations' such as 'equal right', 'the free state', 'fair distribution', 'undiminished proceeds of labour', etc., which Marx and Engels exploded by showing that they were 'objects' as inconceivable as the proverbial 'knife without a blade which has no handle' (the example might have been Marx's or Lenin's – in fact it is Freud's, 1960, p. 60n.).[10] During the First

10. Here is an example from the *Critique of the Gotha Programme*; Marx is commenting on Lassalle's positions on the 'iron law of wages': 'It is as if, among slaves who have at last got behind the secret of slavery and broken out in rebellion, a slave still in thrall to obsolete notions were to inscribe on the programme of the rebellion: Slavery must be abolished because the feeding of slaves in the system of slavery cannot exceed a certain low maximum' (Marx

World War a struggle for peace which was not also *at the same time* a struggle for socialism was a nonsense, because pacifism is an illusion so long as socialism has not been established. This is what Lenin said and explained in a thousand ways, with a bitter irony that occasionally made him say 'This would be funny if it were not so tragic' (1964a, p. 322), for example vis-à-vis the 'unanimity' with which the socialists of each combatant country opposed annexations . . . which were directed against 'their own' imperialisms: Lenin did not need to be a grammarian to see the political operation of this *restrictive clause*, which explains the blindness of the Kautskyists to the *symmetrical character* of inter-imperialist war, *in the context of the world economic and political system*.[11] It was just this interimperialist chain that the October Revolution was to break, and the resultant asymmetry led – among other things! – to the formation of new political expressions ('the USSR, the country of all working people'; and also 'Communists, not Frenchmen', or 'Communists are not to the left but to the East', etc.) and the disappearance of other expressions, to be replaced by others ('the world economic and political system' becoming 'the socialist economic and political system'/'the imperialist economic and political system'). Naturally, expressions like 'the world economy' and 'the world political system' did not simply disappear: *they shifted* from a discursive formation articulated to Marxism-Leninism, in which they designated conceptually the world imperialist system, into another discursive formation, ideologically bourgeois or reformist in nature, which occults the asymmetry introduced by the Soviet socialist revolution by means of a notional pseudo-universality of economic and political behaviour 'over and above the systems'.

This suggests a comment on the notions of penetration and inculcation: given, on the one hand, that the formation of historical materialism represents the opening up of the new theoretical continent of *history*, and on the other hand, that Marxist-Leninist political practice, in its first experiment, allowed access to the new political continent of *the socialist transition to communism*, then the

1970, p. 24). This is very reminiscent of the 'funny story' cited above (p. 107n. 3) about the tribe in which there haven't been any cannibals since they ate the last one last week.
11. See Lenin's article 'The Junius Pamphlet' (Lenin 1964b), in which he sets out the conditions under which an interimperialist war can become a war for socialism, in the context of a national [liberation] war.

conditions of ideological struggle have been transformed thereby. And one might propose that the ideological forms of fascism constitute one of the effects of the ideological 'upheaval' caused by the conjunction of these two events. Let me explain.

Before the concrete existence of the combination *science of history + historical experimentation of the socialist revolution*, the *penetration* of bourgeois ideology into the proletarian masses took place 'blindly', as it were, via the spontaneous operations of reversal-rejection I have set out above. Of course, this penetration presupposed a class ideological practice, i.e., an *inculcation*, but it depended above all on the exploitation by the bourgeoisie and imperialism of the then universal *ignorance* of the *laws of history*, linked with *the absence of any concrete realisation of the 'socialist dream'*.

Since the appearance of socialism and its different concrete historical forms, the *mortal danger* that it constitutes for the capitalist bourgeoisie and for imperialism as a whole has led to the appearance of 'new' political and ideological practices (although their novelty does not of course go so far as to leave the circle of bourgeois ideology!), intended to simulate proletarian ideology and politics in order to disguise, disfigure and occult the concrete existence of socialism, by ceaselessly taking advantage of the 'errors' committed in the name of socialism. Those whom Marx called the 'professionals of ideology' therefore take on directly political functions within fascism, and the renewed interest in the study of rhetoric, 'mass manipulation' and 'mass psychology' is only a symptom within the class struggle of this new bourgeois political and ideological division of labour, which constitutes the impossible and unthinkable 'symmetrical' partner to Marxist-Leninist practice:[12] 'psychology' is therefore not just the raw material of humanism. It is also one of the instruments that the bourgeoisie and imperialism try to use politically against proletarian politics, relying on the fact that the bourgeois ideological state apparatuses always 'work by psychology', by reason of their very *representative structure*. By this I mean that they are based on the deployment of three elementary 'loci', namely:

12. Rhetoric, mass manipulation and mass psychology: what we have here might be said to be a *locum tenens* for a Marxist theory of ideologies, in other words: an ideological theory of ideologies. Note that for bourgeois political 'liberalism' they provide the excuse to lump together fascism and Marxism-Leninism, both equally guilty of violating the universality of the laws, equally psychological, that govern Civilisation and Man.

(1) *The auditorium* (the crowd, the 'people' in the Christian sense, spectators, onlookers, participants, etc.);

(2) *The stage* (the altar, the rostrum, the witness box, the demonstration bench – of the 'scientist', the conjurer or the juggler – the blackboard, etc.);[13]

(3) *The wings* (the vestry, the 'back room', etc.),

and that it is in the relationship between these three loci that the elementary ideological effects of identification-interpellation of subjects, imputation of responsibilities and distribution of meanings are realised. It is a signature of this arrangement that it produces and reproduces the *separation* between the withholding of hidden intentions, goals and strategies, etc., and the appearance which is mounted on the stage, in the form of a psychological 'depth' of the characters. That is why the proletarian struggle *inside* the ideological state apparatuses is at the same time also a struggle *against* their structure and their operation, in so far as the subjective appropriation of proletarian politics paradoxically implies, as we have seen, a disidentification, linked to a subjective transformation in imputation, representation and meaning: the relationship to history as a process, to the masses making history and to the Communist Party as a political organisation of a new type, cannot be a relationship of identification (compare Althusser's remark as to the impossibility of designating the masses 'subject' by saying 'that's it!'), because this relationship tends to abolish the link of representation dividing representatives from those represented (cf. on this point the disidentificatory operation of a mass demonstration).

Let me finally specify that this relationship, the core of proletarian political and ideological practice, is not 'outside ideology', which means that no *subject* can be established as such in this 'third modality' constituted by disidentification, and that, by the same token, proletarian ideology, 'distorting but not mystificatory' as Karsz says, is constantly threatened internally (in the work it does on the subject-form) by the bourgeois mystifications inherent in the operation of the ideological state apparatuses.

13. Cf. for example the ideological use made of the blackboard by Giscard d'Estaing in his television 'demonstrations'.

Conclusion

I have repeatedly stressed that I am here addressing both *specialists* in linguistic science (with the specific type of practice required by that discipline) and *non-specialists* who, in philosophical practice itself, are faced with questions of 'language', 'meaning', etc., imbricated into various specifically philosophical problematics, and especially into what is customarily called the 'theory of knowledge'. Thus I have had to overcome two kinds of reservations (obstacles to a reading):

from the philosophical side, an impatience bound up with certain necessarily 'technical' aspects of my investigation ('technical', i.e., deriving in fact from the specificity of a relatively autonomous field of scientific problems); this impatience was based on the illusion that the heart of the matter could have been reached more quickly if the latter had been dealt with on its own;

from the linguistic side, an embarrassment at the appearance every now and then of elements which, in the present state of things, the linguist cannot but consider foreign to his domain (and therefore 'philosophical' importations) even if, of course, he has 'heard of them' in another connection, i.e., precisely not as a linguist but as an intellectual who tries at least to keep abreast of the latest developments in theory and philosophy, and has his own overall assessment of them, his likes and dislikes, as one says of someone that he has his opinions and perhaps also his prejudices.

I hope I have helped to dispel these various reservations as they have arisen in the course of this work, by making two points plain:

(1) The *philosophers* will have understood that they were not dealing with a philosophical reflection *on* linguistics and/or 'language', using them as raw material, spring-board or jumping-off-point for an 'intrinsically philosophical' result (which would in any case be a misconception of the nature of philosophy, because, since the latter has no object, it cannot, properly speaking, produce intrinsic results).

(2) The *linguists* will have recognised that in no way was I importing 'philosophy' into a field in which it is by nature foreign, but that quite to the contrary, 'the philosophical' was already well and truly installed at the heart of the problem I was raising, in the form of evident propositions about the 'speaking-subject', 'meaning' and 'communication', evident propositions so tenacious that they are invisible to the 'naked eye', I mean the unapprised, unarmed eye of the pure linguist.

I think I have also demonstrated that this philosophical material, already installed as a strangely familiar evidentness at the heart of the question posed, represented quite precise ideological, and in the last instance political 'interests', namely, those of the reproduction of the existing bourgeois relations of production, against which I set out to defend other 'interests', i.e., another position which combines the interests of the scientificity of the discipline of linguisitics– and hence the interests of all those who are really concerned for its scientific development – AND the ideological, and in the last instance political, interests of the proletariat and its allies, whose aim is the transformation of the relations of production inherent in the capitalist mode of production. Let me finally recall one point which is not unimportant if I am to be properly understood here, viz., the fact that this struggle does not involve the terrain of *linguistics in general*, as a supposedly homogeneous discipline comprising phonology, morphology, syntax and semantics (according to the traditional classification, repeated even today in every good text-book of 'general linguistics'), but quite precisely *the relationship between the last mentioned 'constituent', semantics, and all the others.* To sum up in the form of an observation this first point, which I think that what I have argued up to now will support, I shall say:

OBSERVATION 1: *What is designated by the term semantics is not part of the discipline of linguistics in the same sense as phonology, morphology and syntax are and constitutes a point of re-entry for philosophy into that discipline.*

By this I do not of course mean that semantics has 'nothing to do' with linguistics, but rather, as will be realised, that the way in which it 'has to do' with it is radically different from the case of phonology, for example. As an incidental consequence of this, let me recall the genuinely imaginary character of every 'semantics' supposedly constituted according to the structural model of phonology. A glance at the 'semiological' avatars of the work of a Hjelmslev is enough to show that the project itself is not at all imaginary: its imaginary 'reality' still obsesses the undertakings of 'semanticists' today. As I have said, the way in which semantics 'has to do' with linguistics is to constitute the point at which the relative autonomy of the latter comes to an end: in other words, I argue that in order to resolve the questions which are (not) posed in the sector of 'semantics', in order to clear away those obstacle-questions which are 'answers in advance' preventing any progress, hence in order to go forward from this point – even holding to the strictly 'professional' interests inherent in the development of linguistics as a science, i.e., the 'professional' interests of the linguists who are working in this sector and trying to go forward – it has now become possible and necessary to overturn-rearrange the problematic still designated by the word 'semantics' today, by allowing the concepts of historical materialism and the categories of dialectical material-ism to 'take up the cudgels' in that problematic.

In using these terms to designate the necessity for this theoretical alliance (the conditions of which I have tried to expound, and what is at stake in which I shall recall in a moment), I have taken care not to repeat the common confusion of proposing that semantics 'gets by' by allying itself with psychology, sociology, anthropology, even a certain structuralist variety of history. For, as we have seen, there is no need to recommend such an alliance to those linguists preoccupied by semantics, given that it coincides precisely with the very *act of birth* of that same semantics, that the latter's whole career can be traced in it, both at the 'fundamental' level of 'theories of knowledge', theories of language as a relationship between men and as a relationship between subject and object, and at the 'applied' level of 'concrete' investigations into the psychopedagogy of mathematics and modern languages (native and foreign), into sociolinguistics and political vocabulary, even computerised docu-mentation and translation. I give this far from exhaustive list simply to show the extent of the current pretensions of *semantics in alliance with the human sciences*; obviously I cannot show in each case 'where the shoe pinches' scientifically and politically, but I believe I have provided above the principles capable of guiding such investigations.

In short, the resort to historical materialism and dialectical materialism is not to be confused with the spontaneous cohabitation of semantics and the ideology of the 'human sciences', disguised in expressions whose ambiguity must one day be dissipated, such as the expression 'social relations', for example: on the distinction between *materialism* on the one hand and the counterfeit represented by what could be called a *social realism* on the other depends, and will long continue to do so, the possibility of any real advances in this domain. Everything is at stake here, including the very future of the scientific path opened up by Saussure.

In fact, in the course of this study I have shown that the Saussurian notion of *parole* constituted precisely the 'weakest link' of the scientific apparatus set up in the form of the concept of *langue*: *parole* is in no way the concept of a contradictory element dialectically linked to the concept of *langue*, and all the theoretical acrobatics in the world will not change this; Saussure's *parole* is, quite the contrary, the very type of the anti-concept, i.e., a pure ideological excipient 'complementing' in its evidentness the concept of *langue*, i.e., a stop-gap, a plug to close the 'gap' opened up by the scientific definition of *langue* as systematicity in operation. Of course, this does not signify that I am imputing goodness knows what theoretical responsibility to Saussure for an 'error' he should have avoided; I simply want to designate the point of fragility in the Saussurian edifice, its constitutive chink, the central emplacement at which Saussure's thought has been swamped and covered up by the unthought from which in other respects it had separated itself; I shall sum this up in the following observation:

OBSERVATION 2: *The opposition between system of the* langue *and* parole *of the speaking-subject is the contradiction by which linguistics has lived since Saussure,* and I add that *this opposition is the displaced readoption of the pre-Saussurian oppositions between logic of reason and rhetoric of the passions, on the one hand, between existence of language and use of language on the other.*[1]

In other words, I am arguing that, being unable to accede to this central contradiction and to treat it appropriately, (Saussurian) linguistics is in the end condemned to regress *behind the break which inaugurated it,* by a kind of 'return of the repressed' whose central element (forming its weakest link) is located in the region of semantics and articulated around the *langue/parole* couple: it can be taken as a proof of this that Saussurian structural linguistics having given rise both to the glossematics of Hjelmslev on the one hand and

---

1. I.e., a repetition of the oppositions characterising the 'general grammars' of the seventeenth century on the one hand and on the other of those constituting the armature of historical linguistics (above all the use of language as simultaneously wear and 'creation').

to functionalism (and distributionalism) on the other, the first of these currents has led, in the context of European philosophical structuralism, to the emergence of the 'semiology' represented above all by the works of Barthes and Greimas, while the second current evolved, via Harris and Chomsky, to the terrain at present occupied by 'generative semantics', according to which propositional structures (in the logical sense of the term) are supposed to constitute the 'deep structures' of language. It is surely clear that we can begin to detect the outlines today, in the ecumenical guise of great international congresses, of an opportunistic reunification of these two currents in a real ideological 'melting-pot' in which semiological, logico-linguistic and rhetorical 'points of view' are exchanged to everybody's satisfaction, *the occasional waving of the Saussurian flag concealing what is in fact a regression to the pre-Saussurian myth of 'general grammars'* a privileged example of which we have seen in the works of the Port-Royal.[2]

In reality, therefore, the theoretical situation in the sector which constitutes the object of this study is characterised by the fact that the question of its relationship to 'logic', 'science', 'ideology', etc., has been resolved even before it had been posed: I have tried to show that this *'solution-in-advance'* could take the form either of what I have called *metaphysical realism* or that of *logical empiricism*, each of these forms implying a kind of *mixed separation* between logic on the one hand and rhetoric, poetics and politics on the other. The analysis I undertook allowed me to show that the theoretical obstacles which pile up in these two *dead ends* derived in the last instance from reasons of a philosophical kind. Of course, the fact that these two paths are *theoretical* dead ends (i.e., *theoretically blinded*) does not prevent them from having a certain future of academic repetition, authorising the arrangement of new *trompe l'oeil* perspectives, new 'vanishing points', etc. But basically the time is near when researchers in this sector will experience disillusion and thereby come to feel the pressing need for some *explicit* 'philosophy' to enable them to see *where matters really stand* and to determine where it is, as I have said, that *'the shoe pinches'*.[3] It would not be wrong to regard as one index

2. By the same token, the questions raised by historical linguistics have been somewhat too rapidly *liquidated*.
3. The history of the sciences shows that philosophy inevitably *surfaces* inside a scientific practice when the latter is undergoing a 'crisis'. That is why I think it is essential for the linguist working in this domain to know his way around philosophy. I hope I have helped a little in this. It is up to linguists themselves to go further.

of this evolution the fact that, in investigations currently being conducted, anti-philosophical empiricism, armed with mathematical 'instruments' (as for example in the tradition of Harris's early distributionalism), is giving way today to a logical formalism (cf. the avatars of Chomskyism today) that openly admits a shameless philosophical idealism. So it is not useless to bear in mind what sustenance, philosophically speaking, linguists will find the day they turn explicitly to 'philosophy' in order to understand and transform their current situation. Because one can say that they are going to get some surprises, and often rather disagreeable ones!

Undoubtedly the first of these surprises in their exploration of the equipment of the professionals of the dominant philosophy (philosophical anthropology) will be to find that from the very beginning they are on *familiar ground*, to the point that they will be both delightfully reassured – to find philosophers expressing loudly and clearly the very basis of what they have always taken for granted – and at the same time secretly disappointed, with the impression that 'it was hardly worth going out of their way just for that'. Everything I have said so far is intended to prepare those linguists who have taken the trouble to read my book for this exquisite philosophical surprise, so that, *having been alerted to the fact that the evident truths of philosophical anthropology* ('there are subjects and objects, the subjects know those objects by extracting their properties by abstraction and associate words with a meaning to the generalised result of that abstraction, the subjects, being several and "having things to say to one another", communicate with one another using the words, etc.') *are simply the same thing as the spontaneous philosophy of semantics, they do not stay theoretically paralysed by this surprise, because for them it is no surprise.*

One other surprise, perhaps even more paralysing, awaits those linguists who, for theoretical, philosophical or political reasons, ignore the platitudes of bourgeois philosophy and turn to Marxism-Leninism, confident that 'that's where it's all happening' because the materialism of our age is the ally of the sciences, including those sciences in 'crisis' which are struggling to overcome their difficulties. They will in fact find amongst the contemporary studies that are carried out under the banner of Marxism a good number of declarations, analyses and arguments that rely on *certain* quotations from the classics which once again will give them a strong sense of *déjà vu*: once again the subject and the object, the 'theory of knowledge' and the role of abstraction and generalisation, etc., with one difference, that the whole is immersed in a socio-historical ether in which the technical division of labour and 'social relations' (understood as relations between men) form the backdrop, usually graced with one reference to *The German Ideology* (Marx and Engels 1976b) –language as a means of communication between men – and another to Engels's text on 'the part played by labour in the transition from ape to man' (Engels 1970).

In all this we are still dealing with 'the given cognising subject' as Adam Schaff says (1973, p. 136), even if this subject, being the 'ensemble of social relations' wears 'social spectacles' (Schaff again, 1973, p. 137); we are still inside the space which bears the philosophical name of *anthropology* and the less learned political name of *humanism*. Here, too, my aim has been to spare those linguists who are prepared to read this work, and especially those who are turning today to Marxism-Leninism in the hope of learning something that might be of use to them as a weapon, the disagreeable surprise of not being 'surprised' but simultaneously reassured and paralysed by the repeated evocation of the themes of humanist anthropology *even inside Marxism*. That is why I was in a sense *anticipating* when I posed the question of semantics *by way of reflections written in the 1960s by a Communist philosopher*, a specialist in logic and language. But, as the reader will have gathered, Adam Schaff is not alone: he is even, as Althusser said of another Communist philosopher, in the company of many Communists. Without developing this further, and restricting myself to the sector that concerns me here, I can say that the (idealist) theory of knowledge which I have examined at length in its two forms – metaphysical realism and logical empiricism – has fairly extensively infiltrated contemporary Marxism, to the point that it constitutes a veritable epistemological 'commonplace' justifying some rather strange rapprochements under the banner of Marxism and transcending political differences which are often much more than mere nuances: the commonplace designated for example by the couple situational/generic as a representative of the series concrete/ abstract, contingent/essential, irrational/rational, etc., provides a justification today for the coexistence in 'Marxism' of Pavlovism, cybernetics, semiotics, applications of formal logic to the theory of language, psychology (behaviourist or gestaltist), 'scientific propaganda', etc.[4] This rapprochement produces a kind of *marginalisation of the dialectic* in Marxism-Leninism, in favour of formal

4. Obviously I cannot develop these different points here. In Appendix 1 the reader will find certain suggestions as to the question of 'scientific propaganda'.

logic and psychology, which constitute, in different forms, the double motor of 'Marxist' anthropology. Hence the ground is prepared for various *reversing operations*, paradoxically performing this work of marginalisation of the dialectic in Marxism-Leninism in the very name of a 'return to the dialectic'. Thus our addressee, the linguist uneasy about philosophy and politically convinced that he must 'go into philosophy', is more and more surprised!

One of these reversals consists of *the presentation of the dialectic as a way of making formal logic more flexible and fluid*, in the name of the struggle against fixism and metaphysics: to think reality 'dialectically' is to think it full of changes and contradictions, of changes *hence* contradictions. Some hopefuls have even tried to import the mathematical notion of the 'fuzzy set',[5] which is supposed to bridge the artifically rigid frontiers of logical classifications; why stop there, halfway, why not also invent rubber concepts, soft logic and elastic proofs as the *neo plus ultra* of the dialectic?

By a reversal which retains the identity between science and logic and their coupling together in opposition to 'poetry', with 'ordinary language' as the middle term in the series ('poetry' being to 'ordinary language' what 'ordinary language' is to 'science'), 'the imperfections of human language' can become the sign of its 'richness'. In his *Introduction to Semantics*, Schaff appeals to Russell's notion of *vagueness* and argues as follows:

> If we disregard scientific terms, the meanings of which are established by convention, vagueness is a property of practically all words. That property is a reflection of the relative character of all classification which takes the form of general names or, more broadly, of general words. Things and phenomena that belong to objective reality are much richer and much more many-sided than can be rendered by any classification, and by the words which express such a classification. In objective reality, there are transitions between the classes of things and phenomena, represented by words, and these transitions, these "boundary phenomena", account for the fact which we call the vagueness of words. Such is the meaning of the statement that the vagueness of words is an *objective* phenomenon (1962, pp. 356f.).

5. I am not challenging the intra-mathematical forms of this new theory, but its ideological re-inscription in semantic preoccupations. Cf. Zadeh (1971).

There then follows an argument in which Schaff shows that 'science' uses arbitrary, though very useful, conventions, for example to distinguish between *rivulet* and *river*. He goes on:

> Therefore it can be said that a complete elimination of the vagueness of words would make our language a great deal poorer. This is not a declaration against precision in making statements, and against the endeavour to eliminate the vagueness of words and the resulting misunderstandings, but it does draw attention to the objective limits of such a procedure. It is only against this background that we can fully understand the failure of the conception of an "ideal" language (1962, p. 357).

Once again we have the disturbing impression that we have seen all this somewhere before; for example in the form of the famous 'hypothesis' well-known to linguists under the joint names of Sapir and Whorf, according to which language, *by virtue of its conventional nature*, determines for each linguistic community what man can perceive and think. Schaff does in fact refer to this hypothesis and makes a moderate and, in his own words, 'friendly' criticism of it; and he treats Korzybski's 'general semantics' in more or less the same way. In the end he is willing to accept the price of an undeniable *relativism of knowledge* in exchange for the comforting idea that man only knows what he makes, and he thus has the satisfaction of not having forgotten the 'human factor' in 'knowledge'. Anthropology again, as ever!

Faced with such a dead-end situation, a moment comes when one sets aside one's old fears and doubts and bets everything on a single card. After all, 'language' has been fashionable ever since the episode of philosophical structuralism in the 1960s, and the linguist I am addressing has certainly 'heard about it', as I have already said: he will suddenly remember that in brilliant works which he has never read, there is often talk about Saussure, and also about Marx, and Freud; so he wonders whether it is not time he had a closer look, overcoming a certain suspicion of those notorious Parisian philosophico-literary monsters, and also overcoming his fear that he will not be able to understand a word of it all, because he knows that 'it's pretty stiff stuff' in any case, and not within everyone's reach.

It does seem undeniable that there is here a *threshold* to cross if one wants to keep 'up to date', to gain access to the Marxism and Freudianism of our day; and so to put dialectics back 'in command'.

And indeed, having crossed this threshold, because he has after all been to university and knows how to read, the new initiate will undoubtedly come across *traces* in the new field of *the materialist work* that has lately been carried out in Marxism-Leninism and Freudianism. But (decidedly, surprise follows surprise!) he will also not be long in discerning that *these traces are increasingly being covered up* by elements whose new and progressive forms only too often conceal the old content of neo-Kantian and Hegelian idealism. The situation was not so clear a few years ago, but today the signs are multiplying to the point where there can be less and less doubt: with the reappearance of the themes of 'fetishism' and 'the negation of the negation', with the metaphorical use of Marxist economics, accompanied by plays on the words value and circulation, savings and expenditure, the return of 'negativity' as something beyond logical negation.

Now, by surreptitiously re-installing the *Hegelian* dialectic, the various perspectives that come together today on the 'battle field' of Writing, the Text, etc., have little hope of taking further part in these struggles, it seems to me, except in the form of the commentary, which is *the only form of a Hegelian politics*, if there is such a thing. To consider only the theoretical and political interests of Marxism-Leninism, they cannot really be said to have been defended in a discourse which, while speaking of Marx, was in fact giving sidelong glances in the direction of Husserl, Hegel or Heidegger;[6] as far as one can see, this has not helped overcome any obstacles, and one can even wonder if, after having provided, with its 'excesses', 'overflowings' and 'transgressions', a supplementary pretext for humanism, whether 'Marxist' or otherwise, to cling to the sheltered stability of its evident truths, this discourse will not end up in a new anthropology which will eventually find *its place* in the semiological international I mentioned above; as Étienne Balibar and Pierre Macherey have reminded us, inversion is 'a privileged figure of ideological conservation'.

At the end of this tour, let me sum up the 'travel diary' of the linguist uneasy about philosophy in another observation:

---

6. As for the effect that this slide has on Freudian theory, it, too, is not without its consequences; on this point there is a remarkable analysis of the slide and its effect in Roudinesco (1973) – see especially the chapter 'Inconscient et archaicité', pp. 131–58.

OBSERVATION 3: *Until proof to the contrary, the philosophy of the philosophers can be said to reproduce and nourish in various forms the spontaneous philosophy of those linguists working in the domain of 'semantics', such that there is no chance that the contradiction system/ speaking-subject by which linguistics lives – i.e., through which are perpetuated and exacerbated the difficulties afflicting it – will be really tackled, in the empirico-formalist framework of philosophical anthropology, whether the latter presents itself in its bourgeois form or in some 'Marxist' form.*

It will already be clear that this study seeks to intervene in this situation, by showing, as far as I am able at present and in a form which I have already called scientifically embryonic, how the philosophical positions of Marxism-Leninism (on the class struggle, materialism and the process without a subject) constitute precisely that 'proof to the contrary', that philosophical exception by means of which the vital core of the contradiction just mentioned can be attained and worked on. For my part, I hope I have isolated some elements which might contribute to a materialist study of discourse, and I shall be pleased if this work enables others to save time and go further *without retreating*. For it is not easy – as anyone who works in this field will know only too well – to avoid retreating into sociologism, historicism or psychologism: one does not placate historical materialism merely by referring to the socio-historical *conditions of production* of discourse,[7] one also has to be able to make explicit the uneven and contradictory complex set of discursive formations at work in a given situation, under the domination of the set of ideological formations, as determined by the ideological class struggle. In *The Archaeology of Knowledge* (Foucault 1972), a book in many respects of extraordinary interest for the theory of discourse, Michel Foucault 'retreats' from the progress he himself makes, he regresses into the sociology of institutions and roles, because he fails to recognise the existence of the (ideological) class struggle.[8]

Nor does one placate historical materialism simply by inverting the 'communicationist' theory of language into an instrumentalist and pragmatist theory in which language is used first of all to act on others. I insist on this point because Anglo-Saxon analytic philo-

7. For example, this is one of the most serious theoretical failings of Pêcheux (1969). For a critical discussion of the various aspects of this work, see Pêcheux and Fuchs (1975).
8. On this point, see Lecourt (1975).

sophy today easily lends itself to a theory of language which, via the notions of presupposition, performative and speech act (*énonciation*), tends to 'explain' legal-political and ideological relationships as a *word game* in which subjectivities confront one another *in actu*, each trying to *catch* the other, in all the senses of the term: in a word, the struggle to the death of speaking-subjects!

In this book I have several times criticised the theses of Oswald Ducrot, who, apart from a few superficial differences, is an active proponent of this tendency, for at first sight his work might seem to contain certain linguistic elements capable of fitting as such into a theory of the legal-political and ideological apparatuses, but on closer examination it turns out to be just a new form of the logico-rhetorical linguistic complex, with the accent shifted onto the rhetorical aspect.

In reality one never placates historical materialism, or dialectical materialism, and above all one cannot get round them by putting them in the *forefront*, i.e., by posing them *before* starting to work: one must work with them. This is what I have tried to do here, vis-à-vis the vital core of the linguistic contradiction, and this has led me

(1) to develop certain philosophical 'theses' of *dialectical materialism*, especially in respect to the relationship between being and thought, the subject-object duality and the process without a subject;

(2) to advance in the form of 'propositions' certain elements which could provide the basis of a scientific analysis of discursive processes, articulating in *historical materialism* the study of the ideological superstructures, psychoanalytic theory and linguistic research.

I shall draw together below the main aspects of what I think I have thereby achieved; I venture to expose them thus in order to submit them to the discussion and criticism *first of all* of those who are trying today, as I am, to make headway in this domain in the light of Marxism-Leninism, and *also* of all those who, in their research work and in different 'professional' forms, experience as an obstacle the effects of the semantic aporiae which I have examined at length above, and are attempting to remedy this state of affairs.

I shall start by stating a (philosophical) thesis concerning *the real and necessity*: this thesis, which strictly speaking constitutes the *basis* of everything that has been said in this book, can be stated as follows:

THESIS 1: *The real exists necessarily independently of thought and outside it, but thought necessarily depends on the real, i.e., it does not exist outside the real.*

This non-symmetry in the link between the real and thought thus makes it clear from the start that there can be no question here of two 'regions', which immediately rules out of court the question as to which of the two regions 'contains' the other, and on what conditions (and in what space) one might try to make them coincide. This non-symmetry designates in reality the 'primacy of being over thought' in so far as *the real as necessary* ('necessity-real') *determines the real as thought* ('necessity-thought'), and this in such a way that it is a matter of *the same necessity*.

The question of the objectivity of knowledges, which Dominique Lecourt has shown (1973) is inevitably subordinate, for a materialist position, to that of the primacy of being over thought, then becomes the locus of a scientific problematic, i.e., that of the historical forms of the process of the production of knowledges: the propositions with scientific pretensions that I shall put forward below are *in part* situated at this locus, in this 'district' of historical materialism, a district often invoked but still little explored; they are situated in it to the extent that they concern the historico-material modalities in which the real determines the forms of existence of thought. More explicitly, the historico-material modalities in which 'the real determines the forms of existence of thought' are themselves determined by the ensemble of economic, political and ideological relations as they exist at any given historical moment, i.e., as they are organised by the class struggle which traverses them in various forms.

This implies that these historico-material modalities cannot in any way correspond to the idealist structure of knowledge, which presupposes a distribution into objects to be known and knowing subjects endowed with the correlative possibility of attaining (in truth) or missing (in error) the objects in question: *it is one and the same necessity* which, in determinate historico-material modalities, is realised both as 'blind necessity' (i.e., necessity-real in so far as it is not thought) *and* as necessity-thought.

Consequently necessity-thought must not be conceived as a space *enclosed* within the space of blind necessity, an 'empire within an empire' (Spinoza); as I have said, there are not two regions each with its own necessity – the *logical* necessity of 'science' and the *ideological* necessity of non-science, illusion, error or ignorance – so one never *leaves* one region to *enter* the other: one never breaks with ideology in general, but always with some particular ideological formation, historico-materially inscribed in the complex set of the ideological formations of a given social formation. This enables me to suggest that the motor role of contradiction in the practice of the appropriation of the 'external world' (the real) by thought is marked in the form of *the division into two opposing operations* (which in this book I have called respectively notional-ideological operation and conceptual-scientific operation) *of the complex unity of the process of necessity-real* i.e., in their division within the unity of this process.

This makes it possible for me to lay down in a series of *propositions* the historical-material modalities in which necessity-real determines, within the complex unity of its process, the contradictory forms of existence of thought.

PROPOSITION 1: *The historical-material modalities in which necessity-real determines the contradictory forms of existence of thought are constituted by the complex whole in dominance of the discursive formations, or interdiscourse, imbricated with the set of ideological formations which characterise a given social formation at a given moment in the development of the class struggle which traverses it.*

Thought is a special form of the real and, as such, it is an integral part of the objective and necessary movement of the determinations of unevenness-contradiction-subordination which constitute the real as a process without a subject. Consequently 'thought' has by no means the homogeneity, the connected continuity, the transparency – in other words the subjective interiority of 'consciousness' – that all the varieties of idealism vie with one another to attribute to it: 'thought' does not exist in reality except in the form of *regions of thought*, disjunct from one another and subject amongst themselves to a law of distributed exteriority not unrelated to the general exteriority of the real in respect to 'thought'; more precisely, it is in this law of disjunction, of contradictory exteriority immanent in the historico-material forms of existence of 'thought', that is expressed the general dependence of thought with respect to an *outside* which determines it. Hence 'internal' laws whose operation refers to an 'exterior'.

Let me say straight away what this 'exterior' of thought *is not*, to reply to the (idealist) philosophy of language which has a ready-made solution in the form of *the exteriority of language with respect to thought:* the discrepancy between 'the structure of language', and 'the structure of thought' constantly dwelt on by idealist philosophers (and by logic, psychology and rhetoric) would however provide an elegant solution to this problem of exteriority. First because the two are neighbours: mutual attraction, betrothal, marriage, domestic quarrels, divorce, etc., between pure thought on the one hand and language with its moodiness (for it can be 'elegant', 'crude', 'rigorous', 'poetic', etc.) on the other. Second and most important, because this solution is, when all is said and done, the promise of a 'happy ending' in which the exteriority of language will be reabsorbed into thought in the form of an ideography which will finally universalise the field of 'symbolic language' and thereby *reunify thought.*

An elegant solution, therefore, but an idealist one . . . *the* idealist solution I have been fighting throughout this work. And in fighting it I have had occasion to show why this 'happy ending' will never come: essentially because the effects of exteriority, anteriority and independence which represent inside thought itself the primacy of the real over thought *have nothing at all to do with purely linguistic properties, but concern a completely different 'exterior', which is the whole range of the effects, in the 'ideological sphere', of the class struggle in its various economic, political and ideological forms.*

Thus the discursive processes do not in any way constitute a 'district' isolated in its autarchy and subject to a specific necessity. In particular, what I have called the relative autonomy of the *linguistic basis* cannot, on the pretext that it is their basis, confer on the discursive processes which develop on that basis *their form*; the terms interdiscourse, intradiscourse, effect of the preconstructed and transverse-effect, which I have introduced in the course of this work and which, I believe, precisely characterise the form of discursivity, do not therefore correspond to linguistic phenomena: *they represent, in relation to the linguistic basis, the determinant existence of the complex whole of ideological formations*, subject, in always specific historical conditions, to the 'general' law of unevenness which affects those formations (as practical ideologies *and* theoretical ideologies, and via their simultaneously 'regional' and class characteristics) in the process of reproduction/transformation of the existing relations of production. In saying that *the complex whole of discursive formations (interdiscourse) is imbricated with that of ideological formations*, I want to stress that the former is not the general form of the latter (discursivity is not the 'general form of ideology'!), but rather *one of its specific forms* (I shall return in a moment to the specificity of this imbrication with respect to ideological interpellation). Hence I have precise reasons for asserting that the historico-material discursive modalities in which the real determines the forms of existence of 'thought' impose on the latter the form of non-connexity and disjunction, and this 'for ever and ever', irreconcilably, as truly as that the class struggle is the motor of all human history, and that there is no 'end of ideologies'.

Let me linger a moment here on this law of non-connexity inherent in the thought process: in stating such a law, it is not just a question of smashing the evident character of the discursive linearity of thought (the thread of discourse – the train of ideas) on the pretext that that linearity conceals 'in reality' something else instead, for example a tree structure, which is, be it said in passing, the solution of the Chomsky school. In fact, such a solution preserves the connexity between the constituents of the sentence as the form of thought, i.e., the essentials of the consciousness form; it is content to introduce different levels (of 'depth') in the consciousness of the speaking subject, with the result that it can inevitably go no further than *a Leibnizian conception of the subject-monad in which the phenomena of involution and explicitation may be taken for 'unconscious' effects, but only on the strict condition that the content of Freud's discovery be completely ignored.* For Freud, in *The Interpretation of Dreams* (1953) for example, precisely provides a quite different conception of the non-connexity of the thought process, one in which the unifying role of consciousness completely disappears. Re-read one of the superb analyses contained in Chapter VI of that book, for example the analysis of the 'botanical monograph' dream, and you will notice that the thought process as Freud describes it exists in the form of disjunct regions of thought (cocaine, Flora, artichoke, etc.) *none of which can be associated as such with a subject who is enunciating them*: each of these regions, separated from the others as it were by pauses, interruptions and blockages of thought, has the status of a *representation*, in the sense of a picture in which there are no discernable marks of enunciation or assertion, as is clear from *nominalised phrases* such as 'the blooming looks of Professor Gärtner's wife', 'Doctor Königstein, the eye surgeon', etc. One cannot say *who* sees, thinks or speaks about these representations. No subject as such is their cause:[9] quite the

9. It is in this that Freud distances himself from the raw material/obstacle (produced by bourgeois ideology) constituted by the category *representation*.

contrary, it is in these representations that the subject will arrive, finding himself 'hooked' on to them, identified with them, with all the strangeness of an evident familiarity. As I have already emphasised, *the unasserted precedes and dominates the assertion.*

I am quite aware of the specifity of the object of Freud's research, and I do not claim that it is possible to apply his results in detail directly to the problem I am discussing here. Even so, I think that what we have here is by no means simply a fortuitous analogical similarity: the historico-material character of the non-connexity of thought is surely one of the points via which the question of the relationship between *unconscious and ideology* can advance towards the solution which it is still, in my opinion, impossible to formulate today.

Nevertheless, what I am now about to argue concerns this question in certain respects, but in a very special way. Therefore, I shall go on having pointed out the limited and necessarily incomplete nature of the approach undertaken here.

PROPOSITION 2: *A meaning effect does not pre-exist the discursive formation in which it is constituted. The production of meaning is an integral part of the interpellation of the individual as a subject, in so far as, amongst other determinations, the subject is 'produced as cause of himself' in the subject-form of discourse, under the influence of interdiscourse.*

I have just recalled the fact that the historico-material modalities of the existence of thought, in so far as they are realised within the determination of interdiscourse, constitutively impose on thought its disjunction into 'regions of thought': in short, I am maintaining the paradox that thought exists only within a determination which imposes edges, separations and limits on it, in other words, that 'thought' is determined in its 'forms' and its 'contents' by the unthought. I must now recall how *this determination produces its own disappearance from thought* as a necessary effect: in the course of this work I have set out why the obliteration of this determination involved both the question of *meaning* and that of the *subject*. I shall summarise that exposition here and make a few clarificatory points in passing.

The main thesis is that the interpellation of the individual as the subject of his discourse is achieved by an identification of the subject with the discursive formation which dominates him, an identification in which, simultaneously, meaning is produced as evident for the subject and the subject is 'produced as cause of himself'. Let me try to explain this simultaneity by returning for a moment to my claim that 'the unasserted precedes and dominates the assertion'. This signifies that it is in the non-sense of representations which 'are there for nobody' that a place is marked out for the subject who takes up a position in relation to them, accepting them, rejecting them, casting doubt on them, etc. In short, 'subjecthood' is produced *in* the 'non-subjecthood' constituted by a heap of representations 'devoid of meaning', and this production is accompanied precisely by an *imposition of meaning on representations*.

Let me go further: the imposition of meaning on representations presupposes a division between what Freud calls 'thing representation' and what he calls 'word representation', precisely in order that the occultation of that imposition can be carried out. But what Lacan's development of psychoanalytic theory teaches us here is that this division is carried out in *the element of the Signifier* which is as such neither 'word representation' nor 'thing representation': unlike the sign which 'represents something for someone' – and which one can also represent to oneself – the signifier 'represents the subject for another signifier', which I believe has two extremely important consequences:

(1) The first of these consequences lies in what can be called the *primacy of the signifier over sign and meaning*: the signifier which is not the sign, and as such has no meaning, determines the constitution of the sign and of meaning. Hence meaning cannot be a 'property' of certain signifying letters (which would thereby ineluctably be reduced to a sign), it is the effect of a relationship in the element of the Signifier, a relationship that Lacan has named *metaphor*, saying 'one word for another, such is the formula of the metaphor' and adding something exceptionally illuminating for our purposes: 'Metaphor is situated at the precise point where sense is produced in non-sense.'

On this conception of metaphor I based the suggestion, above, that a word, expression or proposition *does not have a meaning of its own*, a meaning attached to its literality, nor, let me add, does it have *several meanings* that can be derived from that literality by a logico-linguistic combinatory which masters its ambiguity by constructing the various possible cases, as generative semantics proposes today: meaning is always a word, expression or proposition *for* another word, another expression or another proposition, and this juxtaposition, this superimposition, this transfer (meta-phor), by which signifying elements are brought together so as to 'take on a meaning' cannot be pre-determined by properties of the *langue* (for example the 'linguistic' connections between syntax and the lexicon); that would in fact be to suppose precisely that the signifying elements are already as such endowed with meanings, that they have *some* meaning at least, or *several* meanings, before having *a* meaning. In fact meaning does not exist anywhere except in the metaphorical relationships (realised in substitution effects, paraphrases, synonym formations) which happen to be more or less provisionally located historically in a given discursive formation: words, expressions and propositions get their meanings from the discursive formation to which they belong. At the same time, the transparency of the meanings which are constituted in a discursive formation masks the latter's dependence on interdiscourse. In fact, metaphor, which is constitutive of meaning, is always determined by interdiscourse, i.e., by *some* interdiscourse. A word of explanation here: interdiscourse never intervenes as a global entity, a gestaltist 'whole' omnipresent in its homogeneous causality. Like the 'complex whole in dominance of the ideological formations' in which it is imbricated, interdiscourse is fundamentally marked by what I have called the law of non-connexity. To this extent, one can say that what makes metaphor possible is the local and determinate character of what falls in the reach of the unconscious as locus of the Other, in which, as Lacan says, 'is located the chain of the signifier which governs all that will be able to be made present of the subject' . . . and of meaning, I would add. In other words, no discursive formation, in that it is the *locus* of realisation of the transfer I have been describing, can be its *cause*, because meaning or sense does not generate itself but 'is produced in non-sense', according to the Lacanian formulation just quoted, which goes on:

i.e., at that frontier which, as Freud discovered, when crossed the other way gives rise to that word that in French is the '*mot*' *par excellence*, the word that has no other patronage than the signifier 'esprit', and at which it is palpable that it is his very destiny that man is defying when he derides the signifier (Lacan 1966a, p.508; 1977a, p.158).

(2) Here we reach the second consequence, strictly coeval with the first, which I have summarised here as *the primacy of the signifier over sign and meaning*. I shall formulate this second consequence by

saying that *the signifier is a participant in the interpellation-identification of the individual as a subject*: 'a signifier represents the subject for another signifier', which implies that *the signifier represents nothing for the subject, but operates on the subject outside any grasp of his*; 'the subject, . . . if he can appear to be the slave of language is all the more the slave of a discourse in whose universal movement his place is already inscribed at his birth, if only in the form of his *proper name*' (Lacan 1966a, p.495; 1977a, p.148): the 'proper name' is not a 'property' like any other, and it designates the subject without representing him. As we have seen, logicians have usually restricted themselves to noting this, discussing under the heading of 'convention' the effect of exteriority, the non-sense exhibited in it. I believe I have begun to elucidate certain aspects of this mystery by basing myself on what, following Paul Henry, I have called the 'preconstructed': it is surely clear now, given what goes before, that the imposition of the 'proper name' constitutes the form princeps of the *effect of the preconstructed*, representing the discursive modality of the discrepancy by which the individual is interpellated as subject of his discourse (that by means of which he says, 'I, Mr. So-and-so'), while remaining 'always-already' a subject, i.e., the discursive modality in which he is *produced as cause of himself*, with his world, its objects and subjects, in the evidentness of their meanings.

One last point about the term identification: the fact that the evidentness of meaning (the production of sense in non-sense) is strictly coeval with the interpellation of the individual as subject of his discourse is expressed, as I have already said, in his identification with the discursive formation that dominates him, where he is 'pinned down' as subject, and this 'pinning down' shifts along with this dominance itself during the 'formation' of the subject. Hence it is a question of an *imaginary identification* bearing on the 'genesis of the ego', the subject's always imperfect attempt to get into coincidence with himself, via his relationships with other subjects each of whom is one of his alter egos, his identification with the features of the object in the representation the subject 'possesses' of the latter. In the domain which concerns us here, I have characterised as *the intradiscourse effect* one of the springs of this imaginary identification, linked to 'forgetting no.2', and I shall say no more about it here. However, I do not think I can leave matters there, in the belief that Ideology interpellates simply the 'ego', leaving the 'subject' to the mercies of the Symbolic. Ideology and the Symbolic are not the same thing, but their difference is not inscribed in such a differentiation of functions:

> All the mirror identifications that are performed in the line of the ideal ego and shunt the subject from capture to capture are entirely dependent on another identification, a repressed, symbolic, non-mirror identification constitutive of the ego ideal, which . . . presents itself in the unconscious in the form of a thought, of a wish (Safouan 1968, pp. 267f.)

This remark of Moustafa Safouan's finds an application here which seems to me by no means out of place in so far as imaginary identification is, as I have shown, dependent on the question of *identity* (the basis of imputation and responsibility) and, by the same token, touches on the symbolic through its reference to the proper name and the Law (and the pact, the debt which result for the subject are indeed present in the unconscious in the form of a 'thought' or a 'wish'): this reference makes manifest the fact that interpellation is at one and the same time ideological *and* legal, i.e., it does not act in the closed and empty sphere of the 'cultural', but in the imbrication of the ideological state apparatuses and the (legal-political) repressive state apparatus.

To sum up, I shall say that *the subject-form of discourse*, in which interpellation, identification and the production of meaning coexist indissociably, realises *the non-sense of the production of the subject as cause of himself in the form of immediate evidentness*. We are here dealing with a causality which effaces itself in the necessary effect it produces in the form of the relationship between subject, centre and meaning, something I have called in condensed fashion the 'Munchausen effect'.

PROPOSITION 3: *The conceptual-experimental (scientific) operation which, in forms specific to each branch of the production of knowledges, materialises necessity-real as necessity-thought (and to that extent locally forecloses meaning and the subject) never exists 'in a pure state', in a form disjunct from its notional-ideological counterpart. Consequently the appropriation of the real by thought cannot consist of a desubjectification of the subject, but presupposes a work of subjective appropriation in and on the subject-form, i.e., amongst other determinations, in and on the subject-form of discourse.*

My starting-point here will be some recent formulations proposed by Dominique Lecourt on the question of 'the concrete historical forms in which is realised that endless process, the production of scientific concepts' (1974, p. 95):

> Once it has been established that the sciences are obedient to a dialectical process which cannot be based on any empirical or transcendental subject, there does indeed remain the very real problem of the effects of this process on the concrete individuals who are summoned to be its agents (p. 111).

Hence a first, very important observation: the practice of the production of knowledges is *in no way an exception among practices as a whole*, it works, like any other practice, 'by interpellation'. Lecourt continues:

> As one can see, the solution to this problem – but also already its posing – presupposes a theory of the various ideological formations, a theory of the 'subjection' of the individual to ideological social relations, so as then to be able to settle the question of the repercussions of this process (without a subject) of scientific knowledge on the effects of that subjection (p. 115).

I shall try to show how the (scientifically embryonic) elements I think I have disengaged in this book concerning discursive processes can help *pose* this question by designating certain conditions of its solution.

Note first of all that the *notional-ideological operation* is realised within the domination of the subject-form and specifically, in what concerns us here, within the domination of the subject-form of discourse. Consequently the *notions* inscribed in that operation *have a meaning* because that operation is itself coextensive with the effects of paraphrase-reformulation, of intradiscourse and 'forgetting no.2' which characterise as such a discursive formation, with the *mirror* phenomena which necessarily accompany it: the notion has a meaning which represents a 'figurative-concrete' directly accessible in the imaginary identification of *Erfahrung* in the form of the 'givenness' of an *object* for a *subject*; the representational character of the notion ensures the evidentness of its meaning within the 'consensus'.

I must add straight away that it is not sufficient for the autonomy of a discursive formation in interdiscourse to be broken for 'concept' to irrupt by that very fact; similarly, any reconfiguration of the relationships between different formations does not in itself constitute an 'epistemological rupture', for that would be to take the effect for the cause. Furthermore, the process of production of knowledges cannot be the object of a 'general theory', since the conditions in which an uneven-contradictory-overdetermined set of theoretical ideologies (and of the corresponding discursive formations) 'works' is always historically specified. So I shall restrict myself in this matter to designating some formal conditions characterising what might be called the modalities of existence of the concept-form, taking care to stress that these are in no way internal, legislative, 'epistemological' conditions of the process of knowledge, as if that process were isolated, i.e., primary: rather they are modalities which the process without a subject of necessity-real, the objective natural-social process – economic, political and ideological – imposes on necessity-thought.

Some formal conditions, therefore, and first that of the meeting-effect between ideological (and, specifically, discursive) elements, an effect which is special in that the occultation of the meeting cannot be carried out completely in an ideological reconfiguration,[10] so it disengages something that might be called free signifier, corresponding to 'representations without a subject' which lose their representational character and are re-inscribed in the symbolic, where *they designate without representing*; like a proper name, a concept designates without representing, but, unlike a proper name, it designates through constructions which are both a construction of statements (construction of necessity-thought) and a construction of devices (in necessity-real). One of the conditions of realisation of the concept-form thus consists of a special relationship between necessity-real and necessity-thought, such that necessity-thought is not 'something different' from necessity-real: *a concept represents*, one might say, *necessity-real in the network of concepts* that constitutes, for a given region of knowledge, necessity-thought, in

10. Indeed, interdiscourse is the locus for a perpetual 'work' of reconfiguration in which a discursive formation, as a function of the ideological interests that it represents, is led to absorb *preconstructed* elements produced outside it, linking them metonymically to its own elements by *transverse-effects* which incorporate them in the evidentness of a new meaning in which they are 'welcomed' and founded (on a new ground of evident truths that absorbs them) by what I have called a 'return of the known in thought': in other words a 'work' of unification of thought, in which subordinations are achieved and simultaneously effaced in the synonymic *extension* of paraphrase-reformulation.

the form of couplings between statements and between experimental constructions. Thus the conceptual-experimental
(scientific) operation affects the relationship between naming-
designating on the one hand and stating-constructing on the other,
by an integration that is not an identification: another 'formal
condition' which one can suspect concerns especially the relationship between effect of the preconstructed and transverse-effect.

I shall go no further into this point, in the estimation that the
'formal' remarks I have just made can only be developed in the
concrete analysis of determinate conceptual operations. I am
content here to note that *the conceptual is not articulated in the subject-
form of discourse*, which is to say that *no subject is as such the bearer of
necessity-thought*: to this extent one can assert that the conceptual
operation locally forecloses meaning and the subject-form of
discourse. In my opinion this foreclosure constitutes one of the
'repercussions' (to return to Lecourt's expression) of the process
(without a subject) of scientific knowledge on the subjection of the
subject: what I should like to show is that this repercussion cannot
be interpreted as a 'de-subjection', a de-subjectification or an
obliteration of the subject; meaning does not 'die', the subject does
not 'disappear'. The repercussion consists of a work in and on the
subject-form, and in particular in and on the subject-form of
discourse.

This calls for some explanation, on the basis of what has been set
out above, and first of all a clarification concerning the fact that this
'repercussion' is not an 'after-effect': there is not *first of all* the process
without a subject of the production of knowledges in so far as it acts
'in itself' *in a first moment*, and then *afterwards* a reprise reinscribing
'some subjects' who appropriate the results of that process *in a second
moment*; the paradox that must be grasped is that the work of
subjective appropriation in and on the subject-form is strictly
coextensive with the process without a subject of the production of
scientific knowledges, and cannot therefore be confined to a sector
that is subordinate to it, for example, to that of 'educational
reproduction': 'agent-individuals always act in the subject-form',
and the production of knowledges is no exception to this. As we have
seen, the historical agents of this production are 'interpellated' in
the specific form of theoretical positions for which they take sides (in
which they recognise themselves) in a given conjuncture, in the face
of other positions which they oppose, and I have suggested (cf.
pp. 140f.) how discursive elements intervene in these confrontations;

indications can be discerned *in the preconstructed* (confrontations over names and expressions) and in the *transverse-processes* (confrontations over the order and concatenation of statements, propositions and theorems).

The paradoxical result of this repercussion of the process without a subject of knowledge on the individuals who are its agents is therefore that it realises in the subject-form a challenging of the subject-form. What I called above (p.158) *the third discursive modality of operation* (i.e., neither identification nor counteridentification) partakes of this 'repercussion'. Dis-identification (and the resulting non-subjective takings of positions) is effected paradoxically in the subject by a subjective process of appropriation of scientific concepts (representation of necessity-real in necessity-thought), a process in which ideological interpellation continues to operate, but as it were against itself.

Thus the production of knowledges consists of the transformation of ideological 'raw material' into materialist objectivities *through the development of new ideologies and new forms of ideological interpellation,* and I have already observed that this transformation has its strict political correlate in what Étienne Balibar, discussing proletarian political practice, has called 'the transformation of the struggle into non-struggle by the development of a new struggle' (1974, p.82). The common point constituted by *ideological interpellation* and *its operation 'in reverse' in dis-identification* explains why this is not a matter of two parallel and symmetrical questions like 'knowledge' and 'action' in an idealist conception of philosophy; the primacy of the real over thought, which is also a primacy of practice over theory, suggests that everything I have just recalled about the subjective appropriation of the real concerns not only the (ideologico-practical) conditions of the production of scientific knowledges *in general*, but also and especially the ideological and political conditions (proletarian political practice) which govern the *specific* setting to work of the scientific knowledges of *historical materialism*.

To sum up this point, I shall say that proletarian political practice breaks with the spontaneous operation of the subject-form, in so far as the empirico-subjective forms of political practice become the raw material for a transformation which, bearing on the (legal-political) state apparatus and the ideological state apparatuses, in the same moment affects the subject-form: the dis-identificatory work of proletarian ideology, an integral part of proletarian political practice, develops paradoxically through new identifications in which interpellation operates *in reverse*, i.e., with reference to 'non-subjects' such as History, the masses, the working class and its organisations.[11] It is this specific determination of proletarian politics in particular that governs the operation of the discursive processes inscribed in it, for example the operation of a *slogan* adopted in a given political conjuncture.

The three propositions I have just been discussing form, I believe, a *basis* for further scientific investigations concerning discursive processes, though I would not claim that I have posed, still less solved, the problems that may develop on that basis. In Appendix 2 I shall evoke some of these problems, in the form of the repercussions they may have in contemporary linguistic research.

But first I think I must condense in one (philosophical) thesis the position that has gradually been defined in this book in relation to the category of Ideology.

THESIS 2:

'*Ideology has no outside for itself*' = the universality of the Subject of Ideology;

'*Ideology is nothing but outside for the sciences and the real*' = the process without a subject of the real, of knowledge of the real and of the transformation of the real.

To state these two theses at the same time is to pose the contradictory existence of the two tendencies (idealist and materialist) which run through all thought, to designate their

---

11. The fact that these 'non-subjects' can be taken for subjects is a very important point in a theory of proletarian ideology. On this point, see Plon (1976b), pp. 185–96. In this same work (p. 189) there is also a clarification of the specificity of revolutionary political practice in its antagonistic relationship with the subjective appropriation of politics: 'This [revolutionary political] practice implies the recognition of a primacy of the class struggle, its motor role in the process without a subject or goal of history; these points make impossible any recourse to the full subject of psychology, installed in a centre from which emanate orders, acts and decisions, the fruit of a clever calculation of intentions or anticipations. But at the same time, this practice cannot exist without the *concrete* presence of individuals constituted as subjects by Ideology; it is specified, no doubt, as a process without a subject, but finds that its existence is bound up with the active presence of subjects: posters have never yet been seen to have the power to stick themselves up without a billsticker or a brush, or computers to manage to simulate a mass meeting or a demonstration. No doubt we are approaching the specificity of that revolutionary political practice based on contradiction and articulated to a theory bearing the same name and charged to think its terms.'

struggle vis-à-vis what is at stake in their mutual identification for idealism and their disjunction for materialism.

Several times in the course of this work, and in different forms, we have encountered an effect which, for lack of anything better, I have called *simulation*: we have seen that this effect of simulation was the occultation of a relationship of *exploitation of scientific knowledges by a universal theory of ideas* which aimed to present itself (in the forms of metaphysical realism or logical empiricism) as the condition, the basis or the envelope of those knowledges. By that very fact, I have argued, this universal theory tends to mask their existence, obliterating the distinction between science and non-science. And I have made it plain that the current aims of 'semantics' are inscribed in the space of this universal theory. We have also seen, while studying the manoeuvres in which logic, law, politics and the spontaneous philosophy of the scientists (including a certain conception of poetic fiction) were intermingled to this end, that this *exploitation-simulation* was not just *theoretical* (in the form of a pseudo-science of Everything, a science of the other sciences and itself, locus of Knowledge and of what purports to be such, to adapt Paul Henry's expression): it maintains a privileged link with the bourgeois form of the legal-political in so far as law and judicial-administrative procedures in general are a *practical* realisation of this 'universal theory' in their explicit operation.[12] This has enabled us to understand that the interpellation of individuals as subjects (and especially as subjects in law) *takes place in the name of the universal Subject of Ideology*: the Subject 'recalls itself' to the subjects, as I have said, and causes them to be what they are, to act as they act and in particular to speak as they speak). In other words, the universal Subject of Ideology *represents* to the subjects 'the cause that determines them', and it represents this cause to them *in the boundless sphere of the subject-form*. It can therefore be said that the universal Subject of Ideology represents *in the subject-form* the process without a subject (in so far as the latter is the cause of the subject) such that the one passes spontaneously for the other, a mere 'nuance' separating them. Yet it is on this 'nuance' that the division between idealism and materialism is built 'in thought': the idealist tendency tends to reduce the two to one, the process without a subject being identified with the Subject (tendentially: Plato, Descartes, Hegel, etc.); the materialist tendency tends on the contrary to dissolve the unity of this identification, revealing the Subject as an effect of the

12. On this point Edelman (1979) casts a very illuminating light.

process without a subject (tendentially: Lucretius, Spinoza, Marx, etc.).

Let me linger over this 'nuance' for a moment: in the terminology I have used here, it can be said that *a mere nothing separates the 'Munchausen effect' from the process without a subject, origin or goal(s)*. A 'mere nuance' disjoins *the perpetual movement of matter* (Engels) and *the motor which moves itself* (be it Aristotle's God or the mechanical phantasy seeking to realise perpetual motion!); a 'mere nuance', too, between *the class struggle which has its locus, i.e., cause and effect, in the capitalist mode of production* and *the circle of the Hegelian dialectic*; a 'mere nuance', again, between *the process without a subject of the production of knowledges* and *Bachelard's 'quasi-subject'*, about which Lecourt remarks:

> Bachelard has produced the category of dialectical process by posing the thesis of objectivity and as a result ruining the category of the Subject; however, retreating from his own discovery, he tries to find in this process without a subject . . . a subject. The sense in which I use the term 'quasi-subject' is clear: 'Subject' of a process without a subject . . . This 'quasi-subject' is mathematics (1974, p. 103).

A 'mere nuance', then, initially, between idealism and materialism; but a nuance on which everything depends, and continuously: this nuance lies in the discrimination between *identification* (of the subject with the object, of the subject with the Subject, of the Subject with the objective process, etc.) and what I have called *disidentification* (disjoining thing-objects from the objectivity of processes, substance and the subject from the cause, etc.). And this discrimination is never, in any concretely existing thought, definitively achieved. It is all 'a question of tendency'.

To illustrate this point, let me borrow the following example from Lacan, ironically directed at the circularity:

> Christopher carried Christ
> Christ carried the whole world
> Tell me, pray, where Christopher
> Was able to place his feet?'
> (Lacan 1966b, p. 377)[13]

13. One might also cite Lenin on the 'circle' by which sensation is the basis of

What is challenged here is the *exceptional* status of this object the subject-Christopher who, absurdly, must be *in the world* in order to be able to *sustain it*: a critique of religious mythology on the basis of that mythology, taking it at its word in order to denounce its 'circularity'. The outline of a materialist dissolution within religious idealism. Now we know how the scientific practice of astronomy 'resolved' this circle by demonstrating that if 'everything' rests on 'the earth' *except* 'the sky' (and the earth itself), it is because of that pure *non-sense* which has it that 'the earth' is in 'the sky', such that the *exception* of *the earth as support* turns into a new *rule* in which the earth is inscribed as a *celestial body*. What should be clear here is the fact that this rule of astronomic laws (a rule to which the earth is no exception) cannot be formulated in the element of pre-Copernican thought in which, precisely, the exception appears.

A 'nuance', then, in the treatment of the exception: the idealist tendency tries to fix the exception as an object and to reintegrate its meaning in a Subject, so it confirms the rule by providing it with its foundation; the materialist tendency, on the contrary, *starts from the exception* as from the symptom of an unknown 'rule', disjoined from the ground of evident truths in which that exception arose. Think for example of the way Marx came to formulate the laws of the capitalist mode of production by starting from that *exceptional* 'commodity' constituted by labour power, in the space subject to the 'universal' rule of value.

Ideology as a philosophical category – as distinct from the scientific concepts of historical materialism, such as ideological superstructure, ideological formation, ideological state apparatus and ideological practice, dominant ideology, ideological class relations, etc. – is thus not the 'Marxist' equivalent of error, illusion or ignorance. This category designates the space of the 'eternal' struggle between two tendencies:

the idealist tendency, aiming to identify the process without a subject with a subject – cf. Hegel's delightful complaint against Spinoza in *The Science of Logic*: his 'Substance lacks the principle of Personality' (1929, vol. II, p. 168)! – the 'target' being the unification of the real in the form of the unification of thought;

the materialist tendency, aiming to disjoin this identification by positing the real (including thought which, in a specific form, is

---

matter (1962, p. 93): 'The waters rest on the earth, the earth rests on a whale, and the whale rests on the waters.'

determined by it) as a non-unified process, traversed by unevennesses and contradictions.

This point implies, let me stress, one last consequence, i.e., that the two tendencies are not symmetrical: idealism *never* meets anything other than itself, even when it is 'opposing' materialism; the latter, on the contrary, *always* recognises the existence of idealism, because it is for ever dissociating itself from it.

Appendix 1 A Scientific Theory of Propaganda?

In a study entitled *Sprache der Politik* (The Language of Politics) and published in the GDR (Klaus 1971), the Marxist philosopher and logician Georg Klaus has recently remarked 'unfortunately, no theory of agitation has come down to us from the Marxist classics' (p. 203). He undertakes to work out the fundamentals of such a theory on the basis of the scientific principles of historical materialism, while at the same time using notions borrowed from semantics, semiology and cybernetics. Unlike Adam Schaff, who prefers a place above politics and the class struggle, Klaus states his position clearly: *the language of politics is an element of the class struggle* in presocialist modes of production and an instrument for the development of socialism in socialist societies. He therefore excludes on principle the neutralism that reduces the conditions of political discourse to mere rhetorical technique; he rightly insists that *words are weapons, poisons or tranquillisers*, and reflects, vis-à-vis the example of German fascism, on the conditions in which it is possible for certain expressions (for example that of *Volksgemeinschaft*, 'popular community') to be *turned against* the proletariat and the German people.

His answer to this question is that of *The German Ideology*, i.e., the distinction between essence (*Wesen*) and appearance (*Schein*), with the idea that capitalist exploitation relies on an ideological manipulation designed to present the appearances to the exploited masses in such a way that they take them to be reality itself: under capitalism (that of the 1930s and also that of West Germany today), 'the working masses are unable to see behind the scenes, they are reduced to the use of primitive means of testing (*primitive Testmittel*)' (1971, p. 56). A commentary might express this as follows: *the masses are prisoners in the capitalist cave*, according to the threefold division of ideological space I had occasion to set out above (the auditorium, the stage and the wings, cf. p. 170) as the structure of representation peculiar to bourgeois and pre-capitalist ideological state apparatuses. And indeed, 'that's right', Klaus 'sees the truth': there are wings to the capitalist world, with *officials* who pull the puppet-strings, there is the tableau of the appearances, the screen of the *Schein* and the illusions, there are the people in chains . . . that is right, indeed, except that Klaus does not go so far as to recognise explicitly that it is *in part* the 'illusions' themselves that keep the masses 'in chains', implying that Ideology is not a pure non-being but a material force, and also that it is in the element of that very material force that the people 'throw off their chains', using that material force, which, as such, has neither history nor end, against itself. Having failed to recognise this essential point, Klaus is forced into adopting the Platonic separation between *logic* as the locus of truth and *rhetoric* as the locus of lies, error and deceit, which justifies his use of semantics, semiology and also, as we shall see, cybernetics and psychology:

> There are words and expressions that describe and apprehend the appearance (*Schein*) and others that describe and apprehend the essence (*Wesen*). The appearance acts directly and immediately on the broad masses and for that reason constitutes a preponderant theme of political language. The essence on which this appearance is based requires thorough penetration (*verlangt Gründlichkeit*), the systematic illumination in propaganda of the basic social questions, in other words the achievement of a scientific approach (1971, pp. 94f.).

Given this, and the bourgeois political language which spontaneously plays on the appearances and prefers to strike in the 'emotional sphere' (which constitutes one of the mainstays of demagogy), what are the characteristics of the 'language' of the socialist revolution?

Klaus replies: 'A scientifically based politics and agitation will only use words for which this *reduction* can be performed . . . and in which *semantic univocality* is preponderant, excluding those to which no *operation* can be assigned' (1971, p. 110).[1] Klaus explains that the requirement that reduction be possible expresses the necessity 'to use only semantically meaningful signs and series of signs', i.e., ones

---

1. I have emphasised the expressions on which I want to comment.

amenable to an 'operationalist interpretation' guaranteeing their univocality. Much to his credit, moreover, he does add straight away that- this reduction *is only possible on the basis of historical materialism*, and that any other attempt would reduce us either to primitive biological materialism or to objective or subjective idealism. Thus it is not a matter of a purely logical distinction like the one the neo-positivists posit between 'meaningful' (*sinnvoll*) and 'meaningless' (*sinnlos*) expressions, but one of a distinction involving the existence of a science: this logical distinction (*sinnvoll/sinnlos*) is made on the basis of the science of social formations, it is, as it were, its politico-educational application, making it possible *to distinguish between Wesen and Schein* whenever necessary; in other words (and this is the catch!), logic intervenes as the modality of the application, in the political and ideological struggle, of the scientific contents of historical materialism, such that in the last analysis that struggle takes on *the form of an education*, since it is *in the recognition of the true* that theory is supposed to become a 'material force'.

However, things are not quite so simple, for the class struggle does not have quite the characteristics of a lecture theatre (with the professor's cabinet, the rostrum and the audience), and Klaus knows this, he has the 'political instincts' to remember it. *He feels politically that ideologies are not 'ideas', but cannot think it theoretically, because it is unthinkable in the framework of semantics etc.*; so he is led, in order to represent this unthinkable within that framework (in which, as we know, the logic/rhetoric couple is invitingly available), to counter-balance the logicism by juxtaposing rhetoric to it, in the form of a psychology of attitude change: the ultimate objective of political language, says Klaus, is always 'to produce a certain type of behaviour from whoever it is addressed to' (1971, p. 130), and the fact that the tricks of capitalist psychological manipulation are both unacceptable and unusable in a socialist state 'does not mean that we should ignore the objective laws of psychology, or fail to take them into consideration when the point is to produce a receptivity to the truth' (1971, p. 207). This explains the necessity for the existence under socialism of a kind of rhetoric in the service of truth, involving elements which catch the eye and touch the heart before reaching the mind, and partake of what Klaus calls '*ceremonial*', about which he says that, when it is adequate to the historical situation and the existing social conditions, it 'can mobilise more men than a logically self-enclosed and strictly proven political theory (*eine logisch in sich geschlossene und streng bewiesene politische Theorie*)' (1971, p. 75). Surely there is a contradiction here with the formal criterion of *operationality* stated above, which seems to imply the constant possibility of verification and control from 'things themselves' (*Testmittel*), via the reception of the multiple responses (in the cybernetic sense of feedback – *Rückkopplung*), which, according to Klaus, characterise socialist practices as a whole. 'Instinctively' – i.e. in fact politically – Klaus realises that this would be to imprison himself in a false contradiction, foreign to the whole concrete, theoretical and practical development of Marxism-Leninism; but theoretically imprisoned, as we have seen, in the logic/rhetoric couple (the lecture hall and the theatre . . .) he resolves the issue with a rather symptomatic play on words. Immediately after the sentence I have just quoted, he adds: 'And besides, ceremonies are also an element of order. To discover or institute order corresponds to a basic human need, as Gestalt psychology – to the extent that it is scientific – has established' (1971, pp. 75f.)

This play on words, between formal logical order and social order, guaranteed by psychology, might, moreover, be compared with the following remark from the same author's *Moderne Logik*:

> Formal logic has . . . nothing to do with the metaphysical type of thought . . . The need for a rationalisation of our social life (for example through juridical laws, the introduction of methods for fixing earnings and wages, the regulation of our democratic life, etc.) continually requires logical classifications (1965, p. 198).

A play on words like this, in which what I have distinguished above as *Erfahrung* and *Experiment* are superimposed, I regard as a sign that, however much they deny it, formal logic and psychology make good bedfellows, including when they are presented 'under the banner of Marxism'; they both help to marginalise the dialectic (and politics) by posing as the two collusive masters of everyday evident truths, with the result that the dialectic only surfaces exceptionally, when things are 'out of the ordinary'.

In short, Klaus provides *here* (and not in all his work, which of course I do not pretend to 'pass judgement' on in this note) an example of what might be called theoretico-political top-heaviness:

on the one hand, Marxist-Leninist objectives (to understand how the political discourse of fascism came to find 'listeners' in Germany, to determine the nature of the resistances to the *dictatorship of the proletariat* – resistances to the word and to the thing – to understand why, in 1945, the slogan of the immediate installation of socialism in the Soviet occupation zone was rhetorically easy but politically incorrect, to determine how to develop to the maximum among the masses that material force Marxism-Leninism, in a developed country today, etc.);

on the other hand, 'theoretical instruments' (cybernetics, semantics, etc.) which, despite their 'scientific' appearance, usually have the effect, thanks to the theoretical ideologies they carry with them, of displacing and then effacing the very core of Marxism-Leninism;

with the result that this top-heaviness is an unstable equilibrium which must be resolved at any cost, the question always being to know whether this resolution takes place on the terrain of Marxism-Leninism or outside it.

Appendix 2 Some Possible Repercussions on Linguistic Research

As I said at the beginning, this work is intended to intervene in the relationship between *the three main tendencies* whose contradictions traverse and organise the field of contemporary linguistic research, as a French linguist approaches it today. Its attack is therefore directed above all at the theoretical situation of *linguistics in the imperialist countries of the 'West'*, in so far as that situation is at present marked by the domination of the formalist-logicist tendency. Naturally the ideological struggle that is unfolding in the framework of peaceful coexistence necessarily brings this situation into contact – and not only in the framework of great international congresses – with the situation characterising *linguistics in the socialist countries*, where the tendency of *historical linguistics* (often marked by historicist evolutionism, it must be said) is confronting the rise in importance of a tendency quite close to the *logicist formalism* familiar to us.[1] This said, it is difficult for me to appreciate what response the preoccupations I have revealed in this work will find in that situation today: given, among other things, the small number of texts translated from Russian at present, I am reduced to theoretical guesses based on certain clues (e.g., what I know of the studies undertaken in the perspectives of the Soviet linguist Mel'chuk; I shall return to this point).

The remarks which follow try to suggest very schematically the main *linguistic questions* to which this work seems to me to give rise. I say *linguistic questions* in so far as I believe it would be absurd to pretend to have founded a new 'discipline' or a new 'theory', even the 'materialist theory of discourse'. I have used this formulation

1. For example, as I noted earlier, the recent works of the Soviet linguist S. K. Shaumyan, to which a recent issue of the journal *Langages* has been devoted (no. 33, March 1974), are explicitly inscribed in this tendency.

several times, of course, but, as I have said, this was less to mark out the frontiers of a new scientific 'region' than to designate *certain conceptual elements* (above all that of *discursive formation*) which, until they themselves have been 'rectified', may be useful to materialist linguists who want to work *in* historical materialism: the point is, in the end, to begin to formulate the conceptual conditions which will make it possible to analyse scientifically the linguistic support for the operation of the ideological state apparatuses.

I shall rather arbitrarily group these linguistic questions under two heads:

(1) The first question seems to me to be that of *paraphrase*, currently the object of investigations conducted in many very different theoretical perspectives; without pretending to be exhaustive, I might cite the investigations of Zellig Harris[2] in the United States, those of the Soviet linguist Igor' Aleksandrovich Mel'chuk, and also studies undertaken in France (see for example Antoine Culioli, Catherine Fuchs, Judith Milner). I shall not discuss here the French work, nor the recent investigations of Zellig Harris, in so far as both have been treated in the journal *Langages* no. 37, and especially in Pêcheux and Fuchs (1975), by way of a critical discussion of the procedure called the 'automatic analysis of discourse' (cf. Pêcheux 1969)[3] which we are at present correcting and improving.

On the other hand, I shall take this opportunity to evoke, with respect to the question of paraphrase, the works of Mel'chuk and

---

2. For example, see Harris (1970) and *Langages* no. 29, March 1973, an issue devoted to this question.
   'According to certain American linguists grouped around Zellig Harris, the description of a *langue* includes as an integral (and no doubt essential) part the construction of a paraphrastic algorithm, i.e., a mechanical device, a calculus, enabling one to predict all the possible paraphrases of any given utterance. Indeed, they think that this translation algorithm might even have a mathematical structure simpler than the sentence-forming algorithm constitutive of generative grammars.'
   This characterisation of Harris's perspective is provided by Ducrot and Todorov (1972, p. 366). It shows fairly clearly how the perspective I have suggested here is close to that of Harris (rather than to those of Chomsky or Shaumyan, for example), and also how it differs from it (especially in the idea that it is a matter of a description of the *langue* and of properties *internal to utterances*).
3. A recent example of a concrete analysis carried out with the help of this method can be found in Pêcheux (1978).

Aleksandr K. Zholkovskii, works not sufficiently widely known in France: as it emerges from the text from which I learnt about it (a French version of Mel'chuk and Zholkovskiǐ 1970),[4] i.e., in a very schematic and programmatic form, unfortunately, this perspective seems both extremely interesting and profoundly ambiguous. While in fact referring to Katz and Chomsky, these authors at once separate themselves from them by criticising classical Chomskyan theory, in so far as the latter claims (or claimed) to be concerned with the 'mere generation of texts irrespective of an input meaning to express' (1970, pp. 10f.); instead they insist on the necessary relationship between *meaning* and *text*, relying for this moreover on the thesis that *language is a means of communication*, a thesis I have examined at length above. By questioning in this way the idea of a purely syntactic deep structure, they *might appear* to be moving in the same direction as certain students of Chomsky's grouped together in the current of 'generative semantics' (Fillmore, Lakoff, Ross, etc.) and perhaps they have this impression themselves today.[5] As a matter of fact a good many of the formulations used by Mel'chuk and Zholkovskii undeniably go in this direction. Nevertheless, the way in which they define *meaning* seems to me, by its very ambiguity, to stand in a relationship of productive contradiction with the thesis of the ideal pre-existence of meaning:

> Meaning is what all synonymous utterances (accepted and used by speakers as equivalent) have in common; in short, meaning is the invariant of synonymic transformations (paraphrases),

and they add:

> Thus meaning appears as a construct, a bundle of correspondences between actual (content-) equivalent utterances, symbolised, if necessary, in terms of a special 'semantic notation'. (One is tempted to trace an analogy between such a notation and the system of reconstructed proto-forms of comparative linguistics) (1970, p. 11).

4. Cf. also Rozentsveig (1973).
5. Remember that, in *generative semantics*, the idealism of a universal theory of ideas is, as I have said, 'openly admitted', for example in the project of a grammar consisting of a set of transformations leading from each conceptual structure to the wider set of surface structures that may be used to express that concept. In other words, in the beginning was the meaning . . .

Obviously I cannot be sure to what extent, for Mel'chuk and Zholkovskii, this reference to comparative historical linguistics is or is not *incidental*. Let me simply say that, taken at its face value, and rid of the evolutionist aspect ('proto-forms') it might seem to bring with it, this formulation could result in the idea that *meaning exists in the form of historical paraphrastic invariants, i.e., historically variable invariants*. I do not know whether these two authors are in fact thinking along these lines at present; but this brief commentary on one aspect of their work allows me to note, in what concerns me, an *opposition between* a 'purely syntactic' conception of paraphrase, presupposing a non-contradictory unity of the system of *langue* as an eternal reflection of the human mind, *and* a conception which I shall call historical-discursive to mark the necessary inscription of paraphrastic operations in a *historically given discursive formation*. I shall close this first point by asking some questions:

Under what conditions can scientific linguistic practice appropriate theoretically this new object constituted by *the discursive processes of paraphrase in a discursive formation*?

And, in particular, how should one conceive the phonological, morphological and syntactic 'systematicities' which constitute the basic linguistic material conditions on which the discursive processes develop, in such a way that the illusion is dispelled that these systematicities (and above all that of syntax) are homogeneous blocks of rules, logical machines? How should one conceive the obliterations, occultations and partial overloadings which *necessarily* affect these various systematicities?

Finally, how should one conceive what has been called the 'structure of the lexicon' so that it is both the result and the raw material of discursive processes (through the formation of metaphors, metonymies and synonymies, the never unified construction of contradictory lexical subordinations, the always provisional determination of the 'literal' with respect to the 'figurative', etc.) and no longer operates as the circular logical presupposition of all 'speech acts'?

(2) I shall be even briefer and more schematic with the second question, which I have designated in the course of this book by speaking of a *linguistic imaginary* or *verbal body*: 'If the Freudian theory of the unconscious is so largely ignored by linguists', writes Elisabeth Roudinesco (1973, p. 123), 'it is surely because it intervenes in a *critical* way in their presuppositions'. Hence this question about the conditions in which this criticism can become knowledge:

How should one conceive the time (tenses, moods, aspects, etc.) and the space (localisations, determiners, etc.) which are the imaginary time and space of the speaking-subject in such a way that the evidentness of meaning and subject becomes a theoretical object for linguistics, no longer being blindly and spontaneously repeated in it in the form of the dual imperialism of subject and meaning? In short: how can one take the linguistic consequences of the fact that 'the unasserted precedes and dominates the assertion'?

Paris, 1975

Appendix 3 The French Political Winter: Beginning of a Rectification (Postscript for English Readers)

To intervene in Marxism on the question of ideology, interrogating its relationship to psychoanalysis and linguistics, is *ipso facto* to touch on the kind of 'Triple Alliance' in theory concluded, in France at least, between the names of Althusser, Lacan and Saussure during the 1960s. As you will no doubt be aware, today more than ever, the future of this 'Triple Alliance' is highly problematic, and the parties to it have themselves become the object of a real theoretical *and* political shake-up, in which everything is reopened to question.

The reason the triple field of linguistics, Marxism and psychoanalysis is undergoing this shake-up today is fundamentally that something was *wrong* (and hence, no doubt, simultaneously *only too convenient*) in that 'Triple Alliance', with its claim to 'articulate' these three disciplines together and to control the traffic between the three continents of History, the Unconscious and Language: there is no smoke without fire.

And the reason this shake-up has produced the clouds of smoke that are spreading wider and wider today (towards a 'sexology' beyond Freudianism, a concern with language beyond linguistics, a 'new philosophy' beyond Marxism) is also that this shake-up is following its line of least resistance politically and taking shape blindly as the necessary effect of the causes determining it: there is no smoke without fire.

Of course, the two things marked here by the repetition of a single aphorism are but one and the same political contradiction at work in the philosophical element: this can be expressed by saying that the errors, deviations, 'oversights', etc., that took up residence at the heart of the 'Triple Alliance' and played a sometimes fatal theoretical part there, designated the unrecognised presence of the adversary even *inside* the theoretical citadel supposedly organised to resist that adversary's assaults *from without*.

To intervene philosophically one has to take sides: I take sides *for* the fire of a critical work which is only too likely to destroy the 'Triple Alliance' itself, but in which there is at the same time the possibility that something new will be born – and *against* the incinerating fire that produces nothing but smoke.

In order to take sides in this way, it is essential to discern the points in the philosophical battlefield which urgently need to be abandoned and those it is more important than ever to occupy and defend, on condition that they are occupied and defended *differently*. This is a question of precision: the philosophical struggle, a class struggle in theory, is an endless process of co-ordinated rectifications sustained by the urgency of a position to be defended and reinforced in the face of what could be called adversity in thought. It is by going back up that 'line of least resistance' that philosophy makes its specific contact with the real.

I want here to present to English readers a fragmentary sketch of this attempt at adjustment[1] by seizing on one precise point in it and restricting myself to it for now. In the conclusion to the 1975 text (cf. p. 191) there appears the following condensed formulation: 'The subject-form of discourse, in which interpellation, identification and the production of meaning coexist indissociably, realises the non-sense of the production of the subject as cause of himself in the form of immediate evidentness'. Let me emphasise that it is no accident that, in its very formulation, this thesis, which tries to

---

1. This work of rectification implies others, on the notion of the dominated ideology, and also on the term 'disidentification' that I thought fit to introduce in 1975. Here I shall only consider the question of the disjunction between *subject* and *ego* in the problematic of ideological interpellation, in relation to the question of meaning, hence of language and especially of metaphor. This study would have been literally impossible – and this is no mere rhetoric – without a number of recent essays: above all Roudinesco (1977), Henry (1977), J.-C. Milner (1978), Roustang (1976) and Plon's critical review of *Les Vérités de La Palice* (Plon 1976a). Let me add that I also found Jean-Louis Houdebine's rather sharp review (1976) highly illuminating in certain respects and am philosophically grateful to him, however 'Stalinist' I was and remain in his eyes! Finally, the text (unpublished in French) written by Althusser in 1976 to accompany the presentation to a German audience of his 1970 article 'Ideology and Ideological State Apparatuses' (Althusser 1977) has obviously been of precious value in this work which has its very beginnings indeed largely in the 1970 article.

encapsulate a fundamental point of the Althusserian project, sounds odd, recalling both English 'nonsense' humour and the German 'absurd' (to be found in the adventures of Baron Munchausen, for example) as well as, on the other hand, the self-ironising tautologies of the jokes French tradition calls '*lapalissades*' after Monsieur de La Palice: it is no accident because it is precisely at this limit point in Marxist reflection that, 'ideology interpellating individuals as subjects', we run into the impossible fact of a 'subject-form' in History as a 'process without subject or goal(s)'.

It was originally the fact that this materialist point is quite simply incomprehensible to pure 'rationalism' that drew my attention and literally caught my interest. Yet Marxists had long since specifically recognised and expressed this point in a thousand perfectly reasonable common-sensical and obvious ways, when they said, for example, that the material conditions of existence of men determine the forms of their consciousness without the two ever coinciding, that men make history but not the history they want to make or think they are making, etc. These formulations clearly expressed the fact that 'men' are determined in History so that they freely think and do what they cannot not do and think, but always expressed it in the eternal repetition of something *descriptively evident* which ultimately threatened to lock proletarian politics into the dilemma of quietism (the idea that within the revolutionary movement itself time and experience are working for the revolution) and the voluntarist leap (the idea that revolutionary theory has to be imported into the workers' movement to 'put it on the right track').

One could not but realise that at this point reasonable, clear, evident explanations (the 'attainment of consciousness', the 'lessons of experience', the 'penetration of ideas' and even the 'proof of practice') finally marked the site of a long theoretical *and* political blockage. A blockage entailing (among other consequences) the present glaciation of French left-wing politics.

But it was on this in many ways unbearable point in historical materialism that Althusser dared to touch (with the theory of the 'extra-economic' conditions of the reproduction of the relations of production) in order to give this famous singular point a chance to work in Marxism-Leninism: when he said that subjects 'work all by themselves' because they are subjects, i.e. individuals interpellated as subjects by ideology, he was allowing something new to be *heard* within the workers' movement, in both senses of the term.

He was *stating theoretically* vis-à-vis the subject of ideology something which, from outside the workers' movement, played with the idea of a theoretical relationship between Marxism and certain psychoanalytic concepts (on terms like subject, ego, unconscious/ conscious, imaginary, identification . . .), on the lines of his 1964 article, 'Freud and Lacan' (Althusser 1971a).

But more important he was *revealing politically*, in the workers' movement, the urgent need to develop, in unprecedented proportions, the 'fusion' of theory and practice on the terrain of the ideological class struggle in its relationship to the question of the state; and he was implying, from within the practices of the workers' movement, the extent to which the evident propositions and injunctions of the ruling ideology can blind and deafen.

The *political* intervention was probably so unbearable that, in the rebound of a theoreticism willing to recognise in the Ideological State Apparatuses the horror of its own image inverted much more than it found in them its real 'source', 'Ideological State Apparatuses' was read most often and by all sorts of readers as a purely *theoretical* intervention, to be precise as a functionalist thesis, either in order to reproduce it or to condemn it. And despite all Althusser's rectifications, which they regard as null and void, some today are not afraid to go so far as to claim that 'Althusserianism' is a theory of Order and the Master instituted by the dual foreclosure of History (encapsulated in Reproduction) and the Subject (reduced to the automaton that 'works all by itself'). It had to be done!

As if *Ressentiment* would not forgive Althusser for having pointed out politically, and attempted to call by its name theoretically, the Plague of subjection, and avoided the unbearable by denouncing him pure and simple as complicit in what he had named and pointed out. . . . Others in history before him have suffered from the same resentment, in different forms: Spinoza, for example, a real companion in heresy for Althusser, who also knew the art of taking unforgivable questions to extremes.

Oddest of all, here and there (and especially where one would have least expected it!) the same provocative question arose immediately: 'What have you done with the class struggle, M. Althusser?' One way of signifying to him: 'You've gone over to the class enemy who conducts the class struggle in the forms of silence or denegation in the name of Eternity!' A quite natural response, really, for all those Althusser's interpellated individuals and agent-supports had dispossessed of the famous 'political subject' who, in the self-education of the 'attainment of consciousness', of the 'lessons of experience', etc., 'makes politics' and thereby escapes, surely, from interpellation by the ruling ideology as he struggles, if not for the revolution, at least for 'change' . . . What is to be done, if men are only 'supports'?!

Some of us were weak enough to take this provocative question seriously, despite the malevolence of those who asked it, and I still have this weakness, for the risk of a *politically functionalist* interpretation of the Ideological State Apparatuses is indeed too great (the line of least resistance!) for us to neglect the question; and recent studies of ideology and the state (e.g., Santiago Carillo appealing to Gramsci and Althusser in order to preach the 'democratisation of the state apparatus') are not likely to prove me wrong.

So, for my part, I undertook to develop the notion of the ideological class struggle in *Language, Semantics and Ideology* on the basis of Althusser's article and starting from its final remarks characterising the Ideological State Apparatuses as the *seat* and *stake* in a class struggle: it seemed to me at once that it was more correct to characterise the ideological class struggle as a process of the *reproduction-transformation* of existing relations of productions in such a way as to inscribe there the very mark of the class contradiction constituting that struggle (and I hold firmly to this point today).

In my enthusiasm, and in response to attacks against the 'apolitical eternalism' of the Ideological State Apparatuses, I went further and tried to discover how, in that circle of absurd evidentness constituted by interpellation, 'subjecthood was produced' which was capable historically – on certain conditions, essentially linked to the appearance of Marxist-Leninist theory – of turning against the causes determining it, because it could grasp them theoretically and practically: as a result, at the end of *Language, Semantics and Ideology*, whatever my intentions, I eventually outlined the ghost of a strange materialist subject achieving 'the subjective appropriation of proletarian politics'; and despite all the theoretical precautions I surrounded myself with (in particular the notion of 'disidentification', to which I shall return elsewhere), I finished up with a paradoxical subject of proletarian political practice whose tendential symmetry with the subject of bourgeois political practice went unquestioned!

For, faced with the full subject identified in the interpellation of the dominant bourgeois ideology, bearer of the evidentness that makes everyone say 'That's me!', I found support in a *radical exteriority of Marxist–Leninist theory* to reveal the point at which the absurd reappears beneath the evident, thus making possible a kind of *education by breaking with the imaginary identifications in which the subject is caught,* and hence an 'interpellation in reverse' at work in proletarian political practice: the theoreticist exteriority was thus necessarily accompanied by an inverted didacticism; which led to a typically Platonic bent consisting of posing in theoretical succession

(1) the ideological mechanism of interpellation-subjection

(2) the erasure ('forgetting') of any registrable trace of this mechanism in the full subject produced by it

(3) the theoretical remembering of the said mechanism and its erasure, in a kind of Marxist-Leninist-style anamnesis, the notion of 'subjective appropriation' being the practically effective result.

The reader will perhaps be surprised by this insistent self-criticism, to which I reply that an error can never be left to sleep in peace with impunity; what is jarring must be discerned, not so as to guarantee one's definitive location in the true (!) but so as to attempt to go as far as one can in the direction of accuracy.

What is jarring here, with respect to Marxism-Leninism, is, as we have seen, the idealist return of a primacy of theory over practice. But the didacticism which went with this return rebounds to designate another impediment on another scene: there is also something jarring in psychoanalysis, in the reference made to its concepts, and it condenses around the relation between *the ego* and *the subject*. In *Language, Semantics and Ideology*, it is just as if what is said there *about the subject* tended to be confused with the proposition that the *ego* is the 'subject-form' of legal ideology, to the point that functionalism, expelled politically from the door, had managed, despite all denegations, to slip back in through the psychoanalytic window, in the form of a kind of genesis of the ego, by dint of taking the illusions as to the unifying power of consciousness far too seriously.

To allow the installation of such a *Jacobinism of consciousness*, locked up in the evident character of its own control over its acts, speeches and thoughts and with nothing jarring within it (on the pretext of isolating the subjection effects of ideological interpellation), was to let the adversity off too lightly while remaining in a way its prisoner: to take the illusion of a full-ego-subject in which nothing jars far too seriously, there precisely is something jarring in *Language, Semantics and Ideology*!

Thus was evaded, with the utmost philosophical obstinacy, the fact that the nonsense of the unconscious, in which interpellation finds a point of attachment, is *never entirely* covered or obscured by the evidentness of the subject-centre-meaning which is produced by it, because the moments of production and product are not sequential as in the Platonic myth, but inscribed in the simultaneity of an oscillation, of a 'pulsation' by which the unconscious nonsense endlessly returns in the subject and in the meaning which is supposedly installed in it.

There is no cause save for something jarring (Lacan). It is at this precise point that Platonism radically misses the unconscious, i.e., the cause that determines the subject at the point at which it is grasped by the interpellation effect; what is missed is that cause insofar as it is constantly 'manifested' in a thousand forms (the slip, the parapraxis) in the subject itself, for the unconscious traces of the Signifier are never 'erased' or 'forgotten' but work without intermission in the oscillation between sense and nonsense in the divided subject.[2]

It is just this that ultimately disconnects the psychoanalytic concept of repression (*verdrängung*) from the philosophical (Platonic) idea of forgetting or erasure. Hence it remains true that 'some sense' is produced in 'nonsense' by the origin-less slide of the signifier – whence the installation of the primacy of metaphor over meaning – but it is indispensable to add immediately that *this slide does not disappear without leaving traces* in the subject-ego of the ideological 'subject-form', identified with the evidentness of a meaning. To grasp ideological interpellation as *ritual* in all its implications presupposes recognition that there is no ritual without disruptions, lapses and flaws: 'one word for another', that is the definition of metaphor, but it is also the point at which a ritual fractures in the slip (and the least one can say is that there is no lack of examples, whether in the religious ceremony, legal proceedings, the educational lecture or the political speech).[3]

2. Cf. Paul Henry (1977, p. 144): 'The subject cannot be thought along the lines of the unity of an interiority as connected. He is divided as the dreamer is between his position as "author" of his dream and that of witness to it. As Moustafa Safouan remarks (1974, p. 18), "only by doing violence to one's intelligence can the dream, considered from a Freudian point of view, impose the distinction between the subject who *truly* speaks (the one that works in the dream) and the one that could be called the 'locutor' or the 'word-mill', the one that relates this same dream to us when awake". He is divided like someone who has made a slip: he didn't say it, it was his tongue that slipped, etc . . . But dreams, slips of the tongue, blunders, neurosis or psychosis are necessary if this is to appear. Otherwise, I spontaneously think myself the source of my thoughts, my actions and my words.'

3. In this perspective, cf. Gadet and Pêcheux (1981).

In this respect, does not the analytical series dream-slip-parapraxis-*Witz* intersect obliquely with something constantly infecting the dominant ideology, even from within the practices in which it tends to be realised? 'Whoever says class struggle of the ruling class says resistance, revolt and class struggle of the ruled class,' wrote Althusser at the end of his article on the Ideological State Apparatuses . . . The slip and the parapraxis (disruptions in the ritual, impediments for the ideological Order) might well have something very precise to do with this always-already existent point, this unassignable origin of resistance and revolt: fleeting forms of appearance of something 'of a different order', minute victories that for a flash thwart the ruling ideology by taking advantage of its faltering.[4]

To retrace the outcome of the slip and the parapraxis in the disruptions in ideological interpellation does not imply that I am now making the unconscious the source of the dominated ideology, having failed to make it the super-egoic spring of the dominant ideology: the order of the unconscious does not coincide with that of ideology, repression in the psychoanalytic sense (*Verdrängung*) can be identified neither with subjection nor with (political) repression, but ideology cannot be thought without reference to the unconscious register. Hence I am not suggesting that the slip or the parapraxis are as such the historical bases constituting dominated ideologies; the real precondition for the latter's disjunction from the dominant ideology lies in the class struggle as a motor historical

---

4. This *impossible degree* of perfect subjection, in the labour process imposed by the capitalist mode of production, is revealed in these lines from the autobiographical account of an intellectual militant who worked for a year as a manual worker in a Citroën factory. He is speaking of work on the assembly line: 'And suppose you said to yourself that nothing is important, just get used to doing the same thing, always in the same way, always at the same pace; hope for nothing more than the placid perfection of the machine? Death tempts you. But life flickers and resists. The organism resists. The muscles resist. The nerves resist. Something in the body and in the head braces up to fight against the repetition and the emptiness. Life: a faster movement, a burst of irregularity, a mistake, a "speed-up", a "slow-down" – all so many tactics on the job: anything by which, in this pathetic corner of resistance against that empty eternity the work point, there are still events, however minimal, there is still time, however monstrously drawn out. That awkwardness, that extra journey, that sudden acceleration, that miswelding, that hand that has to have two goes, that grimace, that "I've had enough" – they are life itself grabbing on. Everything that in every assembly worker screams silently "I am not a machine!"' (Linhart 1978, p. 14).

contradiction (one divides into two) and not in One world unified by the Power of a Master.

On this question certain of Michel Foucault's analyses provide the possibility of a correction of the Althusserian distinction between ideological interpellation and repressive violence by their revelation of the process of individualisation-normalisation in which different forms of state violence subject the bodies and materially guarantee the submission of the ruled – *but only on the express condition that Foucault himself is corrected on one essential point* – concerning precisely his relation of foreclosure to both psychoanalysis and Marxism: by patiently dismantling the many mechanisms by which the training and regimentation of individuals is achieved, the material devices that guarantee their operation and the normalisation disciplines that codify their performance, Foucault, whether he will or not, has made an important contribution to the revolutionary struggles of our day, but at the same time he has concealed it, making the resistance points and bases of class revolt ungraspable. It is my hypothesis that this concealment lies in the impossibility from Foucault's strict point of view of making a coherent and consistent distinction between the processes of material subjection of human individuals and the procedures of animal domestication. This masked biologism, which without realising it he shares with various currents of technocratic functionalism, does indeed make revolt strictly unthinkable, because there can be no 'revolt of the beasts' any more than there can be any extraction of surplus labour or language in what is normally called the animal kingdom.

The reason revolt in human history is coeval with the extraction of surplus labour is that the class struggle is the motor of that history.

And the reason, on quite another plane, that revolt is coeval with language is that its very possibility rests on the existence of the division of the subject inscribed in the symbolic.

The specificity of these two 'discoveries' will not allow them to be fused in any theory whatsoever, even a theory of revolt. But a glance at the price paid for their foreclosure forces us to admit that they have something to do with each other politically.

There is perhaps a thread that it would be interesting to follow in the historical study of repressive and ideological practices in order to begin at last to understand the resistance-revolt-revolution process of the ideological and political class struggle, without making the dominated ideology the eternal repetition of the dominant ideology or the self-education of an experience progressively discovering the truth behind the curtain of illusions held up by the ruling class, or the theoreticist irruption of an external knowledge alone able to break the enchanted circle of the ruling ideology.

It seems to me today that *Language, Semantics and Ideology* touched on these questions, but in a strangely abortive manner, in a false-sounding recurrent symptom: I mean the systematic, compulsive (and, at the time, incomprehensible for me) pleasure I took in introducing the largest possible number of jokes – something which, to my knowledge, irritated more than one reader.

As I now realise, this was the only means I had to signify, by the steering of nonsense in the joke, what the moment of a discovery has basically in common with the faltering of a certainty: the joke is a determinant fulcrum, for, while structurally analogous with what goes amiss in the parapraxis, it represents at the same time the maximum form of negotiation with the 'line of least resistance', the instant of a victory of thought in its moment of birth, the purest figure of its emergence. This marks the fact that thought is basically unconscious ('it, the id, ça thinks'!), and theoretical thought to begin with (the 'materialism of our day' cannot, without serious risks, remain blind to this). To put it another way: the *Witz* represents one of the visible points at which theoretical thought encounters the unconscious; the *Witz* grasps something of this encounter, while presenting the appearance of mastering its effects.

Althusser's text on the Ideological State Apparatuses, whose analytical range of reference systematically avoided the series dream-slip-parapraxis, remained prudently noncommital here, while pointing towards the *Witz*.

The 'Munchausen effect' is in its turn aimed in this direction, but again prolongs the non-commitment by 'theoreticising' it. Hence, three years later, this little foot-path that I am trying to trace during our political winter, taking my bearings from two fixed landmarks:

There is no domination without resistance: the practical primacy of the class struggle, which means that one must 'dare to rebel'.

Nobody can think in anybody else's place: the practical primacy of the unconscious, which means that one must put up with what comes to be thought, i.e. one must 'dare to think for oneself.'

Bibliography

Dates in round brackets are the dates of the edition referred to. Dates in square brackets are the dates of the original composition, if known, or of the first edition in the original language.

Althusser, Louis (1969), *For Marx* [1965], trans. by Ben Brewster (London: Allen Lane).

——(1970), 'From *Capital* to Marx's Philosophy' [1965], in Althusser, Louis and Balibar, Étienne, *Reading Capital*, trans. by Ben Brewster, pp. 11–69 (London: NLB).

——(1971a), 'Freud and Lacan' [1964], in *Lenin and Philosophy and Other Essays*, trans. by Ben Brewster (London: NLB) pp. 177–202.

——(1971b), 'Ideology and Ideological State Apparatuses (Notes towards an Investigation)' [1970], in *Lenin and Philosophy and Other Essays*, trans. by Ben Brewster (London: NLB) pp. 121–73.

——(1971c), 'Philosophy as a Revolutionary Weapon, Interview conducted by Maria Antonietta Macciocchi' [1968], in *Lenin and Philosophy and Other Essays*, trans. by Ben Brewster (London: NLB) pp. 13–25.

——(1972), 'Marx's Relation to Hegel' [1968], in *Politics and History: Montesquieu, Rousseau, Hegel and Marx*, trans. by Ben Brewster (London: NLB) pp. 161–86.

——(1974a), *Philosophie et philosophie spontanée des savants* [1967], Collection 'Théorie' (Paris: François Maspero).

——(1974b), '[Texte ronéotypé]' [1970], in Saül Karsz, *Théorie et politique: Louis Althusser, avec quatre texes inédits de Louis Althusser* (Paris: Fayard) pp. 321–3.

——(1976a), 'Elements of Self-Criticism' [1972], in *Essays in Self-Criticism*, trans. by Grahame Lock (London: NLB) pp. 101–61.

——(1976b), 'Reply to John Lewis' [1972], in *Essays in Self-Criticism*, trans. by Grahame Lock (London: NLB) pp. 33–99.

——(1977), Introduction [1976] to *Ideologie und ideologische Staatsapparate* (Hamburg and Berlin: Verlag für das Studium der Arbeiterbewegung).

Althusser, Louis and Balibar, Étienne (1970), *Reading Capital* [1965], trans. by Ben Brewster (London: NLB).

Arnauld, Antoine and Lancelot, Claude (1664), *Grammaire générale et raisonnée. Contenant Les fondemens de l'art de parler; expliquez d'une maniere claire & naturelle; Les raisons de ce qui est commun à toutes les langues, & des principales differences qui s'y rencontrent; Et plusieurs remarques nouvelles sur la Langue Françoise* [1660], 2nd edn (Paris; repr. Menston: Scolar Press, 1968).

——(1753), *A General and Rational Grammar, Containing the Fundamental Principles of the Art of Speaking, Explained in a clear and natural manner. With the reasons of the general agreement, and the particular differences of languages* [1660], trans. by Thomas Nugent (?) (London; repr. Menston: Scolar Press, 1968).

Arnauld, Antoine and Nicole, Pierre (1685), *Logic; or the Art of Thinking: in which Besides the Common are contain'd many excellent New Rules, very profitable for directing of Reason, and acquiring of Judgment, in things as well relating to the Instruction of a Man's self, as of others* [1662], trans. into English by Several Hands (London).

——(1964), *The Art of Thinking. Port Royal Logic* [1662], trans. by James Dickoff and Patricia James, The Library of Liberal Arts (Indianapolis: Bobbs-Merril).

Balibar, Étienne (1966), 'Marxisme et linguistique', *Cahiers Marxistes-Léninistes*, 12–13, pp. 19–25.

——(1974), 'La Rectification du *Manifeste Communiste*', [1972], in *Cinq études du matérialisme historique*, Collection 'Théorie' (Paris: François Maspero) pp. 65–101.

Balibar, Étienne and Macherey, Pierre (1974), 'Présentation', in Renée Balibar, *Les Français fictifs: le rapport des styles littéraires au français national* (Paris: Hachette) pp. 7–49.

Balibar, Renée (1974) *Les Français fictifs: le rapport des styles littéraires au français national*, Collection 'Analyse' (Paris: Hachette).

Balibar, Renée and Laporte, Dominique (1974), *Le Français national: politique et pratique de la langue nationale sous la Révolution*, Collection 'Analyse' (Paris: Hachette).

Barbault, Marie-Claire and Desclés, Jean-Pierre (1972), *Transformations formelles et théories linguistiques*, Documents de Linguistique Quantitative, 11 (Paris: Dunod).

Baudelot, Christian and Establet, Roger (1971), *L'École capitaliste en France*, Cahiers libres, 213–4 (Paris: François Maspero).

Belaval, Yvon (1960), *Leibniz critique de Descartes* (Paris: Gallimard).

Bierwisch, Manfred and Kiefer, Ferenc (1969), 'Remarks on

Definitions in Natural Languages', in Ferenc Kiefer (ed.), *Studies in Syntax and Semantics* (Dordrecht, The Netherlands: D. Reidel) pp. 55–79.

Bouveresse, Jacques (1971), *La Parole malheureuse: de l'alchimie linguistique à la grammaire philosophique* (Paris: Éditions de Minuit).

Bruno, Pierre, Pêcheux, Michel, Plon, Michel and Poitou, Jean-Pierre (1973), 'La Psychologie sociale: une utopie en crise', *La Nouvelle Critique*, 62, pp. 72–8, 64, pp. 21–8.

Cavaillès, Jean (1960), *Sur la logique et la théorie de la science* [1939], 2nd edn (Paris: Presses Universitaires de France).

Chomsky, Noam (1966), *Cartesian Linguistics. A Chapter in the History of Rationalist Thought* (New York: Harper & Row).

Condillac, Étienne Bonnot de (1970), 'Cours d'Etude pour l'instruction du prince de Parme, II, Grammaire' [1775], in Charles Porset (ed.), *Varia Linguistica* (Bordeaux: Ducros) pp. 149–211.

Dessaintes, Maurice (1960), *La Construction par insertion incidente (étude grammaticale et stylistique)* (Paris: D'Artrey).

Ducrot, Oswald (1969), 'Présupposés et sous-entendus', *Langue Française*, 4, pp. 30–43.

Ducrot, Oswald and Todorov, Tzvetan (1972), *Dictionnaire encyclopédique des sciences du langage* (Paris: Éditions du Seuil).

Edelman, Bernard (1979) *Ownership of the Image, Elements for a Marxist Theory of Law* [1973], trans. by Elizabeth Kingdom (London: Routledge & Kegan Paul).

Engels, Friedrich (1970), 'The Part Played by Labour in the Transition from Ape to Man' [1876], in Karl Marx and Friedrich Engels, *Selected Works in Three Volumes*, vol. III (Moscow: Progress Publishers) pp. 66–77.

Fichant, Michel and Pêcheux, Michel (1969) *Sur l'histoire des sciences*, Cours de Philosphie pour Scientifiques, vol. III, Collection 'Théorie' (Paris: François Maspero).

Foucault, Michel (1969), 'Introduction', in Antoine Arnauld and Claude Lancelot, *Grammaire générale et raisonnée (1660)* (Paris: Republications Paulet) pp. III–XVIII.

——(1972), *The Archaeology of Knowledge* [1969], trans. by A. M. Sheridan Smith (London: Tavistock Publications).

Frege, Gottlob (1952a), 'Function and Concept' [1891], trans. by Peter T. Geach, in Peter T. Geach and Max Black (eds), *Translations from the Philosophical Writings of Gottlob Frege* (Oxford: Basil Blackwell) pp. 21–41.

——(1952b), 'Illustrative Extracts from Frege's Review of Husserl's *Philosophie der Arithmetik*' [1894], trans. by Peter T. Geach, in Peter T. Geach and Max Black (eds), *Translations from the Philosophical Writings of Gottlob Frege* (Oxford: Basil Blackwell) pp. 79–85.

——(1952c), 'Negation' [1918], trans. by Peter T. Geach, in Peter T. Geach and Max Black (eds), *Translations from the Philosophical Writings of Gottlob Frege* (Oxford: Basil Blackwell) pp. 117–36.

——(1952d), 'On Concept and Object' [1892], trans. by Peter T. Geach, in Peter T. Geach and Max Black (eds), *Translations from the Philosophical Writings of Gottlob Frege* (Oxford: Basil Blackwell) pp. 42–55.

——(1952e), 'On Sense and Reference' [1892], trans. by Max Black, in Peter T. Geach and Max Black (eds), *Translations from the Philosophical Writings of Gottlob Frege* (Oxford: Basil Blackwell) pp. 56–78.

——(1967), 'Rezension von: E. G. Husserl, Philosophie der Arithmetik I' [1894], in I. Agnelli (ed.), *Kleine Schriften*, (Hildesheim: Georg Olms Verlagsbuchhandlung) pp. 179–92.

——(1977a), 'Compound Thoughts' [1923], in *Logical Investigations*, trans. by Peter T. Geach and R. H. Sloothoff (Oxford: Basil Blackwell) pp. 55–77.

——(1977b), 'Negation' [1918], in *Logical Investigations*, trans. by Peter T. Geach and R. H. Sloothoff (Oxford: Basil Blackwell) pp. 31–53.

——(1977c), 'Thoughts' [1918], in *Logical Investigations*, trans. by Peter T. Geach and R. H. Sloothoff (Oxford: Basil Blackwell) pp. 1–30.

——(1979), 'Logic (1897)', in Hans Hermes, Friedrich Kambartel and Friedrich Kaulbach (eds), *Posthumous Writings*, trans. by Peter Long and Roger White (Oxford: Basil Blackwell) pp. 126–51.

Frémontier, Jacques (1971), *La Forteresse ouvrière: Renault* (Paris: Fayard).

Freud, Sigmund (1953), *The Interpretation of Dreams* [1900], in *The Standard Edition of the Complete Psychological Works of Sigmund Freud*, trans. under the general editorship of James Strachey, vols IV and V (London: Hogarth Press).

——(1960), *Jokes and their Relation to the Unconscious* [1905], in *The Standard Edition of the Complete Psychological Works of Sigmund Freud*, trans. under the general editorship of James Strachey, vol. VIII (London: Hogarth Press).

——(1961), 'Negation' [1925], in *The Standard Edition of the Complete*

Psychological Works of Sigmund Freud, trans. under the general editorship of James Strachey, vol. XIX (London: Hogarth Press) pp. 235–9.

——(1966), 'Project for a Scientific Psychology' [1895], in *The Standard Edition of the Complete Psychological Works of Sigmund Freud*, trans. under the general editorship of James Strachey, vol. I, (London: Hogarth Press) pp. 283–397.

Fuchs, Catherine (1970), 'Contribution à la construction d'une grammaire de reconnaissance du français' (Université de Paris VII) Thèse de troisième cycle.

Fuchs, Catherine and Léonard, Anne-Marie (1979), *Vers une théorie des aspects, les systèmes du français et de l'anglais* (Paris: Mouton-EHESS).

Fuchs, Catherine and Milner, Judith (1979), *À propos des relatives, étude empirique des faits français, anglais et allemands, et tentation d'interprétation* [1975], (Paris: Éditions SELAF).

Gadet, Françoise (1977), 'La Sociolinguistique n'existe pas: je l'ai rencontrée', *Dialectiques*, 20, pp. 99–118.

Gadet, Françoise and Pêcheux, Michel (1981), *La Langue introuvable*, Collection 'Théorie' (Paris: François Maspero).

Grize, Jean Blaise (1969), *Logique moderne*. Fasc. 1: *Logique des propositions et des prédicats. Déduction naturelle* (The Hague: Mouton).

Guedj, Aimé and Girault, Jacques (1970), *'Le Monde', Humanisme, objectivité et politique* (Paris: Éditions Sociales).

Haroche, Claude, Henry, Paul and Pêcheux, Michel (1971), 'La Sémantique et la coupure saussurienne: langue, langage, discours', *Langages*, 24, pp. 93–106.

Harris, Zellig (1970), 'The Two Systems of Grammar: Report and Paraphrase' [1969], in *Papers in Structural and Transformational Linguistics*, Formal Linguistics Series, vol. 1 (Dordrecht, The Netherlands: D. Reidel) pp. 612–92.

Hegel, Georg Wilhelm Friedrich (1929), *Hegel's Science of Logic* [1812], trans. by W. H. Johnston and L. G. Struthers, 2 vols (London: Allen & Unwin).

Heger, Klaus (1964), 'Die methodologische Voraussetzungen von Onomasiologie und begrifflicher Gliederung', *Zeitschrift für romanische Philologie*, 80, pp. 486–516.

——(1965), 'Personale Deixis und grammatische Person', *Zeitschrift für romanische Philologie*, 81, pp. 76–97.

Henry, Paul (1974), *De l'énoncé au discours: présupposition et processus discursif*, mimeo (Paris: CNRS-EPHE).

——(1975) 'Constructions relatives et articulations discursives', *Langages*, 37, pp. 81–98.

——(1977), *Le Mauvais outil: langue, sujet et discours* (Paris: Éditions Klincksieck).

Herbert, Thomas (1968), 'Remarques pour une théorie générale des idéologies', *Cahiers pour l'analyse*, 9, pp. 74–92.

Houdebine, Jean-Louis (1976), 'Les Vérités de la Palice ou les erreurs de la police (d'une question obstinément forclose)', *Tel Quel*, 67, pp. 87–97.

Humboldt, Carl Wilhelm von (1906), 'Lettre à M. Abel-Rémusat sur la nature des formes grammaticales en général, et sur la génie de la langue chinoise en particulier' [1826], in Albert Leitzmann (ed.), *Wilhelm von Humboldts Werke*, vol. v, pp. 254–308 (Berlin: B. Behr's Verlag; photomechanical repr. Berlin: Walter de Gruyter: 1968).

Husserl, Edmund (1970a), *The Crisis of the European Sciences and Transcendental Phenomenology, an Introduction to Phenomenological Philosophy* [1936], trans. by D. Carr from W. Biemel's edn, North-Western University Studies in Phenomenology and Existential Philosophy (Evanston, Illinois: North-Western University Press).

——(1970b), *Logical Investigations* [1913], trans. by J. N. Findlay, International Library of Philosophy and Scientific Method, 2 vols (London: Routledge & Kegan Paul).

Kant, Immanuel (1933), *Critique of Pure Reason* [1781], trans. by Norman Kemp Smith (London: Macmillan).

Karsz, Saül (1974), *Théorie et politique: Louis Althusser, avec quatre textes inédits de Louis Althusser*, Série 'Digraphe' (Paris: Fayard).

Katz, Jerrold (1972), *Semantic Theory* (New York: Harper & Row).

Kiefer, Ferenc (1966), 'Some Semantic Relations in Natural Languages', *Foundations of Language*, 2, pp. 228–40.

Kiefer, Ferenc (1973), 'On Presuppositions', in Ferenc Kiefer and Nicolas Ruwet (eds), *Generative Grammar in Europe* (Dordrecht, The Netherlands: D. Reidel) pp. 218–42.

——(1974), 'Quel est l'effet sémantique des transformations?', in *Essais de sémantique générale*, traduction de Laurent Danon-Boileau, 'Repères' (Tours: Éditions Mame) pp. 117–53.

Klaus, Georg (1965), *Moderne Logik* (Berlin: Deutscher Verlag der Wissenschaften).

——(1971), *Sprache der Politik* (Berlin: Deutscher Verlag der Wissenschaften).

Lacan, Jacques (1966a), 'L' instance de la lettre dans l'inconscient ou la raison depuis Freud' [1957], in *Écrits*, Le Champ freudien (Paris: Éditions du Seuil) pp. 493–528.

——(1966b), 'Introduction au commentaire de Jean Hyppolite sur la "Verneinung" de Freud' [1954], in *Écrits*, Le Champ freudien (Paris: Éditions du Seuil) pp. 369–80.

——(1977a), 'The Agency of the Letter in the Unconscious or Reason since Freud' [1957], in *Écrits, a Selection*, trans. by Alan Sheridan (London: Tavistock Publications) pp. 146–78.

——(1977b), *The Four Fundamental Concepts of Psychoanalysis* [1964], Jacques-Alain Miller (ed.), trans. by Alan Sheridan (London: Hogarth Press).

Lecourt, Dominique (1973), *Une Crise et son enjeu (essai sur la position de Lénine en philosophie)*, Collection 'Théorie' (Paris: François Maspero).

——(1974), *Bachelard, le jour et la nuit* (Paris: Bernard Grasset).

——(1975), 'On Archaeology and Knowledge (Michel Foucault)' [1970], in *Marxism and Epistemology: Bachelard, Canguilhem, Foucault*, trans. by Ben Brewster (London: NLB) pp. 187–213.

Leibniz, Gottfried Wilhelm (1896), *New Essays Concerning Human Understanding together with an Appendix consisting of some of his Shorter Pieces* [1702–3], trans. by Alfred Gideon Langley (Chicago: Open Court Publishing Company).

——(1951), *Theodicy: Essays on the Goodness of God, the Freedom of Man and the Origin of Evil* [1710], Austin Farrer (ed.), trans. E. M. Huggard (London: Routledge & Kegan Paul).

——(1973), 'The Monadology' [1714], in *Leibniz: Philosophical Writings*, trans. by Mary Morris and G. H. R. Parkinson, rev. 1st edn, Everyman's Library (London: Dent, 1934) pp. 179–94.

Lenin, Vladimir Il'ich (1962), *Materialism and Empirio-criticism* [1908], in *Collected Works*, vol. xiv (London: Lawrence & Wishart) pp. 17–361.

——(1963), 'Explanation of the Law on Fines Imposed on Factory Workers' [1895], in *Collected Works*, vol. ii (London: Lawrence & Wishart) pp. 29–72.

——(1964a), 'The Discussion on Self-Determination Summed Up' [1916], in *Collected Works*, vol. xxii (London: Lawrence & Wishart) pp. 320–60.

——(1964b), 'The Junius Pamphlet' [1916], in *Collected Works*, vol. xxii (London: Lawrence & Wishart) pp. 305–19.

Linhart, Robert (1978), *L'Établi* (Paris: Éditions de Minuit).

Mach, Ernst (1960), *The Science of Mechanics: A Critical and Historical Account of its Development* [1883], trans. by Thomas J. McCormack (La Salle, Illinois: Open Court Publishing Company).

Macherey, Pierre (1978), *A Theory of Literary Production* [1966], trans. by Geoffrey Wall (London: Routledge & Kegan Paul).

Marx, Karl (1961–2), *Capital: A Critical Analysis of Capitalist Production. Critique of Political Economy* [1867–94], 3 vols (Moscow: Foreign Languages Publishing House).

——(1970), 'Critique of the Gotha Programme' [1875], in Karl Marx and Friedrich Engels, *Selected Works in Three Volumes*, vol. III (Moscow: Progress Publishers) pp. 9–30.

——(1975), 'Economic and Philosophical Manuscripts of 1844', in Karl Marx and Friedrich Engels, *Collected Works*, vol. 3 (London: Lawrence & Wishart) pp. 229–346.

——(1976), 'Theses on Feuerbach' [1845], in Karl Marx and Friedrich Engels, *Collected Works*, vol. 5 (London: Lawrence & Wishart) pp. 3–9.

Marx, Karl and Engels, Friedrich (1976a), 'The Communist Manifesto' [1847–8], in *Collected Works*, vol. 6 (London: Lawrence and Wishart) pp. 477–519.

——(1976b), *The German Ideology* [1845–6], in *Collected Works*, vol. 5 (London: Lawrence & Wishart) pp. 19–581.

Maupertuis, Pierre Louis Moreau de (1970), 'Réflexions philosophiques sur l'origine des langues et la signification des mots' [1748], in Charles Porset (ed.), *Varia Linguistica* (Bordeaux: Éditions Ducros) pp. 25–67.

Mel'chuk, Igor' Aleksandrovich and Zholkovskii, Aleksandr K. (1970), 'Towards a Functioning "Meaning-Text" Model of Language', *Linguistics*, 57, pp. 10–47.

Milner, Jean-Claude (1978), *L'Amour de la langue* [1976], Le Champ freudien (Paris: Éditions du Seuil).

Pêcheux, Michel (1969), *Analyse automatique du discours* (Paris: Dunod).

——(1978), 'Are the Masses an Inanimate Object?', in David Sankoff (ed.), *Linguistic Variation: Models and Methods* (New York: Academic Press) pp. 251–66.

Pêcheux, Michel and Fuchs, Catherine (1975), 'Mises au point et perspectives à propos de l'analyse automatique du discours', *Langages*, 37, pp. 7–80.

Peirce, Charles Sanders (1953), Letter of 14/23 December 1908, in *Letters to Lady Welby*, Irwin C. Lieb (ed.) (New Haven,

Connecticut: Whitlock's Inc, for the Graduate Philosophy Club of Yale University) pp. 22–32.

Plon, Michel (1972), 'Sur quelques aspects de la rencontre entre la psychologie sociale at la théorie des jeux', *La Pensée*, 161, pp. 53–80.

——(1975), *Forme et limite d'une idéologie théorique: la psychologie sociale. Essai sur l'appropriation subjective de la politique*, mimeo (Paris).

——(1976a), 'La sémantique ou le fantasme du cercueil de verre', *La Nouvelle Critique*, 89, pp. 94–5.

——(1976b), *La Théorie des jeux: une politique imaginaire*, Collection 'Algorithme' (Paris: François Maspero).

Plon, Michel and Préteceille, Edmond (1972), 'La Théorie des jeux et le jeu de l'idéologie', *La Pensée*, 166, pp. 36–68.

Raspe, Rudolph Erich (1786), *Baron Munchausen's Narrative of his Marvellous Travels and Campaigns in Russia. Humbly dedicated and recommended to Country Gentlemen; and, if they please, to be repeated as their own, after a hunt, at horse races, in watering-places, and other such polite assemblies; round the bottle and fire-side* (Oxford).

Raspe, Rudolph Erich and Bürger, Gottfried August (1786), *Wunderbare Reisen zu Wasser und Lande, Feldzuge und lustige Abentheuer des Freyherrn von Münchhausen, wie er dieselben bey der Flasche in Cirkel seiner Freunde selbst zu erzählen pflegt. Aus dem Englischen nach der neuesten Ausgaben ubersetzt, hier und da erweitert und mit noch mehr Kupfern gezieret* (London).

Raymond, Pierre (1973), *Le Passage au matérialisme. Idéalisme et matérialisme dans l'histoire de la philosophie*, Collection 'Théorie' (Paris: François Maspero).

Roudinesco, Elisabeth (1973), *Un Discours au réel. Théorie de l'inconscient et politique de la psychanalyse*, 'Repères' (Tours: Éditions Mame).

——(1977), *Pour une politique de la psychanalyse*, Collection 'Action Poétique' (Paris: François Maspero).

Roustang, François (1976), *Un Destin si funeste* (Paris: Éditions de Minuit).

Rozentsveig, Viktor (1973), 'Les Modèles dans la linguistique soviétique', *La Nouvelle Critique*, 68, pp. 77–83.

Russell, Bertrand (1940), *An Inquiry into Meaning and Truth* (London: Allen & Unwin).

Safouan, Moustafa (1968), 'De la structure en psychanalyse: Contribution à une théorie du manque', in Oswald Ducrot et al.,

Qu'est-ce que le structuralisme? (Paris: Éditions du Seuil) pp. 239–98.

Safouan, Moustafa (1974), *Études sur l'Oedipe*, Le Champ freudien (Paris: Éditions du Seuil).

Saussure, Ferdinand de (1974), *Course in General Linguistics* [1906–11], Charles Bally and Albert Sechehaye (eds) in collaboration with Albert Reidlinger, trans. by Wade Baskin (London: Fontana).

Schaff, Adam (1962), *Introduction to Semantics* [1960] (Oxford and Warsaw: Pergamon Press/Panstwowe Wydawnictwo Naukowe).

——(1973), *Language and Cognition* [1964], Robert S. Cohen (ed.), trans. by Olgierd Wojtasiewicz (New York: McGraw-Hill).

Smith, Adam (1767), 'Considerations Concerning the First Formation of Languages and the Different Genius of Original and Compounded Languages' [1763], in *The Theory of Moral Sentiments, to which is added A Dissertation on the Origin of Languages*, 3rd edn (London: A. Millar) pp. 437–78.

Spinoza, Baruch (1928), 'To the very Honourable and Prudent Mr. Hugo Boxel' [October 1674], in *The Correspondence of Spinoza*, translated by A. Wolf (London: Allen & Unwin) pp. 286–90.

Stalin, Iosef Vissarionovich (1951), 'On Marxism in Linguistics' [1950], in *The Soviet Linguistic Controversy*, trans. from the Soviet press by John V. Murra, Robert M. Hankin and Fred Holling, Columbia University Slavic Studies (New York: King's Crown Press) pp. 70–6.

Vax, Louis (1970), *L'Empirisme logique, de Bertrand Russell à Nelson Goodman*, SUP Série 'Initiation Philosophique', 93 (Paris: Presses Universitaires de France).

Vinogradov, Viktor Vladimirovich (1969), 'Triompher du culte de la personnalité dans la linguistique soviétique', *Langages*, 15, pp. 67–84.

Zadeh, Lofti Asker (1971), 'Quantitative Fuzzy Semantics', *Information Sciences*, vol. 3, no. 2, pp. 159–76.

Index

division in the symbolic, 216–7, 217n2, 219
of enunciation, 156–7, 186–7
form (of discourse), 51, 110–129, 133–42, 149–50, 155, 159, 165, 170, 187, 191–2, 194–5, 197, 212–13, 216
ideological notion of, 86, 89–90, 90n5, 176–7
in interpellation, 92, 92n6, 102n5, 105–7, 110, 112–13, 118, 137, 156, 190, 212–13
in law, 101, 105, 110, 110n1
materialist theory of, 91–2, 102
psychoanalytic, 114n11, 214, 217, 217n2
of science, 38, 86, 92n6, 117, 139, 142, 156
speaking, 4, 7, 14, 24–5, 29, 32n4, 33n6, 35–6, 39, 109, 112, 117, 121–3, 125–6, 172, 174, 181–2, 210
   see also under langue as linguistic system
and Subject, 92, 92n6, 113–14, 117, 120–2, 121n22, 149, 157, 197–9, 214
universal, 121, 139, 156–7
see also under real
subjection, ideological, 92, 92n6, 104, 110n1, 121, 156–7, 164, 192, 216, 218n4, 218–19
subjective appropriation, 81n12
of knowledge, 159–64, 159n3, 191, 194–5
of politics, 159, 159n3, 164–70, 196n11, 215–16
subjective/objective, 13, 17n4, 31–6, 33n6, 42–3, 43n3, 50, 77, 84, 136, 176
subjectivism, philosophical, 14, 29, 30–1, 37, 42, 47, 125
subjectivity, materialist theory of, 90–3, 114
substance/accident, 13, 13n8, 23
superstructures, 104–5, 182
see also under language
sustaining effect, 73–4, 84, 114, 116, 118, 162

see also under articulation; transverse discourse
symbolic, 92n6, 125–6, 125n25, 190, 193, 219
see also under identification; subject
symptom, 108, 199
syntactic constructions, 64–5, 70–1, 108
syntagmatisation, 115–16, 115n14, 118
syntax
as component of linguistics, viii–ix, 5, 9–10, 33n6, 37, 55, 58, 112n9, 125, 172, 189, 208–9
and semantics, 90, 125–6

tabula rasa, 27n1
taking up a position, 121, 141–3, 143n2, 152–3, 156–7, 160n5, 194–5, 212
tenses, 33n6, 71, 125, 210
text and writing, 6, 83, 158–9, 180
theoreticism, 146, 214, 216, 220
theory of knowledge, 3, 17n14, 18, 18n15, 24, 29, 32, 32n4, 41, 114, 119, 171, 173, 176–7
see also under rhetoric/theory of knowledge
thought and being, *see under* being
Todorov, Tzvetan, viii
transformational-generative grammar, ix, 6–7, 9, 12, 38, 176, 186, 207n2, 208
see also under linguistics, formalist-logicist
transverse discourse, 116–17, 121–2, 126, 137, 154–6, 162, 185, 193–5
see also under articulation; intradiscourse; sustaining effect
truths of reasoning/truths of fact, 25–6, 31
Twentieth Congress of the CPSU, 1–2, 14, 16n12

unconscious, 92, 92n6, 104, 104n1, 116n15, 121, 123, 125–6, 125n25, 186–7, 189, 191, 209, 211, 214, 216–18, 220

vagueness of terms, *see under* Russell